Re Ingrated

classic recipes, tastes & traditions of

Malaysia & Singapore

classic recipes, tastes & traditions of

Malaysia & Singapore

Sensational dishes from two exotic cuisines, with 150 authentic
recipes shown step by step in 600 beautiful photographs

Ghillie Başan and Terry Tan

LORENZ BOOKS

This edition is published by Lorenz Books,
an imprint of Anness Publishing Ltd, Hermes House,
88–89 Blackfriars Road, London SE1 8HA;
tel. 020 7401 2077; fax 020 7633 9499

www.lorenzbooks.com; www.annesspublishing.com

If you like the images in this book and would like to investigate using them
for publishing, promotions or advertising, please visit our website
www.practicalpictures.com for more information.

UK agent: The Manning Partnership Ltd; tel. 01225 478444;
fax 01225 478440; sales@manning-partnership.co.uk

UK distributor: Grantham Book Services Ltd; tel. 01476 541080;
fax 01476 541061; orders@gbs.tbs-ltd.co.uk

North American agent/distributor: National Book Network;
tel. 301 459 3366; fax 301 429 5746; www.nbnbooks.com

Australian agent/distributor: Pan Macmillan Australia; tel. 1300 135 113;
fax 1300 135 103; customer.service@macmillan.com.au

New Zealand agent/distributor: David Bateman Ltd; tel. (09) 415 7664;
fax (09) 415 8892

Publisher: Joanna Lorenz
Editorial Director: Helen Sudell
Contributing Editor: Beverley Jollands
Project Editors: Molly Perham and Rosie Gordon
Cover Design: Jonathan Davison
Page Design: Mike Morey
Production Controller: Steve Lang
Home Economists: Lucy McKelvie, Bridget Sargeson and Fergal Connolly
Stylist: Helen Trent

Publisher's Acknowledgments
The publisher would like to thank William Lingwood and Martin Brigdale for
their superb photography throughout the book, apart from the following
images: Arcangel Images p.14tr; Nicky Dowey p.18tc; Robert Harding Picture
Library p.20; Superstock Ltd p.19t; Travel_ink pp. 9r, 10t, 10b, 11b, 13t, 15
16, 19b; Photoshot pp. 6, 7t, 8b, 11t, 12, 13b, 14b, 17t, 17b, 18b, 21, 22b,
23r, 28, 53t.

ETHICAL TRADING POLICY

At Anness Publishing we believe that business should be conducted in an
ethical and ecologically sustainable way, with respect for the environment
and a proper regard to the replacement of the natural resources we employ.

As a publisher, we use a lot of wood pulp to make high-quality paper for
printing, and that wood commonly comes from spruce trees. We are
therefore currently growing more than 750,000 trees in three Scottish forest
plantations: Berrymoss (130 hectares/320 acres), West Touxhill (125
hectares/305 acres) and Deveron Forest (75 hectares/185 acres). The
forests we manage contain more than 3.5 times the number of trees
employed each year in making paper for the books we manufacture.

Because of this ongoing ecological investment programme, you, as our
customer, can have the pleasure and reassurance of knowing that a tree is
being cultivated on your behalf to naturally replace the materials used to
make the book you are holding.

Our forestry programme is run in accordance with the UK Woodland
Assurance Scheme (UKWAS) and will be certified by the internationally
recognized Forest Stewardship Council (FSC). The FSC is a non-
government organization dedicated to promoting responsible management
of the world's forests. Certification ensures forests are managed in an
environmentally sustainable and socially responsible way. For further
information about this scheme, go to www.annesspublishing.com/trees©
Anness Publishing Ltd 2008

Parts of this book were previously published as part of another volume,
The Food and Cooking of Malaysia and Singapore by Ghillie Basan.

NOTES
Bracketed terms are intended for American readers.
For all recipes, quantities are given in both metric and imperial measures
and, where appropriate, in standard cups and spoons. Follow one set, but
not a mixture, because they are not interchangeable.
Standard spoon and cup measures are level. 1 tsp = 5ml, 1 tbsp = 15ml, 1
cup = 250ml/8fl oz.
Australian standard tablespoons are 20ml. Australian readers should use
3 tsp in place of 1 tbsp for measuring small quantities of gelatine, flour,
salt, etc.
American pints are 16fl oz/2 cups. American readers should use 20fl oz/2.5
cups in place of 1 pint when measuring liquids.
Electric oven temperatures in this book are for conventional ovens.
When using a fan oven, the temperature will probably need to be reduced by
about 10–20°C/20–40°F. Since ovens vary, you should check with your
manufacturer's instruction book for guidance.
The nutritional analysis given for each recipe is calculated per portion (i.e.
serving or item), unless otherwise stated. If the recipe gives a range, such as
Serves 4–6, then the nutritional analysis will be for the smaller portion size,
i.e. 6 servings. Measurements for sodium do not include salt added to taste.
Medium (US large) eggs are used unless otherwise stated.

Main front cover image showing [...] recipe, see
pages 148–9.

CONTENTS

INTRODUCTION

Wherever your travels take you, there can be few regions where food is as revered and delicious as that you will taste in Singapore and Malaysia. Here, traditions and cooking methods draw on a colourful history of migrant Chinese, Indian, Indonesian, Arab, European and indigenous aboriginal ancestry. Culinary influences are highly reflective of the eclectic mix of these cultures, classic Chinese flavours blending intriguingly well with the spicy nuances in Indian, Indonesian, Arab and indigenous cooking styles.

CULTURAL INFLUENCES

Only 40 years ago, Singapore and Malaysia were one country, and their cuisines evolved in tandem. In essence, the food culture of both countries is not monocultural but plural and polyglot. Singaporean cooking is similar to that of the Malay communities, mainly in the region of Peninsula Malaysia and Indonesia. The original Chinese settlers imbued many a pot with their soy sauces and bean pastes, the legacy of which lives on in a hundred and one

dishes in private homes, restaurants, rustic lean-to food stalls and hawker complexes.

You will no doubt notice many similarities in the dishes within this book. Whether it has high-octane chilli fire or subtle Chinese savoury characteristics, each dish is memorable for the judicious, and often brilliantly inspired, mix of ingredients that is an intoxicating alchemy.

THE IMPORTANCE OF SPICE

Blending spice and seasonings is an art that has evolved through centuries of multiculturalism, and is today integral to the cooking of both countries. Malaysians and Singaporeans have endlessly adventurous tastebuds and experimentation is vital to their kitchens. The keynote of the two cuisines is spice paste, pounded rough or smooth, fried or boiled, rubbed on seafood or meat; each cook does his own fine-tuning to produce dishes of delectable character and taste. Within the Chinese communities, many dishes of the Cantonese, Hakka and Fujian –

the three migrant mainstreams from South China – have retained their intrinsic purity, but some have mutated deliciously to embrace the spicy spectrum. A Fujian soy braised duck is touched with coriander and pepper, a Cantonese noodle dish is liberally spiced up with Indian chilli paste, and Malay desserts are given a fragrant fillip with sesame seeds – this is the beguiling culinary tableau.

Sour Nonya curries rely on the staple tamarind base that typifies Indonesian seafood dishes; meat and poultry cuts are bathed in redolent sambals that speak of South Indian heat; staple rice and noodles from Guangzhou province are flavoured with myriad tropical herbs largely unused in China; and countless cakes and sweet concoctions are spun out of coconut, palm sugar and glutinous rice.

The subtle or robust flavours of Chinese stir-fries take on piquant highlights in the Malay kitchen; for example, Chinese chicken dishes may be perfumed with indigenous herbs such as coriander and lemon grass. Coconut milk – the dairy equivalent in the region – is the liquid basis for many a hybrid creation, reflecting Indonesian, Thai and Indian culinary touches.

A COOKS' HAVEN

Whether in the relaxed ambience of Malaysian villages or the pulsating rhythm of urban life in Singapore, food remains the foundation, with an incredible richness in variety and customs permeating all life. Tantalizing aromas fragrance the region's air, the coastal areas are teeming with marine life and there has always been an abundance of seafood and river catches. Local rice has the best textures, there are bountiful wild and farmed fruit harvests, and of course there is the wonderful herb garden that is Malaysia's natural heritage. The reputation for incomparable culinary skills among Malaysian and

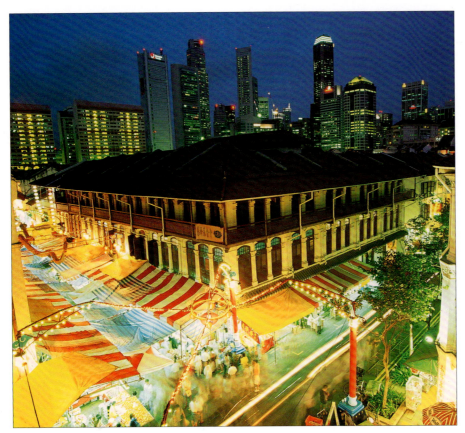

Left: Street stores sell an array of fruits, vegetables, fish, meat and much more, in Singapore's vibrant China Town.

Singaporean cooks – both professional and domestic – has not been earned consciously; it seems inherited by the people from their ingenious and inventive ancestors. Successive generations have adapted, improved and refined dishes, creating a rainbow palette of flavours. Of all the world's cuisines, these are some of the least intimidating, yet the most rewarding. Each is distinctive depending on which state, town, village and ethnic community it comes from. Although Malaysian and Singaporean cuisines share many common threads, each is highly unique in taste and presentation – all the regions have their hallmarks.

Despite their complex flavours, basic cooks can prepare most dishes. There is no need for specialist equipment, as most dishes are derived from traditional and homely recipes across the cultures. Also, no two cooks ever interpret a recipe exactly the same way: ethnic cuisines have evolved over a long period of time and are never an exact science. Every cook or chef, new or established, has free licence to adapt a dish to suit the tastes of his family, community or customers.

TRADITIONAL FOOD IN MODERN LIFE

While the village lifestyle of old is rapidly being left in the past, and the faster pace of city life means that people have less time, the cores of Malaysian and Singaporean food remain sacrosanct. Whether it is a banquet of a dozen dishes, just a few simple ones or rustic offerings by street vendors, visitors to any area will discover that eating and food preparation remain a local obsession.

Living in a highly urbanized city state, Singaporeans have, over several decades, nurtured the love of food to a passionate degree, even though every ingredient is imported from somewhere else. You can scarcely move 50 metres before you come across yet another food court that offers the aromatic promise of dishes from a dozen different regions. This is where you can glean many a culinary trick, to mix and adjust dishes to suit your tastes.

HOW TO USE THIS BOOK

Perhaps you have visited Malaysia and Singapore and long to relive the tastes, colours and scents of the food you ate there. Alternatively, you may enjoy Thai or Indian food and want to discover related cuisines. In either case, you will find the information in this book offers a fascinating insight into the history and people behind the food.

In the following section about kitchen ingredients, you can find out what to look for in Asian markets and how to prepare foods in an authentic way. Many of the ingredients featured may be unfamiliar to Western cooks, but this discovery of exotic vegetables and fruits, beautiful fish and pungent spices is part of the fascination of learning to cook food from other areas of the world.

The recipes aim to immerse you in the true experience of Malaysia and Singapore's food, with classic soups, noodle and rice dishes, fiery sambals, exotic desserts, and meat and seafood dishes with incomparable flavour.

Right: Rice is cooked in many delicious ways in Malaysia and Singapore.

Above: A group setting out to go fishing shade themselves from the heat of the sun on Borneo Island, Malaysia.

These dishes make the most of wonderful fresh ingredients, as well as regional store-cupboard staples, and are easy to prepare quickly and enjoy at leisure with friends and family. Above all, they introduce new experiences; from shopping in the Asian markets to the tantalizing cooking smells and unforgettable flavours of the final meal.

A CULINARY HISTORY OF MALAYSIA AND SINGAPORE

The independent countries of Malaysia and Singapore as we know them today only emerged in the 1960s. Malaysia was born in 1963, with the merging of Malaya, Singapore, Sabah and Sarawak, while the small sultanate of Brunei in north Borneo remained separate. However, Singapore's merger into Malaysia soon proved an unhappy one. Singapore broke free in 1965 and has since then succeeded spectacularly well as a small nation, with an emphasis on hard work and a tight economy.

For centuries before their emergence as independent nations, however, the influxes of traders, colonialists and immigrant workers had been adding to the rich cultural melting-pot that now characterizes these two countries. The cultural mix of Malaysia and Singapore is so diverse that it reads like a recipe in itself. The population of Malaysia is about 60 per cent Malay, 26 per cent Chinese and 7 per cent Indian, with a dash of Peranakan, Eurasian, Indonesian and tribal influences, garnished with a scattering of Vietnamese, Japanese, Filipino and Thai. Most Malays are followers of Islam, as well as adhering to old spiritual beliefs and systems of social law. In the *kampung* (Malay village), the early Hindu-based system of *adat*, with an emphasis on collective responsibility, is part of everyday life. Obligations of kinship and social harmony are at the heart of the Malay psyche, so much so that many urban Malays, caught up in the busy whirl of Kuala Lumpur and Singapore, miss the spiritual simplicity of *kampung* life.

In Singapore, the pace of life is fast and urban. The population is 76 per cent Chinese, 15 per cent Malay and 6 per cent Indian, with a small number of Peranakan, Eurasian and Indonesian, sprinkled with Western influences. This all adds up to one of the most colourful and exciting culinary scenes in the world, made all the more tangible by the fascinating tradition of hawker stalls, where exotic food from all these cultures can be sampled in one place.

Above: Modern-day Malaysia is divided into the two distinct regions of West and East, covering 329,758 sq km/ 127,320 sq miles. West Malaysia (the Malay Peninsula) is joined to mainland Asia with Singapore at the bottom. East Malaysia encompasses the northern part of Borneo and is divided into two states, Sabah and Sarawak.

Above: The busy Johur Bakra causeway that links Singapore to Malaysia.

MALAYAN ANCESTRY

The Orang Asli, the aboriginal Malays, provide us with the most vivid evidence as to early Malay culinary culture. They are believed to have migrated 10,000 years ago from the region in China where the great rivers of South-east Asia meet (today's Qinghai Province). The Orang Asli settled in the forests of the Malay Peninsula, where they led a hunter-gatherer existence. Their numbers dwindled considerably during the 20th century, and some have intermarried with other ethnic groups in the region, but there are still pockets of hunter-gatherer Orang Asli living in the hilly jungles of Pahang in the centre of the peninsula.

Other Malay descendants who settled on the peninsula were said to be of the same ethnic group as their Indonesian ancestors. Culturally they were similar, particularly when it came to food and culinary traditions: this common bond still exists, as the Malays and Indonesians share many of the same spicy dishes. As the Malay ancestors settled on the peninsula, some moved inland and married Orang Asli tribespeople, spreading their knowledge of rice cultivation and the use of the ox and water buffalo as beasts of burden.

Over in East Malaysia, Sabah and Sarawak are still home to numerous indigenous tribal groups, who continue

Right: A traditional fishing boat tied up on the fine sands of Penang, on Malaysia's west coast.

to live by fishing, hunting and collecting wild plants and herbs, most of which are indigenous to those regions.

THE STORY OF MELAKA

A turning point in the region's culinary history came at around 1400, when the small fishing village of Melaka on the west coast of the Malay Peninsula began to grow into a significant port. With Indian ships sailing in on the southwest monsoon and Chinese junks being blown in by the north west monsoon, Melaka was strategically positioned to harbour them and boomed as a multicultural trade centre, drawing traders, merchants and missionaries to its shores.

The local cooking was influenced by the arrival of new cooking techniques, spices such as cardamom, pepper and cloves, and exotic fruits and vegetables. When the Sultan of Melaka converted to Islam in the mid-15th century, there was an increase in trade with other

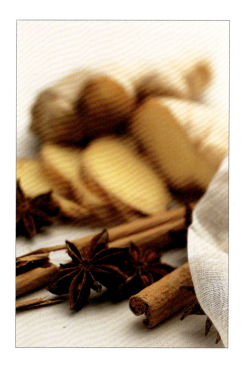

Above: Spices grown locally add unmistakable warmth, sweetness and flavour to the region's food.

Muslim communities in Indonesia and the Middle East, which had a lasting effect on Malay cuisine.

Melaka's colourful history has left it an enviable culinary heritage. Malay, Chinese, Peranakan and Eurasian cuisines all flourish, and many local recipes put a particular emphasis on spices and creamy coconut milk. The sago pudding soaked in palm sugar syrup, *sagu gula melaka*, is a Malay

favourite, as is *satay celup*, an assortment of skewered food such as shellfish, vegetables, fish balls, hard-boiled quail's eggs and chunks of chicken or beef, which is cooked in boiling stock, rather like a Swiss fondue, and served with a peanut sauce. Satay is likely to have evolved from the Middle Eastern kebab, which would have been brought to the region by Muslim Indian or Arab traders.

Right: A stall holder tends his wares in Batu Ferringhi in Penang. Malaysian produce is now widely exported.

PENANG

Off the mainland, the small island of Penang grew as a major trade centre under the rule of the British East India Company in the 18th and 19th centuries, when it was one of the best sources of nutmeg and cloves. At this time it attracted immigrants from China, Sumatra, Thailand, Burma and India. The intermingling of these varied cultures is reflected in the food of Penang, which is regarded as a gastronomic heaven.

INDIA'S INFLUENCE

Traders from India had visited the region long before Europeans set up colonies. However, it was not until the 19th century, when the British brought

Below: Water buffalo are a common sight on Longwaki Island, and are used as beasts of burden as well as for food.

in Indian workers to provide cheap labour in the rubber plantations, that Indian culture had a strong influence on the cuisine of the region. Most of these Indians were Hindus from South India, where rice and dhal (lentils) are the staples, and food is eaten with the hands. Hindus don't eat beef and many are vegetarian, so they introduced vegetable dishes and pickles to Malay cuisine. Southern Indians also tend to cook with coconut oil, contrasting with the ghee-based dishes of North India, such as *tandoori* and *biryani*.

Above: A fish market scene at Kota Bharu in Kelantan.

CHINESE FLAVOURS

Like the Indians, the Chinese had had a long history of trade in the region, but it wasn't until the 19th century that the resident Chinese population grew. With the increase in the region's tin mining and agriculture, the numbers of Chinese grew so quickly that, by 1827, they formed the largest single community in Singapore. By 1845, they made up half the population. Tremendous farmers, the Chinese were responsible for planting many of the rice paddies and vegetable plantations in the region.

Hailing from the provinces of Guangdong, Fujian and Guangxi, they belonged to different socio-linguistic groups, such as Teochew, Hokkien and Hainanese, each of which adheres to its own traditions and cuisines.

EURASIAN HYBRID COOKING

In the 16th century, Portuguese traders and explorers colonized parts of Malaysia, particularly Melaka, and married local women. The descendants called themselves Jenti Cristang

Right: A Chinese market at Penang, known as the "Pearl of the Orient".

(Christian people) and spoke their own language, a kind of Creole Portuguese. They were also called Eurasian, along with the descendants of other European-Malay unions, and developed their own cuisine, a complex hybrid of Malay, Chinese, Peranakan and Indian food, combined with Portuguese cooking methods. The European influence in this food can be detected in their love of roasted cuts of meat, grilled chops and steaks. However, exotic curries, with sour notes of tamarind and lime, are also Eurasian top favourites, including the fiery curry *debal* (devil's curry) and *feng*, the Christmas pork curry. Curries and other savoury dishes are usually served with rice or bread but, unlike the other culinary cultures of Malaysia and Singapore, the Eurasians enjoy a dessert at the end of a meal.

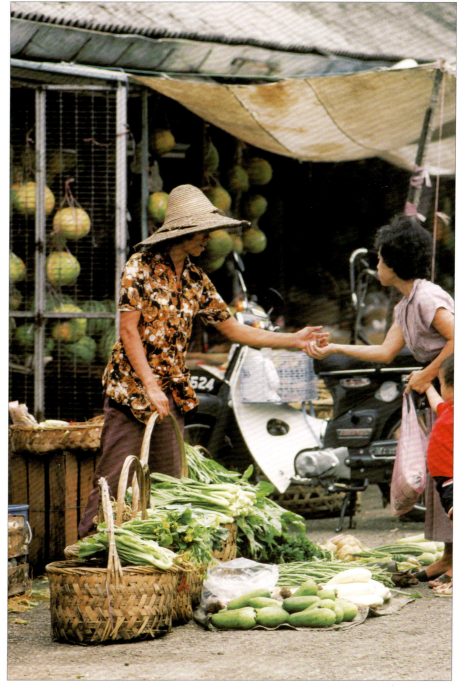

MALAYSIAN CUISINE TODAY

The rich variety of culinary traditions found throughout South-east Asia come together in Malaysia. From Chinese businessmen in skyscrapers in Kuala Lumpur to Orang Asli hunter-gatherers in the jungles of the Malay Peninsula, the people and their eating habits are as diverse as the landscape. Thanks to its location on the sea routes between Asia, India and China, Malaysia has been influenced by merchants and invaders from far and wide.

OUTSIDE INFLUENCES

Bordering Thailand to the north, the states of Perlis and Kedah are known as the region's rice bowl, producing over half the domestic rice supply. Given its proximity to Thailand and the influx of Thais settling in the region, the local cuisine is inevitably influenced by the Thai culinary trademark – hot, spicy flavours paired with sourness.

Further down the west coast, in the states of Perak and Selangor and in the capital, Kuala Lumpur, the food is much more varied, influenced in succession by Indian traders, Chinese merchants, European colonizers, immigrant workers and 20th-century industrialization. Kuala Lumpur, which has grown from a

Above: A modern satay stall in Kuala Lumpar, Malaysia, where street snacking is extremely popular.

19th-century tin-mining town to an affluent, cosmopolitan city, boasts a fascinating mélange of food cultures. You can find regional specialities from all parts of Malaysia as well as from India and China; you can sample French, Vietnamese and Japanese fare in high-class restaurants; seek out old colonial haunts serving British breakfasts and fried chicken with Worcestershire sauce; or simply follow the young crowd and wait at a busy hawker stall for a bowl of noodles with a fried egg on top.

STRONGHOLDS OF TRADITION

Much of Malaysia's tea is grown on the plantations in Perak's highlands, which lead into the Cameron Highlands of Pahang. The area's fertile plateaux attracted tea planters, vegetable farmers and wealthy colonialists retreating from the heat of the lowlands to highland hill stations. However, much of Pahang has remained impenetrable to prospectors and planters, dividing the east and west of the Malaysian peninsula with its high mountain ridges. This is the domain of the indigenous Orang Asli, whose staple foods are tapioca, rice and fish. Malaysia's longest river, Sungai Pahang, flows right through the state and is full of plump carp and catfish.

Over on the east coast, the states of Kelantan and Terengganu are still steeped in traditional Malay culture. The coastline is dotted with thriving fishing villages and idyllic white beaches. Life moves at a slower pace, with fishing as its mainstay. Fish is bought from the nets as the boats come to shore and the local women cook it in inventive ways.

In the south of the peninsula, Negeri Sembilan is known for seriously fiery dishes, influenced by the Minangkabau, who came from Sumatra in the 15th century. The most southerly state on the peninsula is Johor, which has also retained a strong Malay culture and cuisine. Johor provides the crowded island of Singapore with much of its farm produce and water. Linked to Singapore by two causeways, Johor Bahru, the state capital, offers much of the same hawker food, and

Singaporeans often drive over to Johor Bahru to eat cheaper versions of their own delicious seafood dishes.

EAST MALAYSIA

Across the South China Sea, most visitors to Sabah on the island of Borneo go to climb Mount Kinabalu or visit the orang-utan rehabilitation centre. However, Sabah is also home to gorgeous deserted beaches, coral reefs and wild Asian elephants and rhinos, as well as to 30 different ethnic groups who thrive on a diet of fish, deer, wild boar and wild plants, herbs and fruit from the forests. Although rice is grown in the hills, the main staples for the indigenous communities are corn, tapioca (cassava) and, in the swamp lands, pearls from the wild sago palm.

Like Sabah, Sarawak is a world apart from the Malay Peninsula. Covered with dense rainforests, rivers, caves and national parks where wildlife can be spotted, this state is home to the Iban, Melanau and other indigenous tribes. Longhouses and river excursions through the jungles using old head-hunter trails are part of the tourist experience, as is the city of Kuching. Although rice is grown in Sarawak, vast areas of the land are too swampy for paddies, so some tribes rely on the wild sago palm. Wild boar and deer are Sarawakan favourites, roasted whole over charcoal. Most tribes make their own arak, a local liquor, and tuak, rice wine, which are both very potent.

COFFEE SHOP CULTURE

Malaysian coffee shops are friendly and atmospheric. Often occupying the ground floors of old city shophouses, the setup is basic, with minimal decoration and plain tables and chairs. Each neighbourhood has its own Chinese, Malay or Indian coffee shop, where people gather for a chat and a cup of tea or coffee and, frequently, a meal. Meals served in coffee shops are simple and culture-specific, such as the fish head soup served in the Indian and Malay premises, or noodles and dim sum in the Chinese shops. For breakfast, popular choices include *roti kaya* (grilled flatbread smeared with coconut egg jam) and *kuay neng* (runny, soft-boiled eggs cracked open in a saucer and mixed with soy sauce and black pepper).

Tea is generally Assam, made strong and sweetened with condensed milk. Frothy *teh tarik* ("pulled tea") is a Malaysian speciality, and the warm, milky ginger tea known as *teh halia* is regarded as a late-night pick-me-up. Chinese jasmine or lotus teas are served to enhance the appetite, cleanse the blood or aid digestion, but coffee begins and ends the day for many Malays. Brewed strong with earthy and mellow characteristics, it is always sweetened with condensed milk.

Right: Fishing nets dry outside a small house in Kampung, Malaysia. In some areas the traditional ways of life are almost unchanged.

How eateries have changed

Throughout Malaysia there are still many terraced "shophouses" dating back to the years before World War II, with the living quarters upstairs and the ground floor devoted to a small business. Many were turned into eating houses or coffee shops as street hawkers gradually left the streets and started selling their noodles and rice dishes from these small premises. It is a trade that has remained largely unchanged in most urban areas.

In Penang, Ipoh, Malacca, Seremban and villages along the east coast, and in the East Malaysian states of Sawarak and Sabah, coffee shops retain their pre-war ambience, serving basic and inexpensive dishes such as noodles, rice with a plethora of curries, stir-fried seafood and snacks such as curry puffs, Indian breads and other homely offerings.

In other parts of the country many of these coffee houses were abandoned and left to decay, but in recent decades their potential as tourist attractions has been realized.

In Kuala Lumpur, for instance, they have been air-conditioned and made more up-market, with prices to match. Their distinctive marble-topped tables and black bentwood chairs have now become a décor hallmark throughout Malaysia, emulated by interior designers furnishing luxury flats.

Above: The cityscape of Kuala Lumpur indicates this luxurious era.

At the same time there has been an upsurge of shopping complexes in major towns. These invariably feature a "food court", with formerly itinerant street hawkers housed in sparkling new premises. Restaurants from out-of-town areas have also opted to open establishments in these complexes, and they mark a definite change in eating habits among the locals. For Malaysians as well as tourists, they have become comfort zones to escape from the unyielding heat and humidity.

Most menus are still traditional, and serious foodies can find all their favourite dishes, but there are also the Western fast food counters with burgers and pizzas, patronized mainly by younger people. You can see the writing on the wall: it's only a matter of time before the old eating houses go the way of history, to be replaced by food courts with all the benefits of luxury living and dining. But for the moment Malaysia still has much to offer to visitors and locals looking for a traditional experience.

SINGAPOREAN CUISINE TODAY

Often referred to as the "Manhattan of the East", Singapore is a consumer's paradise, and food is a national obsession. Everywhere you go there is something to eat and everywhere you look people are eating. Food is a constant topic of conversation. Like Penang, Kuala Lumpur and Melaka, Singapore is rich in diverse cultures and food traditions, but to many Singaporeans the origin of the dish is unimportant as long as it is tasty. Chinese food dominates, followed closely by Malay and Indian.

Most fascinating of all is how the culinary culture of Singapore has evolved. With no agriculture, but a great deal of affluence so that all manner of goods can be imported, the cuisine of the tiny nation has developed from the humble barrow on the street corner, selling one simple dish cooked on a single burner, to some of the most sophisticated hawker stalls in the world.

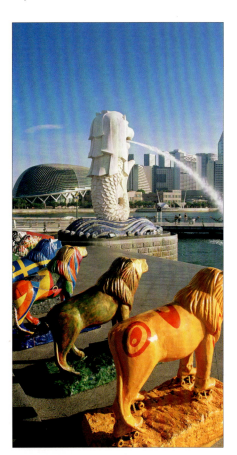

Above: Singapore City is vibrant and colourful, like its cuisine.

For those who wish to dine in style, the Singapore restaurant scene ranks with the best in Sydney, Paris and New York, as the chefs are always creating new recipes and fusions.

The hawker tradition and coffee shop culture are most popular in Singapore, as many people are busy and live in tiny apartments, so eating out is the obvious choice. For some, cooking at home is only a weekend activity. High-class, air-conditioned food courts with tables and chairs are located in shopping malls and at the foot of office buildings. Food halls offer a truly multicultural culinary mix, as adjacent hawker stalls enable diners to taste a bit of Indian, Chinese and Malay at the same meal. But some locals argue that the most authentic food is still to be found at the little stalls on wheels clustered outside markets and coffee shops or by the roadside in more rural areas.

FOOD TO GO

Muslim and Malay stalls are often grouped together, selling *sop kambing* (Indian-inspired mutton soup), *mee siam* (Thai-influenced spicy tangy noodles) and *bubur* (traditional Malay rice porridge), served with side dishes such as fried dried anchovies and a chilli sambal. At grill stalls you will find spicy chicken wings, stingray wings served in banana leaves, and fish, beef, chicken or lamb satay. Rice stalls may offer a selection of dishes or just one with their rice. Some offer specialities such as Hainanese chicken rice.

Cze cha stalls generally display a mix of Chinese and Malay snacks, such as noodles in broth, fish balls, stuffed chillies and dumplings filled with prawns (shrimp) and pork, while noodle stalls lure you with the sweet, spicy aromas of stir-fried prawns and clams, ginger and garlic. Rice cake stalls serve these South Indian specialities, with chutneys and sambals, for breakfast or a mid-morning snack, and the *roti* stalls specialize in more Indian staples such as flatbreads and various *dhals*.

Sweet stalls offer Malay, Chinese, Indian and Peranakan snacks and desserts, such as *gulab jamun*, the

Above: Customers waiting to be served at a street stall in Singapore selling Hainanese specialities.

Indian deep-fried sweetmeats made with coconut milk; *kueh-kueh*, which are Peranakan tea cakes; and Chinese sweet bean soups. Ice cream is also popular, and is sold from stalls and small refrigerators attached to bicycles.

Seasonal fruits are displayed at fruit and juice stalls and can be bought in wedges or blended into a drink. Snack stalls sell roasted chestnuts; salted or sugared *kacang*, which is a mixture of roasted peanuts, peas and beans; deep-fried prawn crackers; deep-fried bananas and *vadai* (dhal fritters).

As Singapore is divided into racial quarters, the hawker stalls and coffee shops follow a similar pattern. In Katong, the Peranakan and Eurasian section, they offer competitive versions of Singapore *laksa* (noodles in coconut milk) right next to coffee shops selling European tea cakes or Chinese chicken rice cafés. In Little India, the warm, spicy aromas of the Tekka Market attract Hindu, Muslim and Chinese shoppers, as well as the Nonyas (Peranakan ladies) and European *taitais* (ladies of leisure) who descend on the Indian coffee shops to tuck into a freshly made *roti paratha* (flaky flatbread), with sweet pulled tea.

The *dosai* shops sell Indian rice crêpes and vegetarian dishes, as they are run by Hindus who do not eat meat. In the same areas you will find Indian "banana leaf" restaurants, where the food is served on banana leaves.

Some dishes are unique to Singapore – they may be versions of traditional dishes from elsewhere that have been given a Singapore twist, or new creations by adventurous chefs. One that has become a Singapore classic is stir-fried chilli crab in a tomato sauce, which is invariably eaten with the fingers and mopped up with a crusty French baguette.

MARKETPLACES

The markets represent the fabulous reality of Singapore's integrated multiculturalism and culinary fusion, with a breathtaking volume and variety of local produce as well as imported fruits and vegetables from Australia, Japan, India and Ecuador, which are all vociferously haggled over. A typical market has wet and dry regions, divided into rows to separate meat from fish, vegetables from fruit, and dried beans and grains from condiments. At the edges, there are stalls selling pots and pans, brooms and mops, clothes and shoes, and makeshift food stalls selling snacks, fruit and drinks. Sweet iced coffee is popular in the Singapore sunshine, and busy workers rely on a crude version of "carry-out" coffee, served in cleaned-out condensed milk cans. The large central markets stay open all day, the local neighbourhood ones close at midday, and the open-air night markets close around midnight, creating a lovely evening throng.

How eateries have changed

Eating is a passion in Singapore, a national pastime quite simply because there's so much food and it's so good. Since Singapore's founding in 1819 by Englishman Stamford Raffles, its cooking has been a delicious amalgam of Chinese, British Colonial, Malay, Arab, Thai, Indian, Indonesian and European food elements.

Until the mid-1980s, hawkers plied their wares in makeshift carts, but government regulations and Singapore's massive urbanization programme then dictated that hawker stalls must be contained within purpose-built food courts. They are no longer termed hawkers, and have been relocated to covered complexes dotting the island. The flavours of street food still abound, but the ambience is more pristine than rustic. Many are air-conditioned with impeccable hygiene standards while others are relaxed, but all are in keeping with strict government health regulations.

One can still dine on a mélange of dishes when along the East Coast or within the plush comfort of five-star coffee-houses, purpose-built complexes in department stores and updated terraced shophouses. Obviously all this is reflected in the prices, though these, while higher than they used to be, are still affordable for most Singaporeans. The food itself has remained largely unchanged. The template for the food courts remains multicultural, a delicious gathering of many different cuisines under one roof. Most open until late at night, offering cheap and delicious ethnic dishes of every type.

Most of the dishes are those that evolved from the original hawkers. They are suited to mass catering and often call for fairly complex preparation, which householders are not inclined to do after a hard day's work. Many dishes require stir-frying in huge woks over roaring fires, which few homes have. It has become something of a national practice to stop by for dinner after work, or to buy cartons to take home.

Right: A statue of Sir Stamford Raffles in Singapore City reminds visitors of the city's colonial past.

REGIONAL FLAVOURS

The people of Malaysia and Singapore are proud of their diverse culinary cultures and regional food. In the cities you can eat just about anything, from traditional Hainanese chicken rice to contemporary chilli crab. At the heart and soul of Malay food is the *rempah*, a spicy mixture made by first pounding wet ingredients such as shallots, ginger, garlic and chilli, and then adding dry spices such as coriander seeds, cardamom and ground turmeric, to form a paste. This mixture is then cooked in oil before any of the other ingredients of the dish are added.

Rice is the basis of many traditional Malay meals, either cooked plain or flavoured with coconut milk or spices. Traditional rice dishes include *ketupat* (pressed rice cooked in coconut fronds) and *lemang* (rice stuffed into hollow bamboo tubes lined with banana leaves and cooked over a charcoal fire). Generally, a Malay meal consists of a fish or shellfish curry or a meat or chicken dish, served with rice, a vegetable dish and a chilli sambal. Bread is often served instead of rice, particularly with dishes in which there is lots of richly flavoured sauce that begs to be mopped up with chunks of fresh, crusty baguette. The Malays also enjoy the Indian flat, flaky bread, *roti paratha*, with curries. They also often eat it as a snack, sprinkled with sugar. Each group eats the same foods in slightly different ways, adjusting the balance to suit their taste, such as the Malay desire for a chilli kick with every mouthful. In rural Malaysia the food is more regionalized.

LOCAL SPECIALITIES

In Kedah and Perlis in the north of the Malay Peninsula, the Thai influence is evident. The fishermen and rice farmers of these two states favour simple fish dishes, flavoured with chillies, lemon grass, kaffir lime leaves, lime juice and fish sauce. These are often tempered with a sweet prawn (shrimp) sauce, *otak udang*, and served with herbs and shredded cucumber.

Ipoh is well known for its authentic Chinese food, introduced by the immigrant population that worked in the tin mines; Penang and Melaka are famed for their delicious Nonya dishes; and Kelantan is regarded as pure Malay.

It boasts some unique specialities, such as *nasi dagang* (glutinous rice cooked in coconut milk and served with fish, grated coconut, herbs and sauces), the famous *nasi kerabu*, a rice dish tinted blue with dye from the pea flower, and *bunga telang*, which is served with fish crackers and fried salted fish.

In Terengganu, the savoury pastries, *epok-epok*, are filled with fish and grated coconut, and the local delicacy, *satar*, is made by stuffing banana-leaf cones with a spicy-sour fish paste and grilling them over charcoal. The Malay speciality, *rendang* (beef cooked in coconut milk), is held to be best in Negeri Sembilan, where it is served with *lemang*, glutinous rice cooked with coconut milk inside bamboo poles positioned over a fire.

In Johor, a local speciality is *satay Johor*, in which skewered meat is continuously basted with a mixture of coconut milk and oil, brushed on with a lemon grass stalk, which imparts a delicate flavour. *Laksa Johor* is also popular: noodles in coconut milk are served with chunks of herring and flavoured with tamarind and mint.

THE TRIBES OF SABAH

Borneo is home to an astonishing number of animal species as well as tribal peoples whose way of life hardly seems to have changed with the centuries. In Sabah, the northernmost state, there are some 30 tribes, speaking 50 or more dialects and languages. Sabah has a huge diversity of ethnic groups who have settled there over hundreds of years and adapted their eating styles to the local habitat. The Kadazans, the main tribal community in the west, favour the sour tastes of unripe mangoes, limes and tangy star fruit and are particularly proud of their fish dish, *hinava tongii*, which combines fresh mackerel with

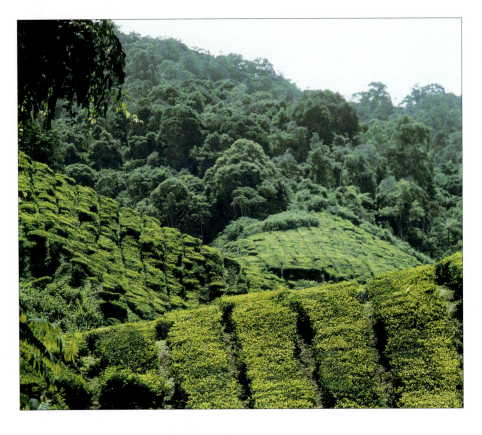

Left: The dense and fertile Cameron Highlands in Pahang have attracted thousands of planters and farmers and, as a result, vegetable crops, flowers and tea bushes still grow in profusion in the plateaux and on the foothills.

Left: Childen of the Orang Asli tribe In Taman Negara, Malaysia.

PENANG: GASTRONOMIC HEAVEN

The varied cuisine of Penang has led to its acclaim as Malaysia's food capital. Specialities of the island include the Indian-inspired *murtabak*, flatbread filled with spicy minced (ground) beef or lamb and vegetables; Peranakan *pasembur*, a salad of yam, bean, tofu, cuttlefish and cucumber tossed with beansprouts and prawn (shrimp) fritters in a sweet and sour dressing; Penang *asam laksa*, the local noodles in coconut milk, with flakes of mackerel, garnished with pineapple, cucumber, chilli, mint and shrimp paste; and *pong piah*, a Hokkien dish of flaky pastry filled with milky syrup.

The Indian coffee shops in Penang are also famous for their pulled tea, *teh tarik*, which is deliciously sweet and frothy. It is usually made by a man, who pours the sweetened tea from a metal pot held above his head into another one held below his waist and repeats the process several times until a layer of froth has formed on the surface and the tea has cooled to drinking temperature, when it is poured into the cup. Also known descriptively as *teh terbang*, or "flying tea", it is an acquired skill, and a spectacle that is just as popular with the locals as it is with tourists.

Below: Penang harbour's ragged stilt houses are the gateway to a "gastronomic heaven".

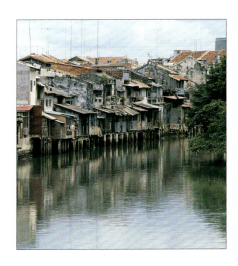

chillies, ginger, shallots and lime juice and one special ingredient that makes all the difference – the grated stone (pit) of a local mango, the bambangan. Dried shrimps and anchovies are added to many dishes.

Sabah's national fish dish, *hinava*, consists of finely sliced raw fish marinated in lime juice and herbs.

The Bisaya, a Muslim group, use the sago to make a thick porridge, *ambuyat*, which they dip into a fiery sambal. In the hilly south-west, the Murut hunt wild boar, chop up the meat and stuff it, with chunks of freshwater fish, jungle leaves, rice grains and salt, into the hollow of bamboo stems, where the mixture is left to ferment for weeks, even months. This pungent speciality, *jaruk*, is eaten with steamed rice or tapioca. A local beverage, rice wine, or *tapai*, is made from glutinous rice and yeast, and is enjoyed by the non-Muslim Sabahan tribespeople. The Murut are traditionally rice and tapioca (cassava) farmers, but are recently expanding to cultivate vegetables, such as aubergines (eggplants) and spinach. Tropical plants and fruits provide spice and sweetness to their cooking.

THE JUNGLES OF SARAWAK

Like Sabah, Sarawak is a world apart from the Malaysian peninsula. Covered with dense rainforests, rivers, caves and national parks, this state is home to the Dayaks, Ibans, Melanau and other indigenous tribes. Longhouses and river excursions through the jungles using head-hunter trails are part of the tourist experience, as is the city of Kuching. Although rice is grown in Sarawak, vast areas of the land are too swampy for paddies, so some tribes rely on the wild sago palm for carbohydrate. A Melanau fisherman's dish, *umai*, consists of finely sliced raw fish, marinated in tamarind or lime juice with chopped shallots, chillies and salt, and served with a bowl of toasted sago pearls. In Sabah the sago pearls are boiled to make a porridge-like paste, usually eaten with a fiery sambal. Sago grubs (young caterpillars found in sago palms) are also popular among tribal peoples.

Wild boar and deer are Sarawakan favourites, roasted whole over charcoal, or used for satay dishes, accompanied by vegetable dishes. Most tribes make their own arak, a local liquor, and tuak, rice wine, which are very potent.

NONYA CUISINE

When the early Chinese traders began to settle in the ports of Penang, Melaka and Singapore from the 15th century onward, a number of them married local Malay women to create an ethnic sub-group of Malay-Chinese. In Malay, this group is called Peranakan, which means "half caste", but they also refer to themselves as Straits Chinese to distinguish themselves from the Chinese immigrant workers who came to the Malay Peninsula later.

Using the Peranakan words for male (*baba*) and female (*nonya*), this group was also referred to as the Baba-Nonyas, and was noted for its distinctive dress, lavishly decorated homes and, above all, for its cuisine. The Peranakans were relatively wealthy,

so they were able to indulge in elaborate meals that were an inspired mix of Chinese and Malay traditions. As the food was prepared by the women, it became known as Nonya cuisine.

To this day, the unique Nonya cooking is highly praised and much sought after, with its lavish use of chillies, lemon grass, galangal and turmeric fused with elements of Indian, Thai, Portuguese and Chinese cooking methods. Classic Nonya dishes include *mee siam*, a Thai-influenced dish of rice noodles in a spicy, tangy sauce, and

Left: A street food vendor fanning the flames at a satay stall.

Below: Pulau Pertentian in Malaysia is one of many unspoilt beauty spots.

creature, and rice can be served with anything from duck's feet, to dog, to sea cucumber. The Chinese communities of Malaysia and Singapore still eat much the same as their ancestors, based on the principles of yin and yang: sweet and sour, hot and cold, plain and spicy.

The Indian and Malay influence has in turn made an impact on some of the traditional Chinese dishes, particularly those served at hawker stalls in Singapore. Spicy favourites include *char kway teow*, stir-fried rice noodles with prawns (shrimp), squid and Chinese sausage, and Hainanese chicken rice, which is served with a dish of chillies on the side to satisfy the Malay taste for hot spicy flavours. A legacy of the 19th-century colonial period, when the British acquired Malaya and Singapore, is the addition of Western ingredients. The British "cookboys" were generally Hainanese, so tomato ketchup and Worcestershire sauce appear among the more conventional ingredients of some of the Chinese dishes.

babi pong tey, a pork stew cooked in an earthenware pot. It is worth looking out for Nonya *tok panjang*, which translates as "Nonya long table". It consists of an elaborate buffet spread of Nonya specialities. The style of eating is similar to Malay, as most dishes are served with rice or bread and are accompanied by a chilli sambal or a bowl of fiery chillies.

Above: A typical Malaysian open air market, full of colour.

Below: Women in Langkawi harvest the rice crops in the traditional way.

INDIAN AND CHINESE STALLS

The most distinctive style of Indian cooking is that found at the *mamak* (Indian Muslim) hawker stalls, particularly in Singapore, where the cooks combine Malay and Indian flavours and techniques. The resulting spicy dishes are in a class of their own, such as *mee rebus* (thick, fresh, egg noodles in a sweet, spicy sauce served with eggs and chillies) and *rojak* (a crispy vegetable salad with fried tofu and fish cakes in a spicy-sweet sauce). A feature of Indian food that stands out from the rest is the use of yogurt as a cooling accompaniment to hot curries, either served plain, or mixed with vegetables and herbs in a *raita* or *pachadi*, or blended in *lassi*, a popular refreshing yogurt drink.

Traditionally, rice has always been the staple of Chinese cooking. The Chinese do not waste any part of any living

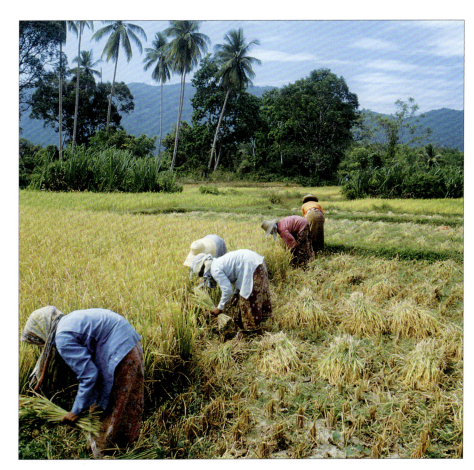

CELEBRATIONS AND FESTIVALS

With such a variety of culinary cultures, every religious or family celebration is a banquet of delights. Traditional weddings involve a great deal of feasting, some of which is symbolic and can span several days. Throughout Malaysia and Singapore, births also require ceremonial feasting, which often takes place on the 100th day of the child's life in Chinese and Peranakan households. Special foods are called for at Chinese New Year, the Muslim Hari Raya Puasa, Indian Diwali, Christmas and other festivals.

WEDDINGS

At Malay weddings, the feasting is on a huge scale, with hundreds of guests who must be served a selection of rice dishes and curries. As they depart, each guest is presented with delicately wrapped gifts of hard-boiled eggs to ensure fertility for the newlyweds. Indian weddings also operate on a large scale, with a vast selection of dishes tailored to the various religious and regional groups, such as Bengalis, Punjabis and Tamils, attending.

Chinese weddings are more restrained, with a traditional tea ceremony and a family banquet. On an auspicious day, the groom visits the bride's house to pay his respects and ask for her hand. When accepted, the groom and his bride return to his home, where they kneel before his parents and older relatives and serve them a specially brewed tea to symbolize that the bride will undertake her new role of serving and caring for her in-laws. The final banquet is usually supplied by the groom's parents, who take traditional gifts of food, such as a suckling pig, to be eaten at the bride's house.

In a Peranakan marriage, the bride's future mother-in-law traditionally cooks a special coconut rice dish, *nasi lemak*, which she takes as a symbolic offering to the bride's mother to reassure her that the bride is still a virgin.

CHRISTMAS

The snow that traditionally accompanies Christmas in northern Europe may not appear in Malaysia and Singapore, but there is no shortage of fake snow, twinkling lights, furs, shiny baubles and silver tinsel. Christmas may be a Eurasian festival, but everyone joins in, from the decorations to the presents and feasting. In Eurasian households, it is common to find roast turkey on the Christmas table – stuffed with glutinous rice, pork and chestnuts. Honey-baked hams keep up the Western tradition, but are often accompanied by chicken or pork curries, such as curry *debal* and *feng*, which is made a day in advance to enhance the flavour. With such a colourful European and Malay heritage, the Eurasians draw from all their different influences at Christmas, adding soy-based dishes, chilli dips, steamed cabbage rolls, fruit cakes and sponge cakes to the feast. As most Eurasians are Catholic, they attend midnight mass on Christmas Eve and return home to a table laden with festive delicacies.

CHINESE NEW YEAR

Shortly after Christmas, preparations for the Chinese New Year begin. Traditionally, this festival marked the advent of spring for the Chinese farmers, but for the largely urban Chinese population the event represents a spiritual renewal rather than a physical one. Houses are cleaned, debts settled, new clothes bought and gifts of money exchanged. On New Year's Day, orange segments are presented to guests for good fortune, and sweets (candy) and cakes are offered to ensure a sweet future.

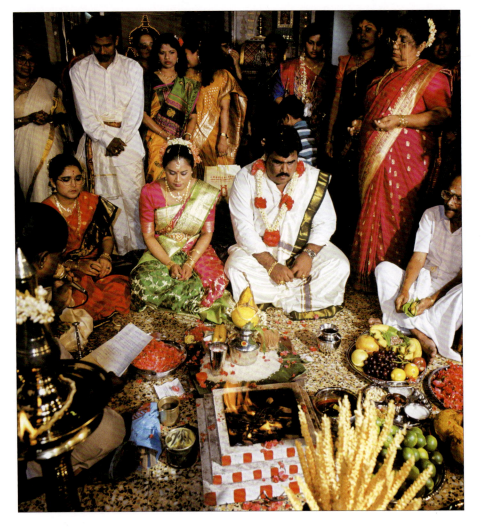

Left: A traditional wedding feast of local fruits and specialities laid out before a newly-married Hindu couple.

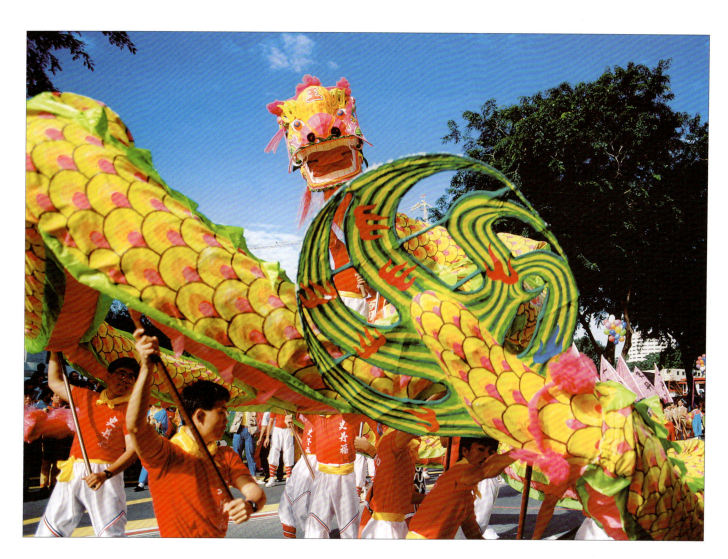

In Malaysia, a Peranakan New Year meal usually includes chicken cooked in a tamarind sauce. In Singapore, on the seventh day of the New Year, Chinese families eat *yu sheng*, a salad of finely sliced raw fish, tossed with shredded vegetables, candied melon, pomelo segments, strips of jellyfish, peanuts, sesame seeds and lime juice, which they believe will bring them prosperity in the year to come.

HARI RAYA PUASA

The third major festival on the calendar is the Muslim Hari Raya Puasa, which marks the end of Ramadan, the month of fasting and abstaining from other sensory pleasures between dawn and dusk. For the men, the day begins with prayers in the mosques; they then go on to the cemeteries to pay their respects to dead relatives. The women prepare the feast at home, making *rendang* (beef cooked in coconut milk), which is served with *ketupat* (compressed rice

cakes) and *serunding*, a side dish of grated coconut fried with chilli. Once this meal is over, friends and family visit one another, bearing gifts of food, cakes and sweetmeats, which are enjoyed with tea and coffee or syrupy drinks.

DIWALI

The Festival of Lights, Diwali, is a Hindu celebration, marking the triumph of good over evil. It takes place on the rising of the new moon in the seventh month of the Hindu calendar, when oil lamps and candles are lit to welcome Lakshmi, the goddess of wealth. To celebrate the occasion, a wonderful array of spicy vindaloo and biryani dishes, flatbreads and chutneys are prepared for gatherings of friends and relatives.

GAWAI DAYAK

In Sarawak, the Dayak (the collective name for all the tribes of the area) celebrate the end of the rice harvest

Above: Chinese New Year celebrations in Singapore involve colourful processions and special feasts.

with a festival, Gawai Dayak. Feasts and a ceremony to cast out the spirit of greediness commence on 31st May, and continue overnight into 1st June. Preparations, cooking and fermenting wine starts well in advance, and on Gawai eve, glutinous rice is roasted in bamboo. The communities celebrate this festival, with a great deal of merry-making and dancing, enhanced by the home-brewed rice wine, tuak.

Cockfights, war dances and blow pipe competitions are all part of the festivities, which are rounded off with local delicacies, such as *ikan kasam* (fermented fish stir-fried with black beans) and a touch more alcohol in the fermented durian pulp, *tempoyak*.

At this time many Dayak weddings take place, as it is the only occasion when so many people get together.

BEVERAGES AND SNACKS

Snacking is a great Malay and Chinese tradition. At times it seems as if the locals never stop nibbling. With such an emphasis on hawker stalls and food centres, there are always delicious cooking odours enticing you to stop and have a little bite to eat. Very often these snacks will be grilled (broiled) or deep-fried, the simplest methods of cooking at a stall. Street stalls still exist in Malaysia so it is possible to snack as you walk through the towns.

At the grill stalls, which are easily identified by the enticing aromas that travel through the clouds of smoke, you can tuck into the tastiest spicy chicken wings, grilled stingray wings, and the ever-popular satay. A great Malay favourite, satay probably evolved from the Arab kebab, which would have been introduced to Melaka by Arab traders once Islam had taken hold of the region. With such an eclectic mix of cultures in Malaysia and Singapore, the traditional tender pork or chicken chunks grilled on skewers has developed, and satay dishes now include every form of fish and seafood, vegetables such as aubergines (eggplants) and sweet potatoes, beef, water buffalo, duck, wild boar in Sabah and mutton or goat in Sarawak. All these different kinds of satay are served with a piquant peanut or pineapple sauce, or a chilli sambal to suit those with a taste for fiery dishes.

Above: Coconut features in many sweet drinks and desserts.

BUFFETS AND ROTI STALLS

Another interesting place to find savoury snacks is the *cze cha* stall, which is a kind of self-service buffet spread. Usually, a stack of bowls flank the appetizing display of tasty delights, such as stuffed chillies, fried tofu, stir-fried kangkong (water spinach), Chinese spring rolls, and the Nonya version, *popiah*, to which diners help themselves.

When it comes to breakfast, Indian *roti* stalls and hopper stands are very popular places for nourishment on the run, as well as for stopping for a sustaining snack. The griddle-fried, flaky flatbread, *roti paratha*, is one of the most popular breads to accompany Malay, Nonya and Indian dishes. In its many guises, it emerges as *roti kaya*, smeared in coconut jam, and *roti telur*, with an egg cracked in the middle, or as a slight variation on the theme, *roti bawang telur*, where the egg in the middle is topped with chopped onions.

Other breads on offer include *murtabak*, which is similar to *roti paratha* but filled with spicy minced (ground) lamb, chicken or vegetables; various forms of *dosai*, which are paper-thin crêpes made with rice and lentils; and *appam* or hoppers, the fermented rice cakes that are cooked in tiny, individual woks and served with sugar as a sweet treat.

Above: A street fruit vendor in Malaysia, where an abundance of exotic fruits makes for exciting drinks and desserts.

Above: Oysters are a snack enjoyed in upmarket seafood bars.

REFRESHING SNACKS

To cool you down in the heat of the day, the Malay stalls have a selection of sweet, refreshing snacks made with ice. *Ais kacang* consists of red beans, seaweed jelly and corn in a pool of condensed milk, topped with shavings of ice and palm sugar syrup, whereas the popular *ais ball* is basically a ball of ice filled with red beans and smeared in rose syrup, condensed milk and palm syrup. Ice cream is served between wafers or tucked into a slice of bread.

JUICE DRINKS

Drink carts are another feature of the street markets, food halls and shopping centres of Malaysia and Singapore. With such a wealth of home-grown fruits, there are plenty to squeeze or blend into refreshing drinks to cool down passers-by in the heat and humidity. Fruits such as pineapples, mangoes and watermelons are blended to make delicious concoctions – the local favourite in Singapore is made with carrots and oranges. Sugar cane is pressed to extract sweet juice, which is served with a wedge of lemon. Lime juice, pressed from the tiny, dark green kalamansi limes with their pale orange flesh, is served in coffee shops as a palate soother and cleanser when eating curry and spicy dishes. Coconut water, served in the actual coconut, is also

regarded as a tamer of the palate. When served at roadside stalls in Malaysia, the tops of green coconuts are carved to a point and the tip is lopped off, enabling you to drink the water and eat the flesh at the same time.

The drink stalls and carts also produce a variety of sweet drinks that are more like snacks. The Malay favourite, *air bandung*, is a sweet condensed milk drink flavoured with pink rose syrup and served chilled. *Air soya* is a protein-rich soya bean milk drink, which can be drunk hot or cold. *Air cincau* is considered a herbal tonic, as it is made with a pandan-flavoured syrup with strands of black agar agar, and avocados are blended with condensed milk to make thick, nourishing milkshakes.

Leaning towards the category of a sweet snack, rather than a drink, is *candol*. This is made by placing fine mung bean noodles in the bottom of a glass, followed by palm sugar syrup and coconut milk, and topping it with ice. Also available at stalls and coffee shops

Above: Many visitors go out for cocktails at the Raffles Hotel in Singapore City.

are *air mata kuching*, a kind of Chinese tea made by boiling red dates and dried longans in water; and *lassi*, an Indian yogurt drink. The Indonesians and Malays also enjoy their own version of *lassi*, sweet or savoury, flavoured with mint, puréed mango or rose water.

ALCOHOLIC BEVERAGES

In general, alcohol is frowned upon in Malaysia, given the predominantly Muslim foundation of the culture. The non-Muslim peoples of Sarawak and Sabah, however, indulge in their local alcoholic beverages of palm-sap and rice wine.

In Singapore, where there is a high Chinese population and a number of Catholic Eurasians and international residents, alcohol is consumed more liberally. Wines, beers and cocktails, such as the famous Singapore Sling, are all available in most of the bars, restaurants and hotels.

THE FOOD AND COOKING OF MALAYSIA AND SINGAPORE

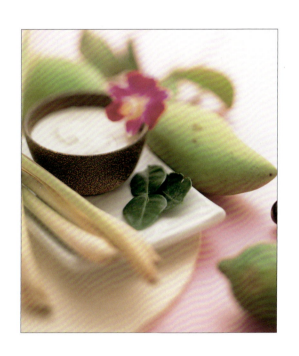

The culinary cultures of Malaysia and Singapore have both been influenced by the cuisines of India, Thailand, China and Eurasia, so there are inevitably many similarities. Fish and rice are the staples of both countries, and there is a strong emphasis on coconut milk combined with spices and herbs, such as ginger, lemon grass, garlic, chillies and coriander.

EQUIPMENT

The traditional Southeast Asian kitchen is basic. Often dark and sparsely kitted out with an open hearth, very little equipment is needed. Food is generally bought daily from the markets, taken home and cooked immediately, so unless you visit the kitchen during the frenzied moments of activity over the hearth, there is little evidence of food or cooking in homes.

In the days when there were no refrigerators, the reliance on fresh produce from the daily markets was vital. For some, two visits to the market were required – in the morning for the ingredients to cook for lunch, and in the afternoon for the evening meal.

Back in the kitchen, the activity begins with the scrubbing of vegetables, the plucking and jointing of birds (if it hasn't been done in the markets), endless chopping and slicing, and the pounding of herbs and spices with a mortar and pestle.

WOK

The wok is the most important utensil for everyday cooking and everybody has one. Without a doubt, there is always something delicious being stir-fried in a home or in the streets. However, woks are not only used for stir-frying, they are also used for steaming, deep-frying, braising and soup-making. The most functional, multi-purpose wok should measure approximately 35cm/14in across, large enough for a family meal or to steam a whole fish. The most common wok is double-handled and made of lightweight carbonized steel. This is ideal for deep-frying and steaming but, for stir-frying, you need the single-handled version.

When you first buy a wok, you need to season it before use. Put it over a high heat to blacken the inside – this burns off any dust and factory coating. Leave the wok to cool, then immerse it in hot, soapy water and clean it with an abrasive cloth or stiff brush. Rinse it well and dry over a medium heat. Pour a little cooking oil into the base and, using kitchen paper, wipe all around the surface of the wok. Now the wok is ready for use.

After each use, clean the wok with hot water only, dry it over a medium heat, and wipe a thin layer of oil over the surface. This will ensure that it doesn't get rusty.

Above: A solid mortar and pestle is an essential piece of kitchen equipment.

MORTAR AND PESTLE

A big mortar and pestle, made of stone, is of particular value, as it is used not only for grinding spices, chillies and garlic, but also for pounding all the condiments and pastes, as well as the meat for pâtés and savoury balls. Some cooks have several mortar and pestle sets, varying in size according to the activity and ingredient. Coffee grinders and electric blenders can be used as substitutes, but they don't release the oils and flavours of the ingredients in the same way and they produce too smooth a texture. It is worth looking for a solid stone mortar and pestle in Asian markets and kitchen suppliers.

BAMBOO STEAMER

Traditional bamboo steamers come in various sizes. The most practical one is about 30cm/12in wide, as it can be used for rice or a whole fish. Generally, the steamer is set directly over a wok that is filled with boiling water to below the level of the steamer. The food is placed in the steamer, either on a plate, or wrapped in muslin (cheesecloth), or banana leaves. The lid is placed on the steamer and, as the water in the wok is heated, the steam rises under and around the food, cooking it gently. A stainless steel steamer is no substitute for a bamboo one, which imparts its

Left: A single-handled wok is good for stir-frying; a double-handled wok is better for steaming and deep-frying.

own delicate fragrance to the dish. Bamboo steamers are available in most Asian stores and some cooking equipment suppliers.

CHOPSTICKS

For cooking, look for long chopsticks made from bamboo. Chopsticks are used to eat with, as well as for cooking, though Malaysian food is often eaten with the hand (always the right hand). Following Chinese methods, many cooks will use a set of long chopsticks for stirring, mixing, tasting, and as tongs. Eating chopsticks are traditionally made from bamboo or wood, but more elaborate ones can be made from ivory, bone, gold, silver or jade.

CLAY POT

Made from a combination of light-coloured clay and sand, these pots come in all sizes, with single or double handles, lids, and glazed interiors.

Right: Bamboo steamers come in several sizes.

Perhaps the oldest form of cooking vessel, these attractive pots are ideal for slow-cooking, braised dishes and soups, as they retain an overall even heat. Generally, they are used on the stove over a low or medium heat, as a high temperature could cause a crack. When you first buy a clay pot, it needs to be treated for cooking. Fill it with water and place it over a low flame, then gradually increase the heat and let the water boil until it is reduced by half. Rinse the pot and dry it thoroughly. Now it is ready for use. Traditional clay pots are available in some Asian markets.

Above: A clay pot can be used in the oven or, with care, on the stove.

Left: Bamboo chopsticks are essential kitchen equipment.

Above: A medium-weight cleaver is a multi-purpose tool.

CLEAVERS

Asian cleavers are the most important tools in the kitchen. There are special blades for the fine chopping of lemon grass and green papaya, heavy blades for opening coconuts, thin ones for shredding spring onions (scallions), and multi-purpose ones for any type of chopping, slicing and crushing. Generally, you use the front, lighter part of the blade for the regular chopping, slicing and shredding; the back, heavier section is for chopping with force through bones; and the flat side is ideal for crushing ginger and garlic, and for transporting ingredients into the wok.

DRAINING SPOONS

Traditional draining spoons are made of wire and have a long bamboo handle; more modern ones are made completely of stainless steel with a perforated spoon. Both are flat and extremely useful for deep-frying, for blanching noodles and for scooping ingredients out of any hot liquid.

Above: Draining spoons are useful for deep-frying and blanching.

COOKING TECHNIQUES

The traditional cooking methods of Malaysia and Singapore require few culinary tools but a great deal of attention to detail. Fresh ingredients are of the utmost importance, followed by the balance of sharp or mild, salty or sweet, bitter or sour, or a combination of all of these flavours. The layering of ingredients is also important, especially in noodle dishes, where flavours and textures should complement each other but remain separate.

Many meals are prepared from scratch, starting with the plucking of chickens and grinding of spices, followed by grilling over charcoal, gentle simmering and steaming, or stir-frying. Armed with the correct equipment, the cooking is easy – most of the work, and the key to culinary success, is in the preparation.

STEAMING

This is a popular way of preparing delicate-tasting foods, such as fish and shellfish, pork-filled dumplings and sticky rice cakes wrapped in bamboo or banana leaves. Place the food in a bamboo steamer, which should be lined with leaves if the food isn't wrapped in them. Put the lid on the steamer and set it over a wok that is half-filled with water. Bring the water to the boil, then reduce the heat and steam the food according to the recipe.

Above: Fish wrapped in banana leaves with spices steams to perfumed perfection on a bamboo rack.

DRY-FRYING

Dried spices are often roasted before grinding to release their natural oils and enhance the aroma.

1 Spread the spices thinly in a wok or heavy pan and put it over a high heat.

2 As the pan begins to heat, shake it so that the spices don't get too brown.

3 Once the spices begin to colour and their aroma fills the air, put them in a mortar and grind to a powder.

BRAISING

The classic slow-cooking method is braising. Oily fish, duck and red meat are often cooked this way, with herbs, spices and coconut milk or juice.

Traditionally, to seal in the moisture, a covered clay pot is used. Placed over a medium heat, or in the oven, cooking can take from 30 minutes to 2 hours, depending on the dish. If you don't have a clay pot, use a heavy-based casserole. The key is in containing the moisture and even heat distribution, so don't use a thin aluminium pot. Simply put all the ingredients in a clay pot and place in a preheated oven. (It can also be placed over a medium heat on the stove if you prefer.)

GRILLING OVER CHARCOAL

As conventional grills (broilers) don't exist in most homes in Southeast Asia, grilling is generally done outdoors over hot charcoal.

This traditional method of cooking not only lends itself to many types of food, it also enhances the taste. Whole fish, pigs or chickens can be cooked this way. Tasty, marinated morsels of food, skewered on bamboo sticks and grilled in the streets, make popular snacks. When cooking over charcoal, light the coals and wait until they are covered with grey or white ashes. If the charcoal is too hot, the food will just burn.

Wooden and bamboo skewers
If you are using wooden or bamboo skewers, soak them in water for about 30 minutes before using to prevent them from burning.

STIR-FRYING

Of all the cooking techniques, this is the most important one in Malaysia and Singapore. The technique is more in the preparation of ingredients than in the cooking process, which takes only minutes. Generally, the ingredients should be cut or shredded into bitesize morsels and laid out in the order in which they are to be cooked. To stir-fry successfully you need a wok, placed over a high heat, and a ladle or spatula to toss the ingredients around, so that they cook but still retain their freshness and crunchy texture.

In stir frying, the key is to work quickly and layer the ingredients according to the length of time they require for cooking. Serve the dish hot straight from the wok into warmed bowls and don't leave the food sitting in the wok – it must be enjoyed fresh.

1 Pour a little oil into the wok and place it over a high heat until hot.

2 Add the spices and aromatics to the oil – it should sizzle on contact – and toss them around to flavour the oil. It is important to keep stirring quickly in order to move the ingredients around the wok and ensure that they do not burn. They will release plenty of aroma.

3 Add the pieces of meat or fish, and toss them in the wok for two minutes.

4 Add the sliced firm vegetables or mushrooms and stir-fry for a minute.

5 Add the leafy vegetables or beansprouts and toss them around quickly.

6 Finally, toss in the herbs, seasonings or sauce, mix well and serve piping hot.

DEEP-FRYING

Use an oil that can be heated to a high temperature, such as groundnut (peanut) oil, and don't put in too much cold food at once, as this will cool the oil down.

1 Pour the oil into a wok or pan (filling it no more than two-thirds full) and heat to about 180°C/350°F. To test the temperature, add a drop of batter or a piece of onion. If it sinks, the oil is not hot enough; if it burns, it is too hot. If it sizzles and rises to the surface, the temperature is perfect.

2 Cook the food in small batches until crisp and lift out with a slotted spoon or wire mesh skimmer when cooked. Drain on a wire rack lined with kitchen paper and serve immediately, or keep warm in the oven until ready to serve.

BLANCHING

This method is often used to cook delicate meat such as chicken breast portions or duck.

Place the meat and any flavourings in a pan and add just enough water to cover. Bring to the boil, then remove from the heat and leave to stand, covered, for 10 minutes, then drain.

RICE

Rice has been a staple crop throughout most of tropical Asia for many generations, and it is around a communal bowl of comfortingly hot, fluffy white rice that most meals are built. Rich in carbohydrate and containing vitamins A and B, rice is one of the healthiest grains. From it comes rice vinegar and rice wine, which are also indispensable to Chinese cooking, which influences dishes in Malaysia and Singapore and throughout South-east Asia. Ground rice flour is made into rice noodles, *dim sum* dumpling skins, and a wide range of sweet puddings.

For good reason,rice is regarded as the "staff of life" and some superstitions connected to its power still hold sway. In every rice-eating household, there is invariably a large barrel or tin in which the raw rice is stored. This must never be completely emptied as it is bad feng shui. As the last few grains are reached families hurriedly top the container up to the brim for fear of attracting bad luck or negative energy. In "rice bowl" areas such as the north Malaysian state of Kedah, rice agriculture is bound up with reverent rites and near mystical rituals, in which offerings are made to the rice deity.

In times past, freshly harvested rice was pounded in an enormous pestle and mortar and then winnowed to

Below: A Malaysian farmer harvests his rice crop.

remove the husk and bran before it could be cooked. Commercial milling of rice began in the mid-19th century. Singapore has virtually no agricultural land and rice has never been grown here to any extent.

All meals are communal, built around rice, and the colloquial greeting among older people is "Have you eaten rice?" which is the equivalent of asking "How are you?" It truly reflects the reverence in which the grain is held. Be it a Chinese, Malay, Peranakan or Indian meal, rice is on the menu.

RICE DISHES

There are only two methods of cooking rice: boiling and steaming. But the precious grain is by no means confined to being boiled and eaten unadorned. Once cooked thus, it can be used as the basis of many other dishes. Indian cooking especially has elevated rice to delicious heights, matched by few others for spicy ingenuity. Rice with saffron, turmeric, ghee and mustard oil, enriched with nuts and seeds, is translated into glorious pilaffs.

Within the Chinese kitchen, rice receives much the same reverence, and special *yang chao* fried rice has become a global culinary favourite. Jasmine rice, also called Thai fragrant rice, is grown widely in China, Malaysia, Thailand and Indonesia and forms the basis of most Chinese and Malay rice dishes in both Malaysia and Singapore. Good quality

Above: Jasmine or Thai fragrant rice has tender, aromatic grains. It is widely available in supermarkets in the West.

jasmine rice has a subtly delicate scent, with dry, thin and firm grains that are translucent when raw. Boiled or steamed, the texture should be firm and still retain some bite. The colour should be a pristine white and when you rake it with a fork, it should fluff up nicely.

LONG GRAIN RICE

Basmati has the longest grain of all in proportion to its size, and peculiarly the grains become longer and not wider when cooked. Long grain and Basmati rice are indigenous to India and Pakistan and are grown mainly in the Punjab. They are ideal for many humble or grand Muglai dishes.

Basmati rice has a distinctive, nutty flavour and is popular among Malaysian and Singapore Indians for cooking their beloved biryanis. It is also becoming increasingly popular with Chinese cooks, as the longer, denser grains lend themselves to frying without clumping together. Both Basmati and American long grain are far less sticky than short grain rice.

SHORT GRAIN RICE

Chinese Teochew families eat a traditional meal called Teochew *mui*, or *congee*, which is made using short grain rice cooked until it resembles porridge, with a lot of milky liquid that is reputed to settle the stomach. *Congee* is served with a wide range of pickles, stir fries and simple dishes.

GLUTINOUS RICE

All types of rice contain a certain amount of starch, though all are gluten free. The varieties imported from Thailand and Laos, whether long grain or jasmine, tend to contain relatively high levels; hence the produce of these regions is known as "sticky rice" or "glutinous rice". There are two kinds of starch in any cereal grain: amylase and amylopectin. Sticky rice is high in amylopectin, and when the rice is cooked, these molecules form a gel, enclosing water within their strands.

Glutinous rice accounts for less than 2 per cent of world output and it is used mainly in desserts, although people in the north of Malaysia serve it in tandem with normal rice. Preference for this rice here is very likely due to the influence of Thai immigrants.

Glutinous rice comes in both long and short grain varieties. The grains have to be soaked for several hours, sometimes overnight, before cooking. For festive dishes such as saffron or turmeric rice for Malay weddings, it is turned out as savoury offerings, often perfumed with rose water, cinnamon and cloves. It is rarely boiled and eaten plain as part of a meal unless for a special occasion such as the Nonya Long Table feast. Glutinous rice mainly lends itself to the making of dumplings, puddings and festive sweets.

In contrast to normal long grain rice, the highly polished, glutinous rice grain is an opaque white colour when raw, and turns translucent when cooked. Although the texture of cooked glutinous rice is quite firm, it is nevertheless sticky and clumps together like a lump of dough. It is this characteristic that makes it popular as a wraparound for a range of filled rice dishes. During the Chinese Dragon Boat festival, also called the Dumpling Festival, triangular dumplings are made with glutinous rice encasing spicy meat or mung bean paste. They are boiled for several hours and eaten as a snack.

Above: Black and white glutinous rice.

BLACK GLUTINOUS RICE

This unpolished, wholegrain glutinous rice is almost exclusively used for sweet dishes. When soaked in water and cooked, the grains turn a deep reddish-purple. In Malaysia and Singapore, black sticky rice is called *pulut hitam*, and in the Nonya dessert of the same name it is served with coconut cream and palm sugar. It must be soaked for several hours or overnight before cooking. Black sticky rice is available in some Asian markets.

Above: Patna rice is one of the many types of long-grain rice.

RICE PRODUCTS

There are many rice products that you will begin to use when you get familiar with the food of Malaysia and Singapore and widen your repertoire.

Ground rice or rice flour

Used in making all kinds of sticky sweets and cakes, such as the Teochew *mua chee* (from which the Japanese derive *mochi*), ground rice is also a thickener for soups and stews. It is mixed with self-raising (self-rising) flour in a batter for banana and sweet potato fritters, which are favourite Malaysian and Singapore snacks. Rice flour is made by grinding the raw grain until it is very fine. All rice grains can be used and the packets are usually labelled accordingly. Long grain and medium grain rice flour is used to make dough for fresh and dried rice noodles, as well as for dumplings, crêpes and buns.

Glutinous rice flour, sometimes called sweet rice flour, is reserved for sweet pastries, pancakes and cakes. Do not confuse this with rice powder, which is much finer ground rice and is used in delicate bakes. Both types are available from Asian stores and should be kept in an airtight container in a dry place.

Rice papers

A large community of Chinese settled in South Vietnam several centuries ago and they still keep to their classical cuisine while adapting many indigenous dishes, and these practices tend to spread. Originally unique to Thai and Vietnamese cuisines, triangular or circular rice papers and wrappers have been adopted by Chinese chefs around the world. Rice papers are spreading in popularity, and are now used in Singapore as a delicate skin for spring rolls. Once deep fried, they make an extremely thin and crispy case.

Made from rice flour, water and salt, 'raw' rice papers are brittle. They need to be soaked briefly in hot water until they are soft and pliant. When each wrapper has softened, lift it out of the water with a chopstick and spread it on a chopping board before topping with filling. Once rolled up, the packets can be eaten as they are or deep-fried. If you are deep frying them do so in small batches, as the delicate wrappers are liable to stick together and break open in a crowded fryer or wok.

Packets of dried rice papers are available in Asian stores and some supermarkets. Do not confuse them with the sheets of rice paper used in baking.

Above and right: Amber and white rice vinegar have a distinctive sharpness.

Above: Rice papers are dried on bamboo mats, which give them their familiar cross-hatch pattern.

Rice wine and vinegar

Throughout China, rice is distilled to make wine and vinegar. The grains are fermented in a process similar to making beer, to produce a highly alcoholic brew. The resulting clear, clean-tasting vinegar is used extensively in Malaysia and Singapore, especially among the Chinese populations, who prefer it to normal vinegar as it has a delicious aroma and is less acidic. Red rice is used to make a distinctive red wine vinegar that is an essential seasoning for northern Chinese casseroles. Black rice vinegar is usually made from black glutinous rice, and is sweet and smoky in flavour. Bottles of rice wine and vinegar are available in Asian and Chinese stores and markets.

PREPARING AND COOKING RICE

Many people find difficulty in preparing soft, fluffy rice. You may get varying advice about this depending on where you are, but there are actually few fundamental rules. Most rice grains are cooked using the absorption method, except glutinous rice, which is soaked and steamed.

Washing rice

In most Asian countries, raw rice is washed several times – traditionalists will insist that it goes through "seven changes of water" but this has more to do with myth than common sense. Most of the rice bought in supermarkets today requires minimal washing to remove traces of husks or discoloured grains. However, long grain rice does benefit from rinsing in cold water to reduce the excess starch, so that the cooked grains are light and fluffy and separate easily.

1 Put the measured quantity of grains into a bowl and cover with cold water. Swirl the grains in the water until it becomes cloudy, then leave to settle.

2 Strain the rice through a sieve (strainer) then return it to the bowl and repeat until the water is clear.

Soaking

Some culinary institutes teach trainee chefs to soak rice before cooking. There are two reasons for this. Soaking is said to bleach the rice so that, when cooked, the colour is more intensely white. The other reason is that increasing the moisture content of the grains in this way means that the cooking water can penetrate more effectively. Consequently the grains are less likely to break up and stickiness is reduced, resulting in fluffier rice.

After rinsing the rice, leave the grains in the bowl and cover with cold water. Leave to soak for half an hour. Drain the rice through a sieve (strainer), rinse it under cold running water, then drain again before you cook it.

Steaming

Rice that is to be steamed needs only the minimum amount of water – just covering it – and it should be steamed in a flat vessel such as a shallow pan or a traditional bamboo steamer. Cover the rice to keep in the steam.

Test if the rice is cooked by eating a few grains. There should be a slight resistance to the bite.

1 Fill a wok one-third full with water. Place a bamboo steamer, with the lid on, over the wok and bring the water underneath to the boil.

2 Lift the lid off the steamer and place a dampened piece of clean muslin (cheesecloth) over the rack. Put the rice in the middle and spread it out a little. Fold the edges of the muslin over the rice, put the lid back on the steamer and steam for about 25 minutes, until the rice is tender but still firm.

Cooking by absorption

Rice soaks up a lot of water as it cooks – 450g/1lb of uncooked rice will absorb up to 600ml/1 pint of water, making enough to feed four moderate appetites (though probably only two hungry labourers). The volume of rice grains doubles when cooked.

The proportion of water required and the cooking time will both vary slightly with different grains, so it is wise to follow the instructions on the packet if you are cooking an unusual variety of rice. Put the measured grains into a heavy pan with a proportionally measured amount of water, and cook the rice until all the water has been absorbed. The age-old method for judging the amount of water is to add enough to come up to two joints of the index finger from the top of the rice.

1 Put the rinsed grains into a heavy pan and pour in the water. Bring to the boil, stir once, then reduce the heat to low.

2 Cover the pan tightly and leave to cook very gently for 15–20 minutes, depending on the size of the grain, until all the liquid has been absorbed. Remove the pan from the heat and leave to stand for 5–10 minutes to allow the residual heat to finish the cooking.

3 When the water is absorbed, fluff the tender rice up with a fork and serve.

Using an automatic rice cooker

Once the preserve of the Japanese, rice cookers are now practically universal and are one of the easiest and most trouble-free methods of cooking rice. Simply wash and drain the rice, place it in the inner cooker bowl with the requisite amount of water, and switch on. When the rice is cooked, it will switch itself off. The cooker works by weight, with the inner pot resting on a springboard. When all the water is absorbed, it switches off automatically as the lighter inner pot springs back to its original position.

Cooking in a microwave

Prepare the rice as for a rice cooker but you should not cover the pot as water will boil over and spill. For 250g/9oz rice you will need 300ml/½ pint water, though long grain rice may need more as it is a denser grain.

ADDITIONAL FLAVOURINGS

Generally, rice in Malaysia and Singapore is eaten plain, and is not salted or seasoned because it acts as a foil to the other flavours in the meal. However, Indian meals may feature rice perfumed with rose water, ghee or saffron to go with curries and sambals.

When coconut rice is called for, especially in the traditional Malay dish *nasi lemak*, the grains are cooked in coconut milk and the rice is served with fried anchovies, nuts and strips of omelette, spiced up with a chilli sambal. For festive occasions, Peranakan cooks prepare yellow rice, which is flavoured and coloured a bright yellow with ground turmeric.

NOODLES

South-east Asian cooking uses noodles in great quantities. If the main dish doesn't contain rice it will consist of noodles. They are eaten at all hours of the day, in soup for breakfast, simply stir-fried for a filling snack, or incorporated into main dishes with meat, fish and vegetables. It is no wonder that most food stalls in Malaysia and Singapore serve both staples in many combinations.

Noodles are made from either rice or wheat flour, and the everyday noodles in Malaysia and Singapore fall into several main types. *Mee* or *mien* are made from wheat flour, sometimes with egg, and are either thin and long or flat, much like tagliatelle pasta strands. Wheat noodles come in a wide range of types, many from China, and are usually sold dried, in packets.

Rice noodles also come in a variety of shapes. Long, flat noodles are called kway teow, and thin versions are called mi fun or bee hoon. Malaysians and Singaporeans prefer to use fresh noodles if the dish calls for kway teow, but the thin variety is usually sold dry.

Noodle stalls are ubiquitous and the hundreds of food courts each have at least three or four noodle stalls. Noodles served with minced pork and fishball soup have become an iconic Singapore dish, as has Singapore *laksa*, a rich, coconut milk-based noodle dish with lashings of chilli paste and aromatic laksa leaves. Penang laksa is different, being cooked in a tamarind-based stock with pungent prawn (shrimp) paste, a black tar-like condiment that can be an acquired taste.

FRESH RICE NOODLES

These are a mainstay among the Teochews who love them in a soup dish called *kway teow th'ng*. The Cantonese have a different use for the same type, known as *hor fun*, either uncooked or stir-fried with meat, seafood and vegetables; and fresh rice noodles are also used in the popular Singapore hawker dish of *char kway teow*.

Virtually every wet market and supermarket sells fresh rice noodles, supplied daily by local manufacturers. They are sometimes frozen but mainly chilled, in packets. Some wet markets in rural areas stock them loose in large basins and customers simply ask for them by weight.

FINE RICE NOODLES

Commonly called rice vermicelli, there are several types of varying thicknesses, all sold dry. A favourite Fujian or Hokkien type called *mee sua* are extremely thin and delicate, and are usually reserved for special birthday dishes as they symbolize longevity. Another even less common type is called *mee teow*, and is used exclusively in Teochew dishes.

RICE STICKS

Though not in widespread use, dry rice sticks are useful because of their long shelf life. They are gradually becoming more popular among busy people who do not have time to buy the fresh variety daily. They are simply briefly boiled or blanched depending on the type. Generally much thinner than the fresh variety, they are ideal for soups but tend to break up easily when fried.

PREPARING RICE NOODLES

Virtually nobody in Malaysia and Singapore bothers to make their own fresh rice noodles because they are so widely available. However, they are worth the effort for special occasions. Fresh rice noodles need to be blanched briefly in hot water and drained before use in soups or stir-fries. Vermicelli, on the other hand, need only to be soaked for about 20 minutes.

Dried rice noodles double in bulk when rehydrated. Once prepared this way, they should not be cooked for too long or they turn mushy and break up. About 150g/5oz of reconstituted noodles are sufficient for one portion, as each bowl will also contain vegetables, meat or seafood.

Throughout the two countries rice noodle soup or fried noodles are daily fare. The added ingredients vary: pork, fish balls, prawns, vegetables, liver, kidneys and beef. Lamb is never used.

MAKING FRESH RICE NOODLES

A variety of dried noodles are available from Asian stores and supermarkets in the West, but fresh ones are quite different and if you want to make them yourself it's not that difficult. For a snack, freshly made noodle sheets can be drenched in sugar or honey, or dipped into a sweet or savoury sauce of your choice. Alternatively, you can cut them into wide strips and gently stir-fry them with garlic, ginger, chillies and *nuoc mam* or soy sauce – a popular snack enjoyed all over South-east Asia.

Left: Different types of dried rice and wheat noodles are used for soups, stir fries, salads and even sweet snacks.

As a guide, to serve four you will need about 225g/8oz/2 cups rice flour and 600ml/1pint/2½ cups water. You will also need a wide pot with a domed lid, or a wok lid, a piece of thin, smooth cotton cloth (such as an old clean sheet) and a lightly oiled baking tray.

Preparing the batter

Place the flour in a bowl and stir in a little water to form a smooth paste. Gradually pour in the rest of the water, whisking all the time to make sure there are no lumps. Beat in a pinch of salt and 15ml/1 tbsp vegetable oil. Set aside for 15 minutes.

Preparing the steamer

Meanwhile, fill a wide pot with water. Cut a piece of cloth a little larger than the top of the pot. Stretch it over the top of the pot (you may need someone to help you), pulling the edges down over the sides so that the cloth is as taut as a drum, then wind a piece of string around the edge, securing the cloth with a knot or bow. Using a sharp knife, make 3 small slits, about 2.5cm/1in from the edge of the cloth, at regular intervals. If you need to top up the water during cooking, pour it through these slits.

Cooking the noodle sheets

1 Bring the water in the pot to the boil. Once it is bubbling and steam is rising through the cloth, stir the batter and ladle a portion (roughly 30–45ml/2–3 tbsp) on to the cloth, swirling it to form a 10–15cm/4–6in wide circle.

2 Cover the pot with the domed lid and steam for 1 minute, until the noodle sheet is translucent. To remove it, carefully insert a spatula or round-bladed knife under the edge of the noodle sheet and gently prize it off the cloth – if it doesn't peel off easily, you may need to steam it for a little longer.

3 Transfer the sheet to the oiled tray and repeat with the rest of the batter. As they accumulate, stack the sheets on top of each other, brushing the tops with oil so they don't stick together. Cover the stack with a clean dish towel to keep them moist.

COOK'S TIP

During the cooking, you may have to top up the water through one of the slits. The cloth might occasionally need to be pulled tight again over the sides of the pot if it begins to sag, otherwise the batter will form a pool and the noodle sheets will be too thick in the centre.

MUNG BEAN NOODLES

Called by many names – transparent noodles, translucent vermicelli, cellophane or glass noodles – these are made from mung bean flour and are always sold dry. They reconstitute rapidly when soaked in warm water and have the peculiar characteristic that they keep their crunch no matter how long you cook them. Usually sold in small skeins, they have a neutral flavour that soaks up seasoning very well, and are often simply cooked in stock.

WHEAT FLOUR NOODLES

Generally pale yellow, these come either dried to be reconstituted or fresh to be blanched before use in stir-fries or curries. There are three distinct types: factory-produced dried skeins of yellow noodles that have to be boiled for a few minutes or longer depending on the type; freshly made and semi-dry noodles usually with a light coating of flour that need only to be blanched; and fresh yellow noodles that need very light cooking.

Some producers oil their fresh yellow noodles, and these must be blanched thoroughly to remove the grease. Dry noodles, like rice sticks and vermicelli, double in bulk when reconstituted but fresh ones remain the same.

Some wheat noodles contain egg and resemble Japanese udon. They are often referred to as Shanghai-style noodles, and are usually sold fresh. They are firmer and denser than rice noodles and are used in stir-fries and soups. Fairly new to the market is a variety infused with spinach, which colours the noodles pale green.

HAND-TOSSED NOODLES

A recent import from north China, these noodles are made fresh, more as a theatrical performance than to meet consumer demand. It takes years of practice before you can knead wheat flour into a firm but elastic dough, then pull and stretch it constantly until fine threads appear before your very eyes. Most restaurants that offer this dish charge a premium price, as only a limited amount can be made each day.

BREAD

The bread that is familiar in the West was not eaten by Malaysians and Singaporeans until the beginning of the British Colonial era in the early 19th century. Nevertheless, the loaf has been adopted and adapted as a part of meals since then. Neighbouring Vietnam and Cambodia had been colonized by the French, who introduced the baguette, but the former British colonies did not embrace the staple with the same passion until relatively recently.

Early Arab traders in Singapore already made their own Middle Eastern loaf and cooks employed by British army families were taught to make basic white loaves and baps. With the increased availability of imported products and baking skills, bread

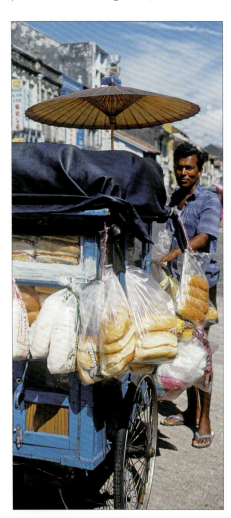

Above: A street bread seller in Georgetown, Penang, with Western-style bread rolls and sandwiches on his cart.

became more accepted. Bakeries began to thrive after World War II and bread became more available. Today, bakers in Malaysia and Singapore produce a wide range of Western-style breads.

BUNS, SANDWICHES AND TOASTS

Visitors to Singapore in the 1950s would have been surprised to find ice cream vendors selling slices of currant bread sandwiching vanilla ice cream. It is still a special treat today.

Buns and dumplings fall into the bread category, as they start with a dough made from wheat flour and yeast. However, following ancient Chinese traditions, they are often stuffed and usually steamed, although some buns are baked after steaming. Flatbreads and wrappers, used for folding around morsels of food and for spring rolls, are made from rice or wheat flour and baked on griddles, or left in the sun to dry.

A Malaysian party favourite, bun Susie, is a small roll filled with spicy prawn (shrimp) sambal, similar to the Singapore sambal sandwich, filled with dried prawn sambal. At picnics and barbecues, small baguettes are eaten. They are affectionately known as *roti pranchis* ("bread of the French").

In shopping malls and food courts all over Kuala Lumpur, Penang and Singapore, there is invariably a bakery that sells many unusual types of bread – buns filled with red bean paste, almond paste and red bean paste; cream-filled rolls and toasted sandwiches filled with barbecued pork and pork floss. The ubiquitous restaurant item of prawns on sesame toast would, of course, not exist without the wide acceptance of bread.

Another culinary phenomenon is the emergence of *kaya* toast. *Kaya* is a Peranakan conserve or jam, made with eggs, sugar and coconut milk and intended to top steamed glutinous rice. Along with imported British jams and butter, it became a favourite spread for toast in the Colonial era. Coffee shops that were once rustic food shops have been upgraded and smartened up to sell coffee and *kaya* toast. There are

Above: Eggs, sugar and coconut make a popular spread, kaya, *for toast and bread .*

now even franchises offering this delicious breakfast fare.

Chinese chefs are also adept at making steamed breads from rice flour to be eaten with braised pork dishes. These fat little buns, which are called *mun dou*, are made to fold over like a balled fist and appear on most Chinese restaurant menus.

INDIAN BREADS

To the Indian community in Malaysia and Singapore, when bread is mentioned it refers specifically to those from the sub-continent. The Indian workers that arrived in the early 19th century brought with them their own breads, which are quite different from the Western loaf. They came from both north and south India and introduced naans, rotis, chapatis, hoppers, puries and parathas to the region.

Although rice is grown in the Punjab and Pakistan, north Indian meals are built around breads, unlike in the south where rice holds away. The mode of eating is with the fingers and breads make perfect edible spoons to scoop up curry and korma gravies.

The chapati is the basic unleavened Indian bread, resembling a Mexican tortilla. Flat, rough and thick, this round pancake is the staple of the community. When made thick, it is called roti. Parathas are heavier, layered and shallow-fried, eaten plain or stuffed with minced (ground) lamb. Naan is a tandoor-baked leavened bread made from white flour although most others are made with wholemeal flour (*atar*) or pounded barley, millet or buckwheat. Channa, also called besan or gram flour, made from chick peas, is also used for breads and dumplings.

From south India comes an incredible range of breakfast breads or "hoppers". Some are made with milk and others with egg and the leavening ingredient is toddy, a coconut water by-product. Thin string hoppers, which are popular in Sri Lanka, are made from Chinese rice flour, as is *puttu*, a steamed, unsweetened crumbly pastry bread with coconut. These are delicious eaten with melted palm sugar. *Iddlis* are featherlight, slightly sour crumpets made with rice flour and lentils, and thosais are like Scottish oatcakes.

How to make chapatis

Unlike the tandoor-baked breads, you do not need any special equipment to make chapatis, as they can be cooked in a griddle or large frying pan.

MAKES 10–12
  250g/9oz wholemeal (whole-wheat) flour
  115g/4oz plain (all-purpose) flour
  pinch of salt
  200ml/7fl oz/scant 1 cup lukewarm water

1 Sift both the flours with the salt into a large bowl and make a well in the centre. Add the water, a little at a time, and stir with a wooden spoon until the dough comes together and forms a ball that is soft and pliant but not sticky.

2 Knead the dough until all the flour is absorbed and nothing sticks to the sides of the bowl. Place the dough on a lightly floured board. With the heel of one hand, knead the dough.

3 Fold and knead again for 10 minutes. The longer you knead the lighter your chapatis will be. Reshape the ball of dough and return it to the bowl. Cover with a damp cloth and leave to rest at room temperature for half an hour.

4 Knead again once or twice and divide the dough into 10–12 even-sized pieces. Use a knife rather than tearing and stretching the dough. Roll each piece into a round ball. Flour the board if necessary to make rolling easier.

5 With a rolling pin, flatten each chapati until you get an even circle about 15cm/6in in diameter. Stack the rounds as you finish them and cover the stack with a clean damp cloth to prevent drying out.

6 Heat a large, preferably nonstick, frying pan or griddle until very hot. Cook each chapati until bubbles appear on the top side, then flip it over. This should take no more than a minute or two.

7 Cook the other side for 40 seconds and remove the pan from the heat. With a perforated spoon, lift the chapati and hold it over the naked flame for a few seconds. It should puff up nicely. Keep the bread warm while you cook the other rounds, and serve them warm and fresh with curry.

VEGETABLES

Shopping for vegetables and fruit is an everyday activity for most cooks. In rural Malaysia, makeshift stalls are set up to sell local vegetables and fruit, but most people head to the wet markets. Every day, vegetables and fruit are taken over the causeway from Johor into Singapore, as the island is totally dependent on Malaysia for its fresh agricultural produce and water. As the wet markets fill up, the stalls begin to transform into a maze of colour and bustling activity.

In general, most vegetable dishes and salads are presented as side dishes to accompany rice or a main dish and grilled (broiled) meats. Some vegetable dishes are served as meals on their own, particularly among vegetarian Indians, who produce exciting dishes that combine Indian and Malay styles. Crisp salads and raw pickled vegetables often accompany grilled meat and fish, and the Indonesian and Malay specialities, such as *rojak* and *kerabu*, are served as snacks at hawker stalls.

AUBERGINE/EGGPLANT/BRINJAL

Technically a fruit, but eaten as a vegetable, the aubergine originally came from India and Thailand. The most common variety in Malaysia and Singapore is long and thin, in shades of pale green and purple. The flavour is sweet, with very little bitterness. Incredibly versatile, it is added to stews, curries and stir-fries, so that the flesh absorbs all the delicious spices and flavours of the dish.

Look for smooth, unblemished skin and firm flesh. Smaller varieties range from green to purple and yellow. Much loved by Thais, they feature in dishes of northern Malaysia and are usually halved and added to curries. Tiny, green pea aubergines are also popular throughout Southeast Asia. The size of garden peas, these grow in clusters and have a slightly bitter taste with a pleasantly crunchy texture.

BAMBOO SHOOTS

A giant grass, indigenous to China and other tropical regions, bamboo has many important uses. The long, thin stems or "trunks" are used for making baskets, furniture and even as containers for roasting rice. They are also made into kitchen utensils, such as steamers, strainers and chopsticks.

The leaves (usually dried) are used as wrappers for Chinese dumplings or steamed rice dishes, imparting their own unique flavour. The small, pine cone-sized shoots that are dug up just before they emerge from the ground have an astringent taste. Fresh, pickled or dried, bamboo shoots are popular throughout both countries, and are the key ingredient in *popiah*, the Nonya spring roll.

The fresh young shoots need only be blanched briefly. With older shoots, the outer sheaths are stripped off and the tough base removed. Once peeled, the pale yellow inner core is sliced and boiled for at least half an hour until tender.

Left: Aubergines may be long and thin or small and round.

The shoots are added to stir-fries, curries and soups. Dried shoots, mainly from China, require long soaking before use. Fresh shoots are available in Asian stores, but cans of ready-cooked shoots preserved in brine can be bought in most supermarkets.

BITTER MELON/BITTER GOURD

This gourd looks like a fat, knobbly pale green cucumber and is, in fact, a bitter relative. The bitterness comes from high levels of quinine, and it is eaten as much for its medicinal value as its flavour. Before cooking, it needs to be sliced into rounds or slit lengthways to remove the red seeds and inner membrane. The pieces can be stir-fried, blanched or pickled, or added to curries. A smaller variety from India and Sri Lanka is puréed as a health tonic by both Chinese and Indians. If you want to remove some of the bitterness, sprinkle on a little salt after slicing, leave for 10 minutes and then squeeze out the moisture.

Bitter melons are sold fresh in most Asian stores. They are best when firm and green. When they turn a little yellow, they should be cooked immediately before they turn mushy.

Above: Long beans taste similar to French or green beans.

LONG BEANS

Sometimes referred to as "snake beans", "runner beans" or "chopstick beans", these long, green beans are the immature pods of black-eyed beans (peas) and can measure up to 60cm/2ft in length. Generally long beans are cooked in curries, boiled and added to salads or stir-fried.

Above: Bamboo shoots are available fresh, but sliced, canned shoots are easier to find.

MOOLI/DAIKON

White in colour, this root vegetable looks very similar to a large carrot. A major feature in Japanese cooking, it is also known as white radish or daikon. It can be eaten raw but is most often pickled in vinegar to bring out its crisp, juicy, slightly astringent flavour. It is popular throughout Malaysia and Singapore for soups, salads and pickles, as well as stir-fries and stews. Mashed and steamed with rice flour it is called *luo bo kau* and is a street food staple in both countries. Mooli can be found in Asian markets and supermarkets.

FUZZY MELON

Also called hairy gourd, the fuzzy melon is about the size of bitter gourd with a fuzzy skin. Peeled and boiled, it is traditionally used in soups with pork ribs. It can also be sliced and stir-fried or added to spicy peppery soups. It is available in Asian markets but is rarely found in supermarkets.

Right: Bitter melon is highly regarded in Southeast Asian cooking.

PULSES

Beans are used extensively in Malaysian and Singaporean Chinese cooking in sweet and savoury dishes.

Red beans

In Malaysia and Singapore these small beans, also called aduki beans, are usually soaked, boiled and mashed as a stuffing for sweet cakes. They are often used as a sweet base in the classic dessert known as *ice kacang* (shaved ice with syrup). *Ang tau thng* (red bean drink), cooked with rock sugar or sweet winter melon slices, is a favourite after-meal drink.

Mung beans

Whole dried mung beans, with husks on, are green, whereas the peeled ones are yellow and sold whole or split. Both require soaking before cooking. The mashed beans are made into a sweet paste that is the key ingredient in the Chinese New Year cake known as red turtle cake: red symbolizes prosperity and the turtle represents longevity.

Above: Yellow split mung beans

Beansprouts

Ubiquitous throughout South-east Asia and Indo-China, beansprouts can be eaten raw but are usually added to stir-fried noodles for their crunch.

Right: Both mung and soya beansprouts are widely used in Malaysian and Singaporean cooking.

The most common sprouts come from mung beans and soya beans. They are similar in appearance, both with white stems, but soya bean heads are green, while those of mung beans are yellow. Soya beansprouts are sturdier and stronger in flavour, whereas mung beans are delicate and watery. Both types are nutritious, rich in vitamins and minerals.

Fresh sprouts can be stored in the refrigerator for up to 2–3 days. Packets of mung beansprouts are available in most supermarkets. Soya beansprouts can be found in Asian stores and some health stores.

Soya beans (dry)

These pale yellow beans are about twice the size of corn niblets and play a much larger role in Chinese cooking than being merely processed into soy sauce. Cantonese and Hakka chefs boil them well to make a subtly perfumed stock that is ideal for vegetarian meals.

For sweet drinks and desserts, soya beans are boiled, drained and sweetened with rock sugar. They make a drink that can be bought just about everywhere in Malaysia and Singapore, called *tau fa sui*, and with a coagulating agent added, the smooth liquid is turned into a super-soft jelly called *taufu fa*. This is a popular hawker treat, served with a syrup and eaten either hot or cold.

LUFFA SQUASH

Dark green with ridges running lengthways, luffa squash has sweet, spongy flesh and is usually harvested when about 30cm/1ft long. The outer skin is tough and inedible and has to be removed to reveal the soft, white flesh. Generally, it is sliced and used in stir-fries, omelettes and soups, in much the same way as you would cook a courgette (zucchini). Luffa squash is available in Asian markets. Unlike cucumber or young, tender courgettes, luffa is never eaten raw. Keep the fresh squash in the refrigerator, but do not store it for too long as within 2–3 days it will start to go limp. The luffa squash is also known as Chinese okra, silk squash and sponge gourd.

MUSHROOMS

Fresh and dried mushrooms are used in many dishes in Singaporean, Chinese and Nonya cooking, but less often in Malay cooking. Dried mushrooms, however, are favoured for stir-fries and savoury fillings because of their texture and delicate taste when reconstituted.

Chinese black mushrooms

Sometimes known as Chinese shiitake, these mushrooms have a distinctive flavour and a chewy texture. They are usually sold dried. After softening in

Below: Sliced straw mushrooms, showing their "umbrella" pattern.

Above: A luffa squash has a sweet, delicate flavour when young.

warm water for about 30 minutes, the stems are removed and the caps are added to stews, stir-fries and fillings. There is a Chinese belief that prominent fissures or cracks on the surface augur good luck and prosperity. They are sold in Asian markets and supermarkets, and are also canned.

Straw mushrooms

Also called bulb mushrooms, straw mushrooms look like glossy quail eggs. Usually sold in cans, the whole mushrooms are excellent in braised dishes for visual appeal and texture. When sliced, they reveal pretty cream stems. Very delicate in flavour and texture, they take to long cooking without turning mushy.

Tree ears

A fungus that grows on trees (hence its name), tree ears are also called cloud ears or wood ears. They are valued for their texture and nutritional qualities and are believed to cleanse the blood. Usually sold dried, they are thin and will swell up to six or eight times their volume to resemble frilly clumps of rubbery seaweed when soaked in water. Reconstitute dried tree ears by soaking for about 30 minutes, then drain and rinse well, and drain again. Remove any hard, woody stalks before cooking. On cooking, the mushrooms become quite translucent and gelatinous, but still retain a bite. Chinese cooks chop them and add them to stuffings for spring rolls and stir-fries. These mushrooms are particularly popular in Buddhist vegetarian dishes.

Oyster mushrooms

In the wild oyster mushrooms grow in clumps on rotting wood. The entire mushroom is of the same colour, which can be pearl grey, pink or yellow. They are now grown commercially and are widely available. Their delicate texture and subtle taste complement stir-fries, noodles and rice dishes. They need to be torn, not cut, and should not be overcooked: add them to the pan in the last few minutes of cooking.

Below: Pale, delicate oyster mushrooms should look and smell fresh, with no damp or discoloured areas.

Above: Tree ears are also known as cloud or wood ears.

ORIENTAL GREENS

Cabbages and greens are grown all over Malaysia but Singapore imports most of its greens, as it has no agricultural industry to speak of.

Pak choi/bok choy

This perennial leafy cabbage is often confused with Chinese leaf. It is popular throughout South-east Asia and is grown widely in Thailand and Taiwan. In fact the Taiwan version has pale green stems while the common variety has ribbed, white stems. All are juicy and crunchy; the dark-green leaves are succulent and tasty.

The tender stems of small cabbages are rarely eaten raw but are often stir-fried with prawns (shrimp) or added to noodles. The leaves, which are mostly composed of water, need very quick cooking and shrink a lot in the process. In stir-frying, it is a good idea to cook the stems first for a few minutes before adding the leaves. These fresh greens are available in Asian stores and supermarkets.

Flowering cabbage

With its yellow flowers, long, slender stalks, and crisp leaves, the flowering cabbage, a member of the rape family, is much prized by the Chinese. When picked young and in flower, at its most tender and flavoursome, it is an excellent accompaniment to noodles while older choy sum are good on their own as stir-fries, especially when cooked with oyster sauce. Bundles are available in most Asian markets.

Green carrot

This is not an unripe "regular" carrot as such but a particular genus grown in China. It tastes much like a carrot and is used primarily as a key ingredient in the Chinese New Year raw fish offering. It can also be grated and used as a filler for spring rolls, or pickled.

Mustard greens

Also called Chinese cabbage, these resemble a head of lettuce such as cos (romaine) but are firmer and thicker. The leaves wrapping the heart have thick stalks and have a mildly bitter flavour. Blanched, they become more subtle. They make a classic Cantonese dish when gently poached with egg white and crab meat.

In Malaysia and Singapore, preserved mustard greens are more common than the fresh variety. The tender hearts and sometimes the leaves are preserved in brine. Quite salty, preserved mustard greens are integral to the Nonya classic Duck and Salted Vegetable Soup. Otherwise, they can be sliced and added to soups or omelettes. They are usually canned or vacuum-packed.

Chinese leaves

Known variously as Chinese leaves, Napa cabbage (mainly in the USA) or celery cabbage, this member of the brassica family has many uses and is widely used, as it is available all year round. There are three common varieties, which look fairly similar.

Chinese leaves have a delicate sweet aroma, with a mild cabbage flavour when cooked. The white stalk has a delicious crunch but becomes custard-soft when cooked. The leaves contrast perfectly with softer noodles and are great in stir-fries, stews and soups, or in salads. They absorb the flavours of meat or fish well, so blanch the leaves in boiling stock before frying them. They are also used for wrapping around minced pork and fish as a festive dish.

Chinese leaves can be stored for up to two weeks in the refrigerator without losing their resilience. If you find tiny black specks on the leaves, do not worry as they are quite normal and will not affect the flavour.

Water convolvulus

Also called water spinach, swamp cabbage or morning glory, this attractive leafy vegetable is traditionally grown in swamps or ponds. It is essential in the classic Nonya dish *kangkung belacan*.

This somewhat rare vegetable is sometimes found in Asian markets. It has hollow stems and tender, light-green, arrow-shaped leaves. When cooked, the stem tips stay firm, but the leaves rapidly become limp. It is highly perishable and must be used promptly.

Preparing water convolvulus

1 Slit the hollow stalks right down their length to check for creepy-crawlies! Separate them from the leaves and split lengthways.

2 Trim off the end bits that usually have a few rootlets. Slice into 7.5cm/3in pieces.

3 Tear off leafy stems or cut into similar lengths so each stem has a few leaves. Individual leaves, if they are small, tend to shrink too much when cooked. Wash and drain thoroughly before cooking. Store in a plastic bag for up to 2 days when refrigerated.

WINTER MELON

Large, mild-flavoured gourds, winter melons can weigh 5.4kg/12lb or more. Egg- or pear-shaped and dark green, they are harvested in the summer (but traditionally stored for winter). The white flesh tastes like marrow or courgette (zucchini) and is believed to cool fevers. It is prepared and cooked like pumpkin, and added to soups and stir-fries. Dried, sugared winter melon slices are used as a sweetener in Chinese drinks.

Winter melons and fuzzy melons are interchangeable in recipes, as they are similar in flavour. Both come in various shapes and sizes.

CASSAVA

Also known as manioc or tapioca, cassava is a large tuber that comes in varying sizes but is usually shaped like a long radish with a thick bark. It originated in South America, and is also popular in Africa and the Caribbean. African cassava can grow as large and thick as a human thigh.

In all types, the starchy root has creamy white flesh and a subtly sweet, almost buttery flavour, sometimes with delicious nuances of almond and new potato. Steamed cassava can be

Below: A large winter melon.

Above: Sweet cassava is a versatile tuber and can be cooked in many ways.

mashed with palm sugar and coconut milk for a sweet, sticky pudding, diced and tossed with desiccated (dry unsweetened shredded) coconut or eaten as a snack.

The bitter and much larger African variety of cassava contains more cyanide compounds, which are present in all cassava at some level. Hence, it must never be eaten raw as it can cause severe reactions.

Tapioca flour

This silky flour is made from the starch of the cassava root. A substitute for cornflour (cornstarch) as a thickener for sauces and custards for ice cream, it is also used to make rice papers and give them a sheen.

Tapioca pearls

Also called sago in Malaysia and Singapore, tapioca pearls are made from tapioca flour and come in various sizes. Sold dried, they have to be boiled until they turn translucent, then rinsed under cold water to wash off the starch. Sago is the key ingredient, with palm sugar and coconut milk, in the famous *gula Melaka* dessert.

Above: Tapioca or sago pearls prepared for drying on trays.

JICAMA

This root vegetable looks like a large turnip or swede and has an apple-like crunch and delicate sweet taste rather similar to water chestnut. Peel and cut into chunks or slices for soups, salads and stir-fries. It is a key ingredient in the Malaysian spicy salad called *rojak*.

LOTUS ROOT AND SEEDS

Held with great reverence since ancient times, the lotus plant is rife with symbolism. It is a beautiful aquatic plant with delicate pink and white flowers, closely associated with the Chinese deity Guanyin, the goddess of mercy and patron saint of sailors, who is always pictured carrying a lotus stem.

The plant is edible in its entirety. The stamens are infused to make a fragrant tisane; the seeds are dried and boiled for sweets and cakes; the leaves are used for wrapping rice and steamed snacks; the stems are added to salads, soups and braised dishes. Lotus roots are juicy and fragrant, and when sliced reveal a lacy pattern of holes.

In ancient Chinese tradition, the nourishing lotus root is believed to aid blood circulation and to improve virility. In Malaysia and Singapore, the lotus

Above: The flesh of a jicama is a cross between an apple and a potato.

Preparing cassava

1 Scrub the root and either peel with a vegetable peeler or run a sharp knife into the skin around the girth at 7.5cm/3in intervals. Then cut down and each piece of skin will come away easily.

2 Cut the white flesh into chunks, removing the fibrous core.

3 Drop the pieces into a bowl of acidulated water to prevent discoloration. Drain, then boil, steam, bake or fry the cassava pieces until tender.

Right: Taro is a rough-skinned tuber used both as a fruit and a vegetable.

root is added to soups with pork ribs, or stir-fried. The roots, stems and seeds of the lotus plant are available fresh, dried and preserved, in most Asian stores. If dried, all of them need to be soaked overnight before being cooked.

TARO

This root, known as taro or yam, comes in varying sizes from little egg-shaped nuggets to barrel shapes the size of grapefruit. All have a fuzzy brown skin with white or purple-flecked flesh.

The Chinese cook taro with duck and chicken. They also steam and mash it to wrap minced (ground) meat for dim sum dumplings. The Teochews make a dessert called *orh nee* from mashed and braised taro paste with a lot of sugar. Nonya cooking also features the tender stalks of young taro in curries. Long and thick, it is peeled and cut into short pieces before being cooked. Its spongy texture absorbs the flavour and sauce of a dish.

Malays tend to use taro as a fruit, to be sliced, battered and deep-fried as a snack or diced and cooked with sweet potato in a popular dessert called *bubur cha cha*. All types have a similar distinctive nutty flavour and crumbly texture when cooked. Taro roots are available in Asian stores as well as in some supermarkets.

Below: Fresh lotus roots, which are in fact rhizomes, look like linked sausages. The papery leaves and light-coloured seeds are also widely used.

WATER CHESTNUT

Water chestnuts are grown in flooded paddy fields but harvested when the soil is dry. When they are sold fresh in the markets, they are often covered with crumbly earth. Each is about the size of a large chestnut and, once peeled, reveals a chalk white, sweet meat. Juicy and crunchy at the same time, the texture is reminiscent of an Asian pear.

Regarded as cooling and beneficial to the digestive system, water chestnuts are also believed to sweeten the breath. They are high in starch and nutrients, including copper. They can be eaten raw in salads, or chopped up and added to fillings for spring rolls or stir-fries. They can also be ground into flour to make water chestnut dim sum.

Fresh water chestnuts have a short life span and must be eaten within 2–3 days of purchase. Cans of peeled and ready-cooked water chestnuts are available in most supermarkets. Once opened, store water chestnuts in water in the refrigerator for up to a week, changing the water daily.

FRUIT

Traditionally, fruit is eaten at the end of a meal to cleanse the palate or aid the digestion, while sweet puddings and cakes are nibbled as snacks. Many of the tropical fruits eaten in Malaysia and Singapore are now available in Asian markets and large supermarkets.

BANANAS

For most Malaysians and Singaporeans, bananas are eaten not merely as a fruit but turn up in many cooked dishes. The most popular type is called *pisang rajah* ("king of bananas"), which has an exquisite perfume. They are sold as fried bananas or made into banana fritters. Other varieties range from finger-length perfumed bananas to the enormous elephant tusk banana, which can be 30cm/12in long. This is sliced and cooked with coconut milk and sugar in a dessert called *penghat*.

The banana plant may look like a palm tree but is in reality a perennial herb. It grows a new "trunk" every year and after blossoming and fruiting, dies back to its roots. Each tree may have up to half a dozen bunches, each bunch containing many "hands" with anything up to a dozen fruits on each hand.

Right: Tiny lady's finger or sugar bananas are often no more than 7.5cm/3in in length.

Right: When very ripe, small apple bananas have a faint taste and aroma of fresh apple.

Above: Banana leaves are not eaten but are often used to wrap food.

Banana leaves

Held in high regard as a natural wrapper, this "green foil" does multiple duty as plates, table mats or shaped into intriguing containers for steaming, baking and grilling (broiling), especially in traditional Indonesian and Malaysian cooking. The leaves are blanched in very hot water to make them pliable and wiped dry before use. Fresh banana leaves are available in Asian and African supermarkets. They do not freeze well as they tend to crack when thawed.

Banana blossom/bud

Each large, deep purple bud of the banana tree contains pale yellow, finger-sized blossoms in thick clusters. They are edible and are enjoyed throughout South-east Asia as a delicate vegetable, especially in Nonya cooking where they take pride of place as a Chinese New Year salad. The purple husks are inedible but make beautiful "plates" for salads and other dishes. The blossoms are

Above: At the heart of the banana flower lies the delicate banana bud.

sliced, blanched and tossed with coconut cream, cooked prawns (shrimp) and chilli and shrimp paste sambal. They can also be eaten raw but are slightly bitter. Soak them in water with lemon or lime juice to prevent them discolouring.

COCONUT

The coconut tree is revered as the "tree of life" and grows prolifically throughout coastal Malaysia. Practically every part is used: the leaves make great wrappers for compressed rice cakes boiled and served as the classic accompaniment to satay; the spines of the leaves are trimmed and made into skewers; the trunks are used as piles in building; and the nut has a myriad uses. The flesh of young nuts is eaten as a sweetmeat and that of older nuts is grated and squeezed for milk, which plays a vital role, like cow's milk in the West.

The outer hard shell is shaped, turned and fashioned into ladles and cups. What we buy is only the stone of the actual fruit; the husk and fibres are removed in the country of origin and used as stuffing for mattresses, as fuel, or woven into ropes. Excess coconut meat is usually smoked into copra for export and for making coconut oil.

When you shake a coconut you should hear the swishing sound of the water inside. Pierce the eyes on top of

Below: Creamed coconut block.

the coconut and pour out the water. To open a coconut, place it on a flat surface and use a cleaver or hammer to tap it hard all the way round. Pull the shell apart and pry the flesh out with a knife or sharp-edged spoon. Slice the thin brown skin off the flesh and chop or grate the pieces for further use. To facilitate extracting the meat, place the coconut in a fairly hot oven for about 15 minutes until it cracks. The flesh comes away more easily this way.

Coconut milk

This is the cream of Malaysia and Singapore and fundamental in most curries and puddings. Its savoury sweetness lends a unique flavour to every dish that is cooked with it, the rich quality blending beautifully with spices, sugar and other aromatics. Its creaminess is much loved by Malays and Nonyas and it is thickened with cornflour (cornstarch) to make a blancmange-like custard. The common practice is to squeeze grated coconut for its "first milk" with a scant amount of water. More water is added to yield a "second milk" to be used in a variety of dishes. Once you have squeezed out all the coconut milk, allow it to settle in the bowl and the cream will rise to the top. This can be skimmed off, if you wish to use it separately. Coconut milk does not keep well and is usually made daily. It can turn rancid very quickly and is best refrigerated if you are not using it immediately. It is widely available in cans and cartons.

Coconut oil

Coconut cream, when simmered for a long time until the milk solids evaporate, renders down to a rich, aromatic oil. This is used mainly by Malays for frying spices to make rich curries. It is a saturated fat that turns solid very quickly.

Green coconut water

The coconut water used for cooking is extracted from young, green coconuts. Each nut yields about 300ml/½ pint of liquid. The slightly astringent water is drunk neat as a cooling thirst quencher. All over rural Malaysia stalls sell young coconut water, which is the most natural of drinks with no additives. It makes an effective rising agent in many Nonya and Malay rice flour cakes, and is used as a tenderizing agent for tough meat. Mild and sweet, it features in a number of braised dishes and Malay cakes. It is even used as a shampoo by Indians. Although you can use the water from ripened nuts, it is best to look in Asian markets for a young coconut.

Above: Coconut is versatile and a valuable crop.

Making coconut milk

While most wet markets sell ready-grated coconut for making milk, or tins of prepared milk, it is easy to make yourself.

1 Grate the flesh from a fresh coconut, or shred it in a food processor.

2 Put the grated flesh into a bowl and knead thoroughly. Squeeze out the creamy "first milk".

3 Pour roughly 600ml/1 pint/ 2½ cups warm water over the shreds. Stir and leave to steep for 30 minutes. Line a sieve (strainer) with muslin (cheesecloth) over a bowl and ladle the coconut into it.

4 Gather the muslin in your hands and squeeze out any excess liquid. This is the "second milk."

Above: The leaves and rind of kaffir limes impart a distinctive, zesty flavour.

CUSTARD APPLE

Originating from tropical America, the custard apple was introduced to Malaysia by the Portuguese. The fruits are heart-shaped, buff or green and about 10cm/4in in diameter. The skin is thick and may have small bumps depending on the variety. The flesh is creamy white and granular, surrounding a fibrous central core. Small black seeds are embedded in the flesh, which has a custard-like consistency and is slightly astringent but sweet when ripe.

DURIAN

This large fruit encased in deep-green armour-like skin with fearsome-looking spikes has had much bad press, often unjustified. Most airlines and hotels ban the fruit but many Malaysians and Singaporeans love it. If you can put up with the strong, indescribable odour, the buttery yellow flesh is delicious, with nut and honey overtones, quite unlike any other fruit.

Durians are much sought after and used to be seasonal but are now available all year round. They are expensive and are only available in some Asian markets. The best ones come from Malaysia and have a slightly bitter edge. Thai durians tend to be woody and dry. Avoid any fruits that have split.

To prepare durian, a wooden blade is forced into the natural seams across the length of the fruit. Inside are four or five indented shells containing large pieces of fleshy pulp. There is no way to eat durian other than with the hands. The flesh is tugged or sucked and licked from the large seeds.

GUAVA

A native of Brazil, the guava was taken by the Portuguese in the 17th century to the Philippines and gradually spread across South-east Asia. Grown widely in Malaysia, the different types vary in shape and size. The thick skin ranges from white to pale green, pink or red, and the flesh may be white, yellow or pink and contain many small hard pips. Guavas have a characteristic aroma ranging from rose blossom to mango. They are eaten mainly as a dessert fruit, but are also sliced and mixed with a sambal for a relish that complements many dishes.

JACKFRUIT

Large and spiky, the jackfruit looks similar to a durian but with short stubs instead of spikes. It can grow as large as two rugby balls. There are two distinct types: *nangka* and *chempedak*. When sliced open, nangka reveals a cluster of yellow fruit, each encircling a large seed. The texture is delightfully crunchy and tastes like ripe mangoes.

Below: A durian and its large seeds.

Chempedak is more fragrant, with nuances of pineapple and apricot, and the flesh is creamy and chewy at the same time. Packed with vitamins, the fruit is enjoyed on its own as well as mixed in a tropical fruit salad. The seeds can be boiled or roasted as a snack. Unripe jackfruit is also cooked in coconut milk curries.

LIME

In Malaysia and Singapore, fresh green limes are generally used for their juice but they are also pickled or dried as sweetmeats. The juice has a sharp tang that enhances the flavour of other ingredients. The rind is grated and added to savoury dishes. The leaves of

Above: Jackfruit are very large, and a single fruit can weigh up to 40kg/88lb.

Above: Mangosteens have a fragrant, delicate flavour and are best eaten raw.

Above: Red-skinned mangoes are eaten as a fruit or in desserts, and green-skinned ones as a vegetable.

kaffir limes are unique in their heady, zesty fragrance and prized in Nonya sambals and curries, shredded and added at the last minute. They are available, dried, in many Asian stores and markets.

Below: Papayas, often known as paw paw, are one of the most attractive tropical fruits.

LYCHEE

Native to the sub-temperate regions of China and north Thailand, lychees have thin, mauve-pink, bumpy skins that are easily peeled to reveal very juicy, white flesh covering a black seed. A superior variety from China, when in season, boasts of very thick flesh encasing one or no seed. Lychees are also available canned in syrup.

LONGAN

These fruits are found in most sub-tropical regions in South-east Asia and have smooth, brown skins with vague black spots. The crisp skin is easily removed and the flesh is firm, crunchy and sweet, covering small black seeds. Longans keep well in the refrigerator and are delicious chilled. They are seasonal, but can be found all year round sold in cans, in their own juice or in a light syrup.

MANGO

Originally from India, several varieties of mango are also grown in Malaysia and Singapore. The sweetest come from Thailand: thick, round and tapered at one end, they are called elephant tusk mangoes. Mango skins may be yellow, pale orange or green and ripened ones are eaten mainly as a fruit. The sweet, yellow or orange flesh is wonderfully

thirst-quenching, with a lovely aroma of pine, and is also a good source of vitamin A. There are also green mangoes that never change colour – these are sliced or shredded and used mainly in salads.

MANGOSTEEN

These handsome fruits are apple-sized with a smooth, thick purple rind. This is partially covered by the flower petals, which remain attached as the fruit ripens. Inside, the pulp is chalk white and divided into five to seven segments. The large segments contain a seed, while the smaller segments are seedless. The flesh is astringent with a delicious perfume. Malaysians and Singaporeans eat them as a cooling treat, especially after a surfeit of durians, as mangosteens ripen just after the spiky fruit.

PAPAYA

Indigenous to South America and tropical Asia, the gourd-like fruit comes in varying sizes, from about 250g/8oz to giants of 1.3kg/3lb or more. The flesh is orange or pale yellow and can have a delicious perfume. Papayas are full of vitamins and honey-sweet.

A favourite Malaysian and Thai salad called som tam uses a variety that remains green and never ripens. Peeled and finely sliced or shredded, it is tossed with ground dried shrimp, lime juice, fish sauce, chillies and garlic.

Below: Pineapples are an important fruit crop in Malaysia.

PINEAPPLE

Grown in both West and East Malaysia, pineapples vary in size, juiciness and sweetness. They do double duty as a dessert fruit, when ripe, and as a sweet addition to Malaysian and Singapore salads and Nonya seafood curries. Look for pineapples with firm skin, with a good orange colouring and a fragrant odour. To prepare fresh pineapple slices, first slice off the leaves, then use a sharp knife to cut off the skin in vertical strips. Make diagonal cuts all along the fruit, removing all the black eyes, then slice the whole fruit lengthways into four quarters and remove the hard, pithy core. Finally cube or slice into rings.

RAMBUTAN

Shaggy-haired and alien-looking, rambutans resemble hairy plums. There are a number of varieties, varying in sweetness and coloured with streaks of gold, orange

Right: Rambutans have a distinctive skin covered in soft spiky hairs. They are available fresh and ready prepared in cans.

Above right: Bright yellow star fruit is used in snacks, drinks and savoury dishes.

and green. The market variety tends to be red. Easy to open, the hairy shells encase a translucent white fruit with a pale stone (pit) in the middle. The flesh is crunchy, cool and sweet.

SAPODILLA

The size of kiwi fruit, these originate from Central America but are widely grown in Malaysia, Thailand and India, where they are variously known as *chiko* or *chiku*. They have a light, slightly fuzzy skin that when peeled reveals a soft, tan flesh with black pips. The texture is luscious, like a soft pear, and tastes of burnt sugar. They are available mainly at Indian greengrocers and in some South-east Asian markets.

SOUR STAR FRUIT

Related to star fruit, sour star fruit is found widely in South-east Asia and other high altitude tropical regions, where it is variously called camia, cucumber tree and tree sorrel. The fruits resemble green or pale yellow miniature cucumbers, up to 10cm/4in long and the thickness of a thumb. They grow in clusters on the tree trunk. The skin is very thin and smooth, and the fruits have very few small seeds.

A favourite ingredient in Malay and Nonya sambals, relishes and pickles, they are very tart with a crunchy texture. They are not widely available but may be found in some South-east Asian markets.

SOURSOP

Often mistaken for a durian, soursop grows widely in humid tropical countries, especially in the coastal regions of Malaysia. The fruit, often kidney shaped, may weigh as much as 3kg/8lb, and is borne on thick, woody stalks. The thick skin is dark green with rows of soft green stubby spikes. The pulp is very soft, white and creamy and very juicy, ranging from tart to sweet flavours. Buried within the flesh are many shiny, black seeds. A rich source of vitamin C, they are often puréed for their juice. They are available in South-east Asian and Chinese markets.

STAR FRUIT

Also known as carambola in South America, this star-shaped fruit has five wedges and is sweet with a slightly astringent taste. In Malaysia and Singapore, the ripened yellow fruit is enjoyed as a juicy snack or pulped for its refreshing juice. The green immature fruit is finely sliced and served as a tangy vegetable, salted and dried as a pickle ingredient, or tossed in salads. Available in some Asian markets, they have a short shelf life: avoid any fruits that have dark spots.

TOFU PRODUCTS

Far from being regarded as a "poor man's meat", tofu or soy bean curd is revered among Chinese communities throughout Asia. Protein-rich and low in calories, tofu is devoid of cholesterol, which is found only in products of animal origin. It also provides essential amino acids, vitamins and minerals. It is made by combining soya bean milk with a coagulant such as gypsum powder to form curds, which are then compressed into blocks of varying densities. While it has a neutral flavour – some call it tasteless – tofu's very blandness is great for absorbing other flavours. It is firm enough to be added to stir-fries and used as a container for various stuffings, and adds healthy bulk to soups, braised vegetarian dishes and spring roll fillings.

FRESH TOFU

These soft white blocks packed in water are available in most Asian markets. The UHT varieties are also available in most supermarkets. Generally, soft tofu is better for soups and steamed dishes, whereas the firm variety is best in stir-fries and fillings. Tofu is best used straight away, but if it is submerged in water, changed daily, it can be stored, chilled, for 3–4 days.

DRIED TOFU

Also known as "bean curd sticks" in Malaysia and Singapore, this product is made by simmering soya milk until a thin skin forms on top, which shrinks and stiffens when dried. Creamy white in colour with a subtle flavour, tofu sticks are sold in Asian markets. They must be soaked in water to soften for about 30 minutes before use.

FRIED TOFU

Firm tofu, deep-fried until it forms a brown skin, is used for the popular Malay street food dish *tauhu goreng*, dressed with shredded cucumber, boiled beansprouts and a spicy peanut sauce. A Chinese variety, called *tau kwa pok*, is tofu that has been rendered completely dry. The light, spongy brown cakes are split open and stuffed with braised duck, chicken or vegetables, with spicy chilli and vinegar sauce.

PRESERVED TOFU

Cubes of fresh tofu that have been preserved in brine for several months have a strong flavour and need to be rinsed before use. They can be used sparingly to add extra flavour to stir fries and other vegetable and meat dishes. Preserved tofu is sold in Asian stores.

Above: Cubes of fermented tofu.

FERMENTED TOFU

Fresh tofu is fermented on beds of rice straw, then dried in the sun before marinating with salt, Chinese grain wine and spices. It is stored in brine in sealed earthenware crocks and left to mature for at least six months. It is a favourite condiment with rice congee and is used in marinating poultry and as a rich seasoning for braised dishes.

TOFU SKINS

These are made by lifting the skin of tofu as it is made and then dried flat as brown, wrinkly sheets. With storage they become brittle and crack easily when handled. If so, they have to be moistened slightly with a damp towel before being used as spring roll wrappers. A classic Nonya spring roll called *bak kng* uses these skins.

TOFU WAFERS

These are light, brown pieces of slightly sweetened, dried tofu pieces that can be fried as crackling to top stir-fried noodles or added to vegetable stews. The Chinese call them *dim choke*.

SILKEN TOFU AND TOFU MILK

Soft, silken tofu, or *tau hu fa*, is a popular dessert in Malaysia and Singapore, where it is served in a very sweet syrup perfumed with pandan leaves. There are vendors in food courts throughout Singapore and on the streets of Malaysian towns selling this cold or warm snack. The tofu is freshly made and entirely different from UHT silken tofu. The same stalls also sell *tou fa shui* – tofu milk or soy bean milk – a hugely popular cooling drink.

Above, clockwise from top: Pressed, silken and firm tofu, all varying in degrees of firmness and suited to stir-fries or soups.

FISH AND SHELLFISH

The coastal waters off Malaysia and Singapore are home to a rich variety of tropical seafood. Malaysia is also blessed with a network of river systems, starting in the mountain ranges and flowing through the rainforests to the sea. Every town and village has a wet market where fishmongers sell absolutely fresh fish that were swimming in their ocean or river habitat just hours earlier. Coastal communities eat more fish than meat, and fish cooking is taken to great heights.

Fish preparation varies from region to region, and even between the races and communities. Indians use a lot of tuna, manifest in the famous fish head curry. Malay and Nonya cooks grind fish into paste, add spices and wrap them in banana leaves for grilling (broiling) or steaming to make a dish called *otak otak*. Malays also deep-fry anchovies until crisp and serve them with coconut rice. Chinese cooks fry large fish whole and bathe them in sweet and sour sauce or black bean sauce.

In the past decade, there has been a trend started among hawker stalls to serve grilled ray fish with *sambal belacan* (spicy chilli and shrimp paste sambal). Singapore chilli crab has also gained a global reputation as an iconic dish, and dozens of stalls and restaurants along the East Coast offer it. Another national dish in Singapore is oyster omelette (*or luak*), in which plump oysters are fried with egg. Some stalls also use barnacles for this dish but both versions are equally delicious. Penang in Malaysia is also famous for its oyster omelette, but there it is called *or chien*.

Fish balls are staple hawker fare, eaten with all kinds of noodles. Prawns (shrimp) and squid are also processed into small balls, each the size of a cherry tomato. Whatever seafood is cooked, it must be absolutely fresh and locals will not buy or cook the frozen variety if they can help it. Until the 1950s, refrigeration was rare in Malaysia and Singapore, and all fish bought had to be cooked on the same day. This has honed the local taste buds to expect nothing but the freshest.

Above: Buy firm fish, such as glossy mackerel, for spicy and fragrant sauces.

ANCHOVY, LONG-JAWED ANCHOVY

One of Malaysia and Singapore's best-loved fish and a well-documented export, anchovies or *ikan bilis* are best known in their dried form, bilis. They form the staple seafood in coconut rice or *nasi lemak*. Fresh bilis are relatively rare these days except in coastal rural Malaysian towns. Steamed whole or deboned and deep-fried, they make delicious crunchy eating.

EELS

Adult eels have almost black backs and silvery bodies. Females tend to be much heavier than males – often three times as heavy – and are highly prized in stewed Chinese dishes with wine and ginger. They are almost always sold live as they deteriorate quickly, especially in the tropics. They are hard to prepare but if you rub the skin with plenty of salt you can grip it firmly. Or you can ask the fishmonger to skin them for you and to chop them into 5cm/2in lengths.

HARDTAIL/TORPEDO TREVALLY

The name of this fish comes from a peculiar hard ridge from the tail to halfway up the body. It can measure up to 50cm/20in and is bluish-green above and silvery below, with dusky grey fins.

Easily recognized because of its torpedo-like body, numerous finlets and stiff thin tail, it is best grilled or steamed. Malays love to grill the fish whole to be eaten with *sambal belacan*. The hard ridge must be sliced off before cooking, so you can remove the meat from the tail end easily.

HERRING

While the common name is herring, these fish are also called sprat or rainbow sardine. Growing to about 15cm/6in with a dark green back and silver belly, they have very fine bones. They are very tasty when fried and eaten with a chilli dip. Larger fish can be gutted and filleted before cooking.

MACKEREL

The mackerel family embraces several species but the most common is known as Spanish mackerel, with dark grey backs, silvery sides and roughly circular spots. They range from 17.5cm/7in long to large fish of up to 43cm/17in. Excellent to eat when very fresh, mackerel has delicate, sweet flesh and is most often fried or cooked in sour fish curries.

Preparing fish

With very few exceptions, this is how any fresh, whole fish should be prepared. The head is generally left on: most Chinese prefer not to behead fish in the belief that no living creature should go the next life decapitated.

1 Wear rubber gloves to protect your hands from the smell of fish if you wish. Holding the fish firmly, make a slit down the belly and remove all entrails.

2 Where the gills join the body at each corner, snip to separate them and remove the gills. With a sharp pair of scissors trim away all fins, cutting close to the body. Wash and pat dry. Coat with a little cornflour (cornstarch) if deep or shallow frying whole, as this gives a crisp coating.

3 To fillet the trimmed fish, lay it on the chopping board and hold it firmly with the tail end towards you. Cut away from you with a sharp knife flat against the central bone. Turn the fish over to cut off the second fillet. Keep or freeze all trimmings as they make excellent fish stock.

POMFRET/PORGY

These distinctively shaped fish have no pelvic fins and come in two main species, black or white. Both types range in size from 12.5cm/5in to as large as 23cm/9in. White pomfrets (porgy) have a delicate flesh much loved by Teochews, and are usually simply steamed with a little ginger. Black pomfret have a robust flavour and firmer flesh and are usually fried or grilled to be eaten with *sambal belacan*.

RED SNAPPER

One of the most important groups of local fish in Malaysia and Singapore, snappers are highly esteemed and easily recognized by their straight ventral profile with pointed snout. These snap when they are caught, hence their name. Most are brightly coloured, ranging from deep red in the larger species to shocking pink, silver and yellow, usually with lines and spots. They are have a delicate flavour and are usually cooked in curries or fried whole.

SEA BASS

A fine fish, sea bass have variable but always striking coloration, from silvery to light brown to orange with large-edged blue spots. They have a sleek shape rather like a salmon, and can grow to a length of 90cm/36in and weigh up to 7kg/15½lb. The white flesh is firm and delicately flavoured and tastes best when simply steamed. Malaysians marinate it with spices and wrap it in a banana leaf before cooking.

SNAKEHEAD

This eel-like fish is highly prized for its meaty flesh and full flavour, and features in Cantonese fish and rice vermicelli soup (*yue tau mifun*). The fish are usually sold live. They have a near-black, slippery skin and are often mistaken for fat eels. Very popular in north Malaysia, they turn up in many guises, in curries, grilled, fried or flaked for relishes.

STINGRAY

Although the normal variety is relatively small, about 30cm/12in across its widest part, stingrays can also grow to enormous size, weighing as much as 200kg/450lb. They may be coloured from sandy to dark brown or marked with numerous spots, but a better recognition point is their whip-like tail. Grilled or fried, they have a similar flavour and texture to skate.

THREADFIN/TASSEL FISH

Probably the most expensive fish of all and quite rare, these fish are almost boneless with a delicate sweet flesh reminiscent of cod or halibut. They are large, up to 120cm/4ft long, and are mostly sold as steaks or cutlets. They are silvery-green above with a creamy belly and the name refers to the four threads on each pectoral fin. Some species have black dorsal tips to their fins and green tassels.

TREVALLY

Not to be confused with torpedo trevally (see facing page), these popular fish range from large yellow-bellied ones to silvery grey small ones, and have a characteristic yellow tail fin. A very meaty fish highly esteemed in Malaysia and Thailand, trevally is also known as kingfish in Africa. It is best simply fried or cooked in a curry.

Below: Sea bass is fleshy and versatile, ideal for stews and curries.

TUNA

While tuna can grow to a very large size, the most popular ones in Malaysia and Singapore are the smaller bluefin tuna, about 50cm/20in long. Characterized by a blue-black top and silvery belly, tuna have to keep swimming continuously in order to maintain a supply of oxygen. This results in strong muscle, the part of the fish that makes the best eating. The flesh is generally pale but can vary from pink to deep red, and is usually sold as steaks because of the fish's large size. The head is highly prized for Indian fish head curry but it also tastes good fried or grilled (broiled).

WOLF HERRING/DORAB

Specimens up to 60cm/24in long have been caught in deep waters off Asian coasts but the market variety is usually around 45cm/18in long. The fish has a bluish-green back with silvery sides that go grey when it has been dead a while.

Preparing fresh prawns

Raw freshwater and saltwater prawns and large shrimp are either peeled before cooking or with their shells left on for certain dishes. If large, peeled raw prawns must have their intestinal tracts removed. It is not necessary to devein small shrimp.

Below: Raw prawns.

The large upturned mouth looks fearsome but the flesh has a delicate, sweet flavour, and the numerous bones cannot spoil the excellent taste and flaky texture. One of the best-loved fish in Malaysia and Singapore, wolf herring is the main ingredient in fish balls and a star item in the Chinese New Year raw fish treat.

ABALONE

Rarely available fresh, abalone is an expensive shellfish that comes mainly from South America and Australia and is usually sold canned. Much prized as a special festive dish during Chinese New Year, dried abalone have to be boiled for at least an hour before continuing to the next step of cooking. Many upmarket Chinese restaurants in Malaysia and Singapore specialize in abalone, either braised in a rich broth or sliced and cooked in Mongolian hotpots or steamboats.

CRAB

There are several varieties, the most common being mottled or flower crabs, named on account of the pale blue mottling on their shells. They are about the size of an adult palm, smaller than the large grey mud crabs. They make good eating, especially in the well-loved Singapore dish of chilli crab.

Preparing crab

Usually sold live, crabs tend to become comatose when chilled for a few hours. Make sure the crab is dry, with no sign of water sloshing around in the shell, which should be firm and contain no cracks or holes. Turn the crab belly up and remove the soft V-shaped flap on the belly. Pull the top shell off, scoop out the soft, yellowish coral and reserve. Discard the feathery gills and snap off the legs and claws. The larger claws should be cracked but not entirely broken, so

Above: Preparing blue mottled crab.

the flesh can be easily extracted when cooked. Rinse the body and cut it into two or more pieces. Alternatively, steam the crabs whole until they turn deep pink throughout.

PRAWNS (SHRIMP)

Both marine and freshwater prawns are highly prized among the Chinese in Malaysia and Singapore for one reason. Their Cantonese name, *ha*, reflects laughter and happiness and they are eaten for symbolic reasons during Chinese New Year. The marine variety is plentiful and comes in various sizes. Prawns have a sweet flavour and turn pink or orange when they are cooked. Buy fresh raw prawns if possible, choosing specimens that are a translucent grey colour tinged with blue. Juicy and meaty, the bigger prawns are often grilled whole, or added to stir-fries or curries; the small ones are dried and added to stocks to enhance the flavour. The small freshwater ones are more delicate and are often steamed briefly, or cooked live in the famous dish called drunken prawns.

SAND LOBSTER

The sand lobster looks like an immature lobster, and has a broad head and tiny claws. Most of the meat is contained within the body section and has much the same delicate, luxurious flavour as normal lobster. When sand lobsters are plentiful, Nonya cooks often use them in place of prawns for spiced or steamed seafood dishes.

SQUID

An important and plentiful food source, squid are consumed widely in Southeast Asia. Along with octopus and cuttlefish, they are members of the cephalopod family. Torpedo-shaped and flanked by two fins, eight short and two long tentacles, the entire body is edible and delicious. Squid is easy to prepare and can be cooked in a variety of ways, such as stir-fried with spices.

If stir-frying, slit the prepared sac from top to bottom and turn it inside out. Flatten it on a board and score the inside surface lightly with a knife, pressing just hard enough to make a crisscross pattern. Cut lengthways into ribbons, which will curl when cooked briefly.

MOLLUSCS

Like other types of shellfish, molluscs are always sold alive but deteriorate rapidly, so always cook them as soon as possible after buying. When you are shopping for bivalves such as mussels, clams and oysters, check that they contain plenty of sea water and feel heavy for their size. Do not buy any that have broken or gaping shells. When you give them a sharp tap, they should snap shut immediately. If they don't, they should be discarded. There will usually be several in each batch that you need to discard, so buy plenty.

Molluscs must be eaten within one day of purchase, but will keep perfectly well for a few hours when stored in the refrigerator. Put them in a large bowl, cover with a damp cloth and keep them

Above: Covering molluscs with a damp cloth will help keep them fresh in the coldest part of the refrigerator.

in the coldest part of the refrigerator (at 2°C/36°F) until you are ready to prepare and eat them.

Oysters can be kept for a couple of days, thanks to the sea water contained in their shells. Store them cupped side down. Never store shellfish in fresh water, or they will die. Ready-frozen bivalves should not be kept in the freezer for more than 2 months.

Preparing molluscs

Scrub bivalves under cold running water, using a stiff brush or scourer to remove any dirt or sand. Open them over a bowl to catch the delicious juice. This will be gritty, so must be strained before being used in a sauce or stock. Cockles usually contain a lot of sand but they will expel this if left overnight in a bucket of sea water or salted water.

Blood cockles

These small bivalves are very popular at seafood stalls and are usually eaten blanched until just cooked and dipped into chilli and garlic sauce. They are also often added to *char kway teow* and *laksa*. They may contain some mud and should be thoroughly rinsed.

Horn shell

Looking like little nautiluses, horn shells are boiled and eaten as a snack with chilli sauce. Peranakans cook them in a rich coconut milk curry. When they are long, you may need to snip away about 1cm/½in of the tapered end to make it easier to get at the meat with a small skewer, or just suck hard to get it out.

Mussels

These are either green lipped or brown with a pale yellow flesh. They are simply steamed or cooked in Chinese wine with garlic and ginger. When buying mussels, allow 450g/1lb per person, as the shells make up much of the weight.

Oysters

Mainly imported from Australia or New Zealand, oysters are more of a Western treat in upmarket seafood places. Those used in omelettes are a smaller variety, or barnacles are sometimes substituted.

Scallops

Served steamed with ginger and garlic, scallops make an elegant starter. As an exception to the rule about buying fresh molluscs, scallops are often sold already opened and cleaned.

Preparing squid

1 Check the squid is fresh and intact. Rinse it well in fresh water.

2 Grip the head in one hand, the body in the other, and tug the head out of the body sac, pulling most of the innards with it. Grip the top of the backbone and pull it out. Rinse the inside of the sac and pat dry.

3 Sever the arms and tentacles from the head and innards and put beside the sac. Discard the rest, including the skin.

DRIED AND FERMENTED FISH

Regarded as natural stock cubes in the kitchens of Malaysia and Singapore, dried and salted or fermented fish products are also frequently served in their own right as side dishes, or even as main dishes with other ingredients. Fried small dried fish and crustaceans, chillied or spiced, are enjoyed as crunchy snacks. Purist cooks still turn their noses up at store-bought stock cubes or seasoning powders and prefer to boil handfuls of dried shrimps, *ikan bilis* (sprats or anchovies), cuttlefish and dried scallops to make the requisite stock for noodles and other dishes.

DRIED SHRIMP

Originating in south India and Sri Lanka, these strongly flavoured shellfish are used in many ways. With a rich, briny flavour and a chewy texture, they have to be soaked or boiled briefly to release their distinctive taste. An important seasoning in many spice blends, especially those meant for seafood curries and *laksas*, dried shrimp are also added to sambals and condiments, usually ground with a pestle and mortar first. They come in many sizes, some so tiny as to look like little commas, others as much as 2.5cm/1in long. Coloured matt pink or light tan, dried shrimp are available in all Asian markets. They can be kept for months in an airtight jar.

Preparing dried shrimp

They should be soaked in warm water for 20 minutes for use in stock or briefly blanched in boiling water if needed as a salad dressing ingredient. This plumps them up and releases their flavour.

Grind them in a pestle and mortar until coarse or fine as required and toss with lime juice and chilli paste for a pungent dip or to flavour fried rice. Deep-fry them and mix with sliced dried chillies to use as a crunchy condiment and topping.

DRIED SQUID

These are widely available in Malaysia and Singapore, and are used as a crunchy ingredient in Malaysian salads, or soaked until soft for Chinese dishes.

Grilled (broiled) or roasted, dried squid (*sotong*) lend pungent sweetness to soups. When soaked in water with borax powder, they turn gelatinous and pale pink. They can be sliced and added to stir-fries or soups. They are available from most Chinese markets.

DRIED ANCHOVIES

Commonly found in all Chinese shops, dried anchovies or *ikan bilis* are integral to Malay cooking. Sold either whole or filleted, these small, finger-length fish are used to make stock for seafood dishes, or fried until crispy to be served as a crunchy side dish with peanuts and coconut rice. When tossed in a rich chilli sambal, they also make a delicious condiment.

SALT FISH

In most coastal regions of Malaysia any excess catch is dried and salted. Various species are preserved in this way, but the most popular and expensive salt fish are made from threadfin. Sold either as fillets or on the bone, they are generally fried to be eaten with congee by the Chinese, or cooked in curries for their rich salty flavour. They are available from all Chinese supermarkets.

SHRIMP PASTE

Malaysia's traditional condiment, *belacan* is essential to Malay and Peranakan cooking. Toasted and ground with chillies to make *sambal belacan* it is central to almost every meal. The best shrimp paste is believed to come from Melaka. It comes in blocks or jars and should be kept refrigerated or in an airtight container.

PRAWN PASTE

Entirely different from shrimp paste, this black, tar-like ingredient (petis-Malay) is made from dried extract of prawns and used mainly as a salad dressing in tandem with chilli paste and lime juice. Extremely thick, it is easier to work with when liquefied with a little warm water. Available in most Chinese stores, it should be kept in an air-tight tin after opening because of the strong smell.

Preparing shrimp paste

Shrimp paste can be used straight from the packet if it is to be ground with other herbs and spices and fried, but it should be toasted or baked to temper its raw taste before using in sambals, dressings and salads.

1 Cut off a small lump of shrimp paste and shape it into a 1cm/½in cube. Mould the paste on to the end of a long metal skewer.

2 Rotate the cube over a low to medium flame, or under an electric grill (broiler), until it begins to char a little along the edges. Ventilate your kitchen to let the strong smell dissipate as it can linger.

3 Alternatively, wrap the paste in a piece of foil and toast in a hot pan, turning occasionally, or wrap it in a microwavable, ventilated plastic bag and microwave for 20–30 seconds.

POULTRY

Although there is a thriving poultry industry in Malaysia, some birds are imported from neighbouring countries such as Thailand, Burma and Vietnam and some from Hong Kong. Many rural Malaysians will have a makeshift coop in their backyards where they rear their own chickens, ducks and geese. Singapore, having no poultry industry at all, imports all its birds.

Chicken is popular among the Chinese community as it symbolizes prosperity and abundance and it is always the featured dish during Chinese New Year and at wedding feasts. Newly married couples are supposed to place a rooster and a hen under their nuptial bed to see which one emerges first. The gender of the first emerging bird is supposed to predict the sex of the firstborn child.

In Singapore, chicken and duck are staple fare, featuring in well-known dishes such as Hainanese chicken rice and Cantonese duck rice. Both birds are frequently roasted, soy braised or barbecued.

CHICKEN

Chickens in South-east Asia are mostly battery-reared today in Singapore and Malaysia and are mainly bought from supermarkets. Free-range birds are more expensive and apart from those bred by rural families they do not feature very much in either cuisine.

There is a breed of black-skinned chicken that practitioners of traditional Chinese medicine advocate eating to alleviate menstrual problems. These chickens taste exactly like any other but are said to contain high levels of an antioxidant. They are not easy to find, but can be bought in some specialist Chinese shops.

DUCK

As with chicken, duck-rearing is confined to rural communities but many are imported from China and Thailand. As it is a tough bird to cook, duck is used in relatively few dishes, such as roast duck, soy-braised duck, Nonya duck and salted vegetable soup and coriander-braised duck.

GOOSE

This is not a common bird in Malaysia and Singapore, but the Teochews excel at cooking geese. In a few restaurants in Singapore and Kuala Lumpur, the large bird is braised in a rich broth of soy sauce, sugar, five-spice powder and galangal called *siew ngor*. It is then sliced and served with a sharp chilli and vinegar sauce and plain rice. Geese are commercially rare and have to be ordered specially from supermarkets.

PIGEON AND QUAIL

Small birds, such as quail and squab, are uncommon, but quails' eggs are sold widely in Chinese stores. They usually end up in soups. The birds used to be popular Chinese restaurant items but have become very rare. They are best marinated in wine and soy sauce and deep-fried. In each case, the birds are killed and then plunged into boiling water to make the feathers easier to pull off. They are then gutted, and the blood and offal are reserved for special dishes. There is little wastage of any bird, fish or animal, especially in Chinese kitchens.

Above: Grilled chickens. Much poultry is sold with its head intact, according to local custom. Western food regulations generally prohibit this practice.

EGG

Hens' eggs are mainstream items, widely available. Duck eggs, on the other hand, are rare and are usually only available salted or as century eggs, which are a special treat eaten with pickled ginger.

Chinese in origin, salted duck eggs are boiled and eaten with rice congee, or in the Singapore dish of oyster omelette that can be found in every food court and hawker centre. The eggs are salted by steeping them in salty water or brine for a few weeks. When boiled, their whites turn opaque and the yolks brilliant orange.

Century eggs are made by coating eggs with a paste made of alkaline clay and rice husks and keeping them in a dark place for several weeks (but not a hundred years) until their whites turn dark brown and their yolks a dull grey, with a creamy texture and a flavour rather like cheese.

MEAT

Malaysia is a predominantly Muslim country with some 80 per cent of the people observing Islam. In Singapore the proportion is reversed, with 20 per cent Muslims. The remainder of the population in both countries is a mix of Chinese, Indians, Eurasians and other migrant races. The types of meat eaten tend to be related to the restrictions of Islam, Hinduism and Buddhism. Among the Christians and Taoists in the region there are fewer taboos affecting the eating of meat.

Muslims eschew pork, and Hindus and devout Buddhists do not eat beef. For this reason, pork is more popular in Singapore than in Malaysia. Mutton is more popular among Indians as both beef and lamb, being imported meats, can be expensive.

Although there are some pig farms in Malaysia, run by Chinese, most of the pork eaten in the region tends to be imported from Thailand and Vietnam, or from Australia, even further afield. Being almost completely urbanized, Singapore imports all its meat.

BEEF, LAMB AND MUTTON

An expensive meat in Asia, beef is eaten as a special treat, mainly in restaurant dishes. Beef satay is quite popular in both Malaysia and Singapore,

but the meat is more often than not taken from cheaper cuts, which are tenderized to make the spicy skewers.

The lamb dishes eaten in the two countries mainly originate from North China. The meat, being imported from Australia or New Zealand, is usually reserved for special occasions or eaten in restaurant dishes. Where you see lamb satay on a menu, they are invariably made of mutton, which is more readily available in South-east Asia and therefore cheaper.

WILD BOAR

This is an delicious meat that can be found only in select areas such as Johor and Kuala Lumpur. It is sourced from rural areas of Malaysia where the animal still thrives in the wild. Wild boar roasted with spices makes a heavenly dish.

PORK

Chinese cooks have many ways to cook pork but the distinctive feature of their cookery lies in the way the pork is cut and sold, which is entirely different from western practice. Leg of pork is preferred for stews, belly for stock, stir-fries and the famous Nonya spiced roast pork (*babi panggang*). Fillets are generally roasted for banquets and

wedding feasts, and suckling pig is a premium restaurant offering. Trotters are popular, ending up in soy sauce stews or slow-cooked in soups. Virtually every part of the pig is eaten and offal (variety meat) is popular despite its high cholesterol content. Foreign visitors are often amused by (and sometimes brave enough to eat) a popular Singapore dish called pig's organ soup, which features practically every part of the animal.

Probably the most high-profile and universally loved pork dish is *char siew*, or Cantonese roast pork, which goes into many dishes, including roast pork rice, a lunchtime staple in Singapore and Malaysia, *kon lo mee* (Cantonese roast pork noodles, *char siew bau* (dumplings) and *bak chang* (Nonya glutinous rice dumplings).

Minced Pork

Minced (ground) pork is used for meatballs and fillings and added to porridge for late-night supper dishes.

Pork and liver sausages are mainly imported from China and are used in Cantonese dishes such as fried rice and dumplings. Pork hams are relatively rare and come mostly from the province of Hunan. These can be expensive and are used sparingly in festive soups and banquet dishes.

Barbecued pork

All over Singapore, and to a lesser extent in Kuala Lumpur and Penang, you can find stalls barbecuing thin slices of highly seasoned pork, which has become a national dish. The strips are given away at Chinese New Year as symbolic gifts and many a Singaporean would not travel overseas without a kilo or so of this special treat.

Preserved pork

Also called wind-dried pork, these strips of pork, usually cut from the belly, are highly seasoned and generally cooked in braised dishes. Some offal, such as liver and tripe, is dried or preserved for soups and stews.

Left: Meats are often marinated to tenderize and infuse them with flavour.

HERBS AND SPICES

Herbs and spices are integral to all Asian cooking, ground up in complex blends or used as top notes in curries, soups and stir-fries. They play a fundamental role in Malaysian and Singaporean cuisines, particularly in those of the Malay, Indian and Peranakan communities. Within the range of dried whole and ground spices and fresh herbs, the varieties are endless. Subtle, pungent or heady fresh herbs such as basil, lemon grass, coriander (cilantro), mint, chillies, lime leaves, chives, pandan and other esoterics are even reputed to have medicinal and restorative properties.

Dried ground spices such as coriander, cumin, fenugreek, aniseed, turmeric and chilli all find a place within the spectrum of spicy cooking. Other flavouring ingredients include tamarind both fresh and dried, in pastes and concentrates, sesame seeds, dried lily buds, sugar cane, palm sugar and limes. It is important to remember that, when using herbs for the preparation of curry pastes and sambals, it is not an exact science. The alchemy between the ingredients is often unfathomable but works brilliantly.

Many of the spices and herbs used in the region have been around for centuries, since the Portuguese first came to the seaport of Melaka, bringing with them many unheard-of ingredients from South and Central America. Today they are grown in every home vegetable plot, on market farms, hillsides and in backyards. Indeed, many a dish would

be a pale shadow of itself but for a herb or two, chopped, torn or added to curries at the last minute to impart their unique, evocative perfumes.

LAKSA LEAVES

With the botanical name of *Polygonum*, this fragrant leaf was adopted by Malaysians and Singaporeans as an essential ingredient in laksa, earning it the name "laksa leaf". The small, thin leaves jutting from slender stalks have a distinct lemony perfume with hints of coriander, mint and basil. A variety grown in Vietnam, where it is called *rau rum*, is also known as Vietnamese coriander or mint.

LIME LEAVES

Also known as kaffir lime leaves (limau perut-Malay), these are unique to the South-east Asian culinary heritage. Grown widely in all tropical regions, the plant is used mainly for its leaves which have a distinctive citrus perfume when crushed. Each leaf is shaped like a guitar or figure eight. The fruit is walnut–sized with a knobbly green skin.

MINT

The most commonly used mint in Malaysia is similar to the garden mint of the West, with furry leaves and a sweet flavour. It is used in salads and as a garnish, often with basil and coriander. There are numerous varieties, including spearmint and peppermint, differing widely in size, shape and flavour.

PANDAN LEAF

One of the most popular herbs in Malaysian and Singaporean cooking, pandan leaves grow like weeds in tropical Asia,

Left: Coriander (cilantro) leaves are used to flavour many savoury dishes and as a popular garnish.

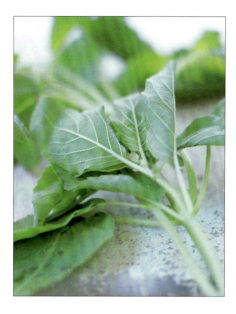

Above: Holy basil is quite pungent with an almost spicy taste.

and the plant from which they come is also known as the screwpine. Used as much for their green colouring as for their perfume, pandan leaves impart a distinctive, vanilla-like scent to puddings. The long, narrow leaves are knotted or bruised to release their unique flavour before being added to dishes. They are also used as a natural wrapper for poultry, meat and seafood for deep frying. The leaves are available fresh or dried in some Asian markets. Some stores also stock pandan essence but if you can't find either, you could use vanilla pods (beans) instead.

BASIL

The basil family is diverse, encompassing different shapes, sizes, colours and aromatic nuances. The types most commonly found in Asia are Thai sweet basil, holy basil and lemon basil. Called *daun selasih* in Malay, Thai sweet basil has the broadest range. Aromatic and reminiscent of anise, it is mild enough to be eaten as a vegetable. In Malay and Nonya cooking, basil is always used raw, sprinkled on noodle soups, tossed in salads or added to curries. Asian basil is found in Asian markets, but the sweet Mediterranean basil found in all supermarkets can be used as a substitute.

CHIVES

Across Asia, chives are found in three forms: green chives, with flat stems and slim-bladed leaves; yellow chives, which are the same variety grown under a cloche, which explains their pallor; and flowering chives, whose round stems are tipped by pointed pale green flower buds. All have a mild spring onion flavour with a hint of garlic.

CORIANDER (CILANTRO)

Ubiquitous in most tropical and temperate countries, originally from Central Asia, coriander is the most common culinary herb, and its seeds are ground into powder as a key ingredient in curries. The feathery, citrus-flavoured leaves are used liberally, especially in soups, Chinese noodle dishes, dumpling mixes and garnishes. Bunches of fresh leaves are available in Asian stores and supermarkets.

Preparing dried chillies

1 Remove the stems and seeds with a knife. Cut into pieces and place in a bowl.

2 Pour over hot water and leave to soak for about 30 minutes. Drain and use according to the recipe.

Right: Red and green Thai bird's eye chillies.

CURRY LEAVES

Very much an Indian herb, curry leaves are diamond-shaped, tough, bottle green and hang in even rows from thin stems. They have a warm peppery scent with citrus notes when crushed and add a distinct flavour to seafood curries, chutneys, rasams (sour soups) and relishes.

CHILLIES

Both fresh and dried chillies are used generously in Malay, Indian and Nonya cooking. Most pastes use dried chillies as they have a more intense red colour, while fresh chillies are the norm for delicate seafood curries, salads and in dips with soy sauce. There are many types of chillies, with fire ranging from barely there to flaming inferno. Green ones are often eaten raw like a vegetable.

Thai bird chillies

These tiny pods have a fire that is disproportionate to their size. They come in many colours, ranging from pale yellow to green, orange and bright red, and are best de-seeded as it is the seeds and pithy flesh around them that are overpoweringly hot. Only two or three are sufficient to give incendiary fire to curries and soups. Thai bird chillies are available fresh and dried in Asian stores and from most supermarkets.

Dried chillies

Also used to make chilli oil, dried chillies are made by infusing them in palm or grape seed oil. Dried chillies can be bought, whole or chopped, from Asian stores and some supermarkets. For most complex curry pastes, they are preferable to fresh chillies. If kept in a dry, cool place, dried chillies have a long shelf life.

Right: Dried chillies.

Preparing fresh chillies

An ingredient called capsaicin found in the seeds and pith gives chillies their fire. Bird chillies can be so hot as to give a burning sensation when merely touched. Always wash your hands after preparing them, or wear gloves.

Slice the chilli in half and run the blade of the knife from stalk to tip to remove all the hottest parts. To seed a chilli without splitting it, slice off the stalk and roll the chilli between your finger and thumb. Hold the chilli upside-down and shake it to release the seeds.

CHILLI PRODUCTS

Sauces and oils made with chilli are great for adding a dash of fire to all kinds of savoury dishes.

Chilli powder

This deep-red powder is made by finely grinding dried red chillies. Any chilli can be used but the hottest powder is made from dried Thai bird chillies.

Chilli paste

This is made by grinding red chillies, seeded or otherwise, into a fine paste. You may add ground garlic, ginger or aromatics depending on what the paste is to be used for. Oil is added if you want a smooth consistency. Versatile and popular, it is used to season sauces, added to curry pastes or as a condiment to salads, relishes and dips for fried snacks. Ready-made chilli paste is sold in jars in Asian markets.

Chilli sauce

This is a smooth, potent sauce used as a dipping sauce on its own, or splashed into fried noodles or *nasi goreng* (Malay fried rice). Many brands are widely available from Asian markets and supermarkets, some with garlic or ginger purée added.

Chilli oil

Used to enhance the colour and flavour of curries, laksas and spicy soups, chilli oil can be made by infusing whole dried chillies, or chilli flakes, in grape seed or palm oil. Heat the oil gently in a very clean pan and infuse the chillies for a few minutes, then strain and store in a glass jar or bottle.

CARDAMOM

Grown widely in the Middle East, India and Nepal, cardamoms come in two varieties – large black and small green pods. They play an important role as a peppery note in rice dishes, soups and curries. Black cardamoms are used sparingly as they are hard to come by. Green cardamoms are added whole to a range of curries but must be discarded before serving as they are not edible, only used for their spicy aroma.

Above: Dried tiger lily buds must be soaked for 30 minutes.

CHINESE FIVE-SPICE POWDER

Based on a mixture of five spices – star anise, cloves, fennel seeds, cinnamon and Sichuan peppercorns – five-spice powder is designed to be pungent. It is used sparingly, mostly in spring roll fillings or in stewed pork dishes, to which it adds a unique flavour. The mixture correlates to the five different types of flavour traditionally said to be at the heart of Chinese cooking – sweet, sour, bitter, hot and salty. In traditional Chinese medicine five-spice powder is often used in relation to the five major organs of the human body – heart, lungs, liver, kidney and spleen. Five-spice powder is widely available.

CINNAMON

A member of the cassia family, the cinnamon tree is grown widely in the Himalayas, Sri Lanka, China and South-east Asia. The most common bark used is that of the Chinese cinnamon, which is thick, rich in oils and a deep brown colour. A warm and pungent ingredient with constituents of volatile oil, cinnamon is added to traditional soups and rice dishes and some cakes, either powdered or in sticks of curled bark. It is available in most Asian stores and supermarkets.

CLOVES

This spice has been known worldwide since the fifth century. In India, cloves are chewed with betel leaves as a digestive aid. They are used primarily as a culinary spice to perfume soups, cakes and stews. They have a warm, spicy aroma and liquorice flavour and are widely available in most Indian stores and supermarkets.

LILY BUDS

Native to Asia, lily buds from the tiger lily plant are prized for their colour and texture in Chinese vegetarian dishes, but are also used in Nonya soups and braised dishes. Bags of dried, tangled buds are sold in Asian markets. They will keep almost indefinitely if stored in an airtight container, away from strong light, heat or moisture. Also known as golden needles, they are light golden in colour. Crunchy in texture, lily buds are floral-scented and earthy in flavour with mushroom overtones.

Preparing lily buds

1 Remove the woody tips of the stems with a sharp knife.

2 Knot the buds in the centre and soak in water for about 30 minutes, then drain and rinse in cold water until clean. This ensures that the lilies remain intact when cooked and retain a slightly chewy texture.

Above: Star-shaped star anise is often used to infuse stocks and medicinal teas.

SESAME SEEDS

These tiny white or black seeds are commonly used in many Chinese dishes. They have a subtle nutty flavour and are most often used to coat meats for deep frying, or sprinkled on stir-fries. Ground up and cooked with sugar as a thick gruel, sesame seeds make a favourite late-night snack.

STAR ANISE

Also known as Chinese anise, this is the dried, star-shaped fruit of a slender evergreen tree that grows in China, India and Japan, where the bark is ground to powder and burnt as incense in temples. Not related to aniseed, star anise imparts a strong liquorice flavour and is generally used in tandem with cloves in aromatic soups and curries. Whole, or crushed, star anise is one of the principal ingredients in five-spice powder. It is available whole or ground from all Asian stores.

GARLIC

Highly prized for more than 5,000 years, garlic is a member of the lily family. Each bulb may contain up to

Above: Cloves of fresh and dried garlic vary in pungency.

10 cloves, which should be firm with a pungent aroma and flavour. Chopped or crushed, garlic is fried in oil to impart flavour to stir-fries, curries, stews and noodles. It is also used in its raw form to flavour pickles, marinades, sauces and dips. Garlic is believed to be good for the heart and circulation.

GALANGAL

While it is a member of the ginger family and similar in appearance, galangal is never eaten raw, unlike ginger itself. The aroma and distinctive pungency of galangal are best harnessed in tandem with shallots, garlic and chillies in spice pastes and marinades. The rhizomes can be sliced or bruised and added to soups and curries to impart a more subtle flavour. When young they are creamy pink in colour with a lemony flavour; the more mature ones are golden and peppery. Fresh galangal will keep for about one week if it is sealed in a plastic bag and refrigerated. It can also be frozen. Both dried and bottled galangal purée are available from Asian stores. Another good way to keep it is to plant it in a pot of moist earth, where it will stay fresh for weeks and may even reward you by starting to grow after a few months.

Above: Beneficial in cooking as well as in the spirit world, garlic is used liberally in South-east Asian dishes.

Above: Galangal comes in both dried and fresh forms.

Below: Fresh root ginger, ginger paste and ground ginger.

Above: Ground and fresh turmeric.

dishes. Pale yellowish-green in colour, the paper-like sheath that encases the stem has to be removed before use. The root end is chopped, pounded or crushed before being added to spice blends, stir-fries, curries and marinades. Lemon grass is one of the principal flavouring ingredients in Malay and Nonya cooking and is available both fresh and dried from Asian stores and some supermarkets.

SHALLOTS

These small, marble-sized bulbs form the sweet basis of many spice blends and when fried in oil make a crunchy garnish in many Malay soups. Spring onions (scallions), which are the young stems of shallots, appear in many dishes. They are often chopped and used liberally as a garnish, added to Chinese spring rolls and tossed into stir-fries at the last minute.

TURMERIC

The fresh root has a subtle, earthy taste and imparts its vivid colour and flavour to spice blends. It is also dried and ground to a deep-yellow powder which imparts colour with only the slightest hint of flavour. Both fresh and dried turmeric are available in Asian markets.

Left: Fresh lemon grass stalks.

GINGER

Indigenous to most of South-east Asia, ginger is the oldest and most widely used flavouring across the Asian region, especially in Indian and Indonesian cooking. A herbaceous perennial plant, root ginger, which is actually a rhizome, is knobbly-looking with a smooth, beige skin. It is sold in two forms. Young, pale yellow ginger is fresh-looking and tender, with a slightly sweet pungency. It can be chopped or shredded for stir-fries, stews, rice, pickles, steamed dishes and puddings. Older, fibrous pieces of ginger are usually ground into spice blends or pickled to make relish.

Ginger is well documented in both traditional Chinese medicine and Indian Ayurvedic practice for its carminative and expectorant action. It is also believed to help with motion sickness and bronchial problems. Choose smooth, plump, fresh-looking pieces and store them in a cool, dry place.

GINKGO NUTS

Also known as the maidenhair tree, the ginkgo plant dates back some two million years. Native to Japan and the central Chinese provinces, ginkgo nuts are used in stir-fries, as a soup ingredient and in desserts, usually in combination with lotus seeds. They have a mild nutty flavour and are available fresh or canned in most Asian stores and health food shops.

LEMON GRASS

A woody, fibrous stalk, lemon grass transcends all South-east Asian culinary cultures. It imparts a fragrant, citrus flavour to

STORE-CUPBOARD INGREDIENTS

A wide range of flavoured oils and sauces are found in Malaysian and Singaporean kitchens, together with staple ingredients such as sugar, salt, agar agar and peanuts.

SESAME OIL

Extracted from sesame seeds, this oil is commonly used in stir-fried dishes. Two types are available: the plain, pale golden oil, which is mildly nutty and good for frying; and the darker, richer-tasting oil made from roasted sesame seeds, which is usually added to dishes in small quantities for flavour just before serving.

FISH SAUCE

More usually associated with Thai cooking, fish sauce is an essential ingredient in some curries, dips and stir fries. Despite its pungent smell, it imparts a superb flavour. Bottles of the sauce, which is made from fermented fish or shrimp, may be kept for up to a year once opened as long as they are kept in a cool, dark place.

ANCHOVY SAUCE

Chinese in origin, this pungent, salty sauce is often used in combination with a sweet, fruity ingredient, such as ripe pineapple. Bottles of this thick, light-grey sauce can be found in Asian stores and markets.

OYSTER SAUCE

This thick, brown sauce is made from dried oyster extract, sugar, water and salt. Strongly flavoured and salty, it is used in moderation as a seasoning agent in Chinese-style dishes. It is available in Asian stores.

HOISIN SAUCE

This is a thick, sweet bean sauce of Chinese origin. Primarily made from fermented soya beans, vinegar, sugar and five-spice powder, it is rich in flavour and ideal for marinades and dipping sauces. It is also used to season noodle soups. Bottles of hoisin sauce are available in most supermarkets.

SOY SAUCE

Probably the most commonly used sauce in South-east Asia is soy sauce, in its various guises, which is made from fermented soya beans, wheat and yeast, Naturally fermented soy sauce will not keep forever; it starts to lose its flavour as soon as the bottle is opened. Try to use it up fairly quickly. In Malaysia it is known as *kicap*. Essential to Malay and Chinese cuisine, it has also been adopted by Indian cooks in Malaysia, who use it to make sweet, spicy sauces for meat stews.

CHINESE WINE

Two types of wine are commonly used in Chinese cooking, called Hsiao Hsing and Hua Teow wines. They are similar in flavour and are used to souse rich stews and stir-fries in northern Chinese cooking. They are made from grain such as sorghum, millet and rye, not from grapes. Cooking sherry makes a decent substitute.

FERMENTED SOYA BEANS

Sometimes called salted beans, this is a condiment (*tuong hot*) made from whole beans. It is used mainly in Chinese-style dishes as a seasoning ingredient.

Left: Oyster sauce.

Right: Palm sugar is sold in blocks, which store well in a cool, dry place.

Right: Toasted sesame oil imparts a rich flavour to many dishes.

PALM SUGAR (JAGGERY)

Widely used in South-east Asia, palm sugar is extracted from the sap of various palm trees. The sap is collected from incisions made in the trunks of the trees. Palm sugar is golden to toffee-brown in colour with a distinctive flavour. It is usually sold in blocks, often referred to as jaggery in Asian stores.

SAMBAL GORENG (FRIED CHILLI PASTE)

Unlike basic chilli paste, this is a master sauce that Malaysian and Singaporean kitchens are rarely without. It goes into a range of dishes, from noodles and rice to curries and salads.

Preparing sambal goreng

> 250g/9oz onions
> 50g/2oz garlic
> 15–20 dried chillies, or to taste
> 40g/1¹/₂oz shrimp paste
> 100ml/3¹/₂oz/scant ¹/₂ cup
>   vegetable oil
> 25g/1oz tomato purée (paste)
> 5ml/1 tsp salt
> 5ml/1 tsp sugar or to taste
> 30ml/2 tbsp tamarind concentrate

1 Grind the first four ingredients until fine and fry for 10 minutes.

2 Add tomato purée, salt, sugar and tamarind and cook for 2 minutes. Remove and store for up to 2 weeks in a refrigerator, in a tightly-sealed container.

SALT

The sea is the main source of salt in South-east Asia, but salty-flavoured soy sauce and fish sauces often replace it as a seasoning in cooking. Salt is combined in equal amounts with pepper to season deep-fried prawns (shrimp) and squid. It is also commonly used as a last-minute seasoning. Mixed with Chinese five-spice powder, or chilli powder, a salt dip is often on the table for roasted or grilled (broiled) meat and poultry or to sprinkle over a meat stew.

AGAR AGAR

Similar to gelatine, agar agar is a gum that is extracted from dried seaweed and processed into white sticks, or ground to a powder. Once dissolved in boiling water, it turns to jelly and is widely used in the jellied puddings of South-east Asia. Agar agar is available in stick or powder form in Asian stores.

Right (clockwise from bottom right): Agar agar is sold in thick and thin strips and as a powder that is used is as a setting agent.

PEANUTS

Important in Malaysian and Singapore cuisine, peanuts are used for richness and texture in a variety of dishes. They are sprinkled on salads and are key to the sauces for *rojak* and *satay*, in which ground peanuts thicken a spicy mix of coconut milk, onions, garlic, belachan and lemon grass.

TAMARIND

The tamarind tree is cultivated in India, South-east Asia and the West Indies. The sticky, tartly flavoured flesh of the tamarind pod is an important flavouring in Indian and Asian cooking. It is strained to remove the seeds and fibrous threads and the resulting paste is available in jars and blocks from Asian markets and supermarkets.

Below: Peanuts are sometimes roasted and crushed for use as a garnish.

Preparing tamarind from paste

Many recipes from Malaysia and Singapore will call for tamarind, so it is worth obtaining tamarind block and having it as a store cupboard staple. You will need warm water and a nylon sieve (strainer) to prepare it.

1 Crumble 300g/11oz of the block and mix with 500ml/17fl oz/ 2 generous cups water. Strain through a fine sieve to obtain a sour, dark brown liquid.

2 Add as much tamarind solution as taste dictates to fish and shellfish curries.

The thick tamarind concentrate can be used straight from the jar or can, again depending on taste. Use it sparingly at first.

BROTHS AND SOUPY NOODLES

Steaming bowls of fragrant, clear broth brimming with noodles, vegetables, succulent seafood and tender meat are the staple fare of hawker stalls and coffee shops in Malaysia and Singapore. They make sustaining lunches and late-night snacks. Years ago, itinerant hawkers used to roam the streets carrying a pole laden with two baskets: one held a stove and a cooking pot, the other held the ingredients for the soup, which could be quickly rustled up for hungry customers.

NOODLES IN SPICY TANGY SOUP

THIS IS A CLASSIC NONYA DISH CALLED MEE SIAM, WHICH HAS BEEN INFLUENCED BY THE FLAVOURINGS OF NEIGHBOURING THAILAND, WITH THE SOUR NOTES EMANATING FROM THE TAMARIND AND SALTED SOYA BEANS. ALMOST EVERY FOOD STALL IN MALAYSIA AND SINGAPORE HAS ITS OWN VERSION OF MEE SIAM, ADAPTED TO SUIT MALAY, CHINESE OR INDIAN TASTES.

SERVES FOUR

INGREDIENTS

vegetable oil, for deep-frying
225g/8oz firm tofu, rinsed, drained
    and cut into cubes
60ml/4 tbsp dried prawns (shrimp),
    soaked until rehydrated
5ml/1 tsp shrimp paste
4 garlic cloves, chopped
4–6 dried red chillies, soaked to
    soften, drained, seeded and the
    pulp scraped out
90g/3½oz/¾ cup roasted
    peanuts, ground
50g/2oz salted soya beans
2 lemon grass stalks, trimmed,
    halved and bruised
30ml/2 tbsp sugar
15–30ml/1–2 tbsp tamarind paste
150g/5oz dried rice vermicelli,
    soaked in hot water until
    pliable
a handful of beansprouts, rinsed
    and drained
4 quail's eggs, hard-boiled, shelled
    and halved
2 spring onions (scallions),
    finely sliced
salt and ground black pepper
fresh coriander (cilantro) leaves,
    finely chopped, to garnish

4 Drain the noodles and, using a sieve (strainer) or perforated ladle, plunge the noodles into the broth to heat through. Divide the noodles among individual serving bowls, sprinkle over the beansprouts and add the deep-fried tofu, halved quail's eggs and spring onions. Ladle the spicy broth over the top, garnish with the coriander and serve immediately.

2 Using a mortar and pestle or food processor, pound or grind the soaked dried prawns with the shrimp paste. Add the garlic and chilli pulp and grind to form a paste.

3 Heat 30ml/2 tbsp of oil in a wok and stir in the prawn, garlic and chilli paste. Fry for 1 minute until fragrant, then add the peanuts, salted soya beans and lemon grass. Fry for another minute and stir in the sugar and tamarind paste, followed by 900ml/1½ pints/3¾ cups water. Mix well and bring to the boil. Reduce the heat and simmer for 10 minutes. Season with salt and pepper.

1 In a wok, heat enough vegetable oil for deep-frying. Drop in the tofu and deep-fry until golden. Drain on kitchen paper and set aside.

COOK'S TIP
This is such a tasty, spicy dish that it is best served on its own as a light meal or nourishing snack so that the flavours can be fully appreciated.

Per Portion Energy 547Kcal/2280kJ; Protein 29.5g; Carbohydrate 42.5g, of which sugars 10g; Fat 29g, of which saturates 4.4g; Cholesterol 48mg; Calcium 389mg; Fibre 3.7g; Sodium 203mg.

PEPPERY VEGETABLE SOUP

OF INDONESIAN ORIGIN, THIS IS A SIMPLE VERSION OF A RICHER SPICED SOUP KNOWN AS SOTO. IT CAN BE COOKED WITH WATER BUT USING A VEGETABLE STOCK, IDEALLY A HOME-MADE ONE, GIVES THE DISH MUCH MORE BODY AND DEPTH OF FLAVOUR. IT SHARPENS THE TASTE BUDS WITHOUT BEING TOO FILLING, AND IS IDEAL AS A STARTER IN A MEAL THAT FEATURES SPICY MEAT OR FISH DISHES.

SERVES FOUR

INGREDIENTS

100g/3¾oz carrots, peeled
100g/3¾oz cucumber
100g/3¾oz French (green) or long
  (snake) beans
5ml/1 tsp black peppercorns
2 shallots
2 garlic cloves
25g/1oz fresh root ginger
30ml/2 tbsp vegetable oil
700ml/24fl oz/2¾ cups water or
  vegetable stock
salt
fried shallots, to garnish

COOK'S TIP
Most supermarkets and ethnic stores now
sell fried shallots in small tubs.

1 Peel the carrots and cut them into
1cm/½in cubes. Trim the beans and
slice them into rounds of a size similar
to the other vegetables.

2 Peel the cucumber and scoop the
seeds out, then dice it.

3 Grind the peppercorns, shallots, garlic
and ginger to a paste. Heat the oil and
fry the paste for 3 minutes. Add the
water or stock and bring to the boil.

4 Add the vegetables and simmer for
15 minutes, until tender. Add salt to
taste and serve in individual bowls,
garnished with fried shallots.

Per portion Energy 72kcal/297KJ; Protein 1.1g; Carbohydrate 4.3g, of which sugars 3.6g; Fat 5.8g, of which saturates 0.7g; Cholesterol 0mg; Calcium 24mg; Fibre 1.5g; Sodium 117mg.

HOT AND SOUR FISH SOUP

IKAN ASAM PEDAS IS THE MALAY VERSION OF THE HOT AND SOUR FISH SOUP FOUND THROUGHOUT SOUTH-EAST ASIA. THE SOUR NOTES ARE DERIVED FROM THE USE OF TAMARIND, WHEREAS THE HOT FLAVOURINGS COME FROM THE CHILLI-BASED REMPAH. THE PERANAKANS SERVE THEIR VERSION OF THIS SOUP WITH STEAMED RICE, BUT MOST MALAYS EAT IT WITH CHUNKS OF BREAD.

SERVES FOUR

INGREDIENTS
30ml/2 tbsp vegetable oil
15–30ml/1–2 tbsp tamarind paste
115g/4oz long beans (snake beans),
    cut into short lengths
450g/1lb fish cutlets (such as trout,
    cod, sea perch, pike), about
    2.5cm/1in thick
fresh coriander (cilantro) leaves,
    to garnish
rice or bread, to serve
For the rempah
8 dried red chillies, soaked in warm
    water until soft, drained and seeded
8 shallots, chopped
4 garlic cloves, chopped
2 lemon grass stalks, sliced
25g/1oz fresh galangal, chopped
25g/1oz fresh turmeric, chopped
5ml/1 tsp shrimp paste

1 To make the rempah, grind all the rempah ingredients to a paste, using a mortar and pestle or food processor.

2 Heat the oil in a wok or heavy pan, and stir in the rempah. Fry it until it is fragrant and begins to change colour. Stir in the tamarind paste and add the long beans, tossing them around the wok until they are well coated in the spice mixture.

3 Pour in 900ml/1½ pints/3¾ cups water and bring to the boil. Reduce the heat and simmer for 5 minutes.

4 Season the broth to taste with salt and pepper, then add the fish cutlets. Cook gently for 2–3 minutes until cooked through, then ladle the soup into bowls. Garnish with coriander and serve with steamed rice or chunks of fresh bread.

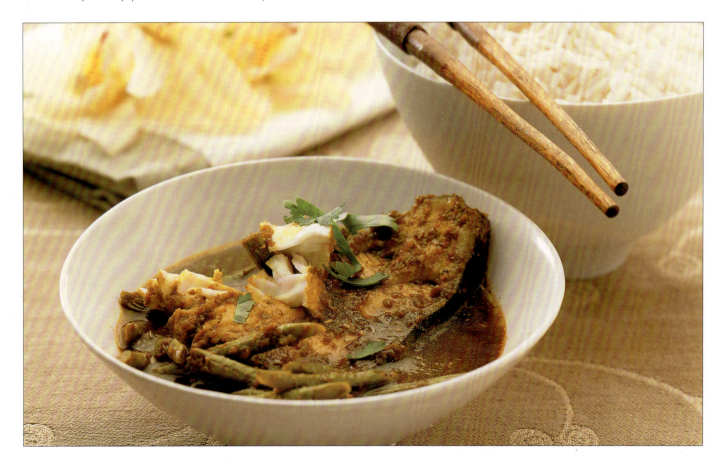

Per Portion Energy 164Kcal/686kJ; Protein 21.7g; Carbohydrate 4.9g, of which sugars 3.5g; Fat 6.5g, of which saturates 0.8g; Cholesterol 52mg; Calcium 33mg; Fibre 1.3g; Sodium 69mg.

CHINESE FISH BALL SOUP

THIS LIGHT CHINESE SOUP CAN BE FOUND IN COFFEE SHOPS AND AT THE TZE CHAR STALLS, WHERE THE FOOD IS ORDERED FROM THE MENU AND COOKED ON THE SPOT. OFTEN EATEN AS A SNACK OR LIGHT LUNCH, THE SOUP IS GARNISHED WITH SPRING ONIONS AND FRESH CHILLIES, AND THE MALAYS OFTEN ADD AN EXTRA DRIZZLE OF CHILLI SAUCE OR A DOLLOP OF CHILLI SAMBAL.

SERVES FOUR TO SIX

INGREDIENTS

For the fish balls
    450g/1lb fresh fish fillets (such as
        haddock, cod, whiting or bream),
        boned and cubed
    15–30ml/1–2 tbsp rice flour
    salt and ground black pepper
For the soup
    1.5 litres/2½ pints/6¼ cups fish or
        chicken stock
    15–30ml/1–2 tbsp light soy sauce
    4–6 mustard green leaves, shredded
    90g/3½oz mung bean thread
        noodles, soaked in hot water
        until soft
For the garnish
    2 spring onions (scallions), trimmed
        and finely sliced
    1 red or green chilli, seeded and
        finely sliced
    fresh coriander (cilantro) leaves,
        finely chopped

COOK'S TIP
This soup is quite quick to make, but if
you wish to do some of the preparation
in advance the fish balls can be stored in
the refrigerator for a few hours.

3 Divide the noodles among four to six bowls. Using a slotted spoon, add the fish balls and greens, then ladle over the hot stock. Garnish with the spring onions and chilli and sprinkle the chopped coriander over the top.

1 To make the fish balls, grind the flaked flesh to a paste, using a mortar and pestle or food processor. Season with salt and pepper and stir in about 60ml/4 tbsp water. Add enough rice flour to form a paste. Take small portions of fish paste into your hands and squeeze them to mould into balls.

2 Meanwhile, bring the stock to the boil in a deep pan and season to taste with soy sauce. Drop in the fish balls. Bring the stock back to the boil, then lower the heat and gently simmer for 5 minutes. Add the shredded mustard greens and cook with the fish balls for 1 minute until just tender.

Per Portion Energy 127Kcal/533kJ; Protein 14.9g; Carbohydrate 14.8g, of which sugars 0.5g; Fat 0.6g, of which saturates 0.1g; Cholesterol 35mg; Calcium 17mg; Fibre 0.2g; Sodium 408mg.

WON TON SOUP

POSSIBLY THE BEST-TRAVELLED CHINESE DISH OF ALL, WON TON SOUP IS NOW UBIQUITOUS IN RESTAURANTS, HAWKER CENTRES AND FOOD COURTS THROUGHOUT SOUTH-EAST ASIA. WON TONS ARRIVED WITH CANTONESE AND HAKKA MIGRANTS FROM SOUTH CHINA AND, IN TIME, WERE ADOPTED BY THE LOCALS. THIS SOUP IS ONE OF THE EASIEST AND TASTIEST STARTERS TO PREPARE AT HOME. ADDING A LITTLE CORNFLOUR TO THE FILLING GIVES IT A SMOOTH TEXTURE.

SERVES FOUR

INGREDIENTS

120g/4oz fresh prawns (shrimp), shelled
100g/3¾oz minced (ground) pork
5ml/1 tsp salt
5ml/1 tsp cornflour (cornstarch)
12 won ton wrappers
600 ml/1 pint/2½ cups water
1 seafood stock cube
1 spring onion (scallion), trimmed and chopped, to garnish
freshly ground black pepper

1 Grind the prawns finely using a pestle and mortar or a food processor and mix with the pork, salt and cornflour.

2 Lay a won ton wrapper flat on the work surface and moisten the edges with water. Place a scant teaspoonful of the mixture in the centre and gather up the sides around the filling to make a tight ball, pressing the wrapper firmly together at the neck to leave a little frill at the top. Repeat with the remaining mixture and won ton wrappers.

3 Bring a pot of water to the boil. Drop in the won tons and cook them for 3 minutes. Drain and set aside.

4 Bring the measured water to the boil, crumble in the stock cube and stir to dissolve. Drop the cooked won tons into the hot stock and cook for 1 minute.

5 Garnish with chopped spring onions and season with black pepper. Divide among four serving bowls and serve the soup immediately.

COOK'S TIP
Won ton wrappers are widely available in Chinese supermarkets.

Per portion Energy 134Kcal/568kJ; Protein 13.6g; Carbohydrate 16.3g, of which sugars 1.9g; Fat 2.1g, of which saturates 0.7g; Cholesterol 52mg; Calcium 42mg; Fibre 0.6g; Sodium 589mg.

HOKKEIN PRAWN NOODLE SOUP

INTRODUCED TO MALAYSIA AND SINGAPORE BY THE CHINESE FROM FUJIAN, HOKKEIN NOODLE SOUP, KNOWN AS HAY MEE, IS SOLD AT THE HAWKER STALLS AND IN THE COFFEE SHOPS. AS MOST OF THE CHINESE POPULATION OF SINGAPORE IS HOKKEIN, IT IS AN ENDURINGLY POPULAR DISH THERE. TRADITIONALLY, PRAWN NOODLE SOUP IS SERVED WITH CRISPLY FRIED CUBES OF PORK FAT, BUT IN THIS RECIPE CRISPY PIECES OF BACON HAVE BEEN USED INSTEAD.

SERVES FOUR TO SIX

INGREDIENTS
For the stock
   45ml/3 tbsp dried shrimp
   1 dried red chilli
   50g/2oz fresh root ginger, peeled
    and sliced
   2 onions, quartered
   4 garlic cloves, bruised
   2 lemon grass stalks, bruised
   2.5ml/½ tsp black peppercorns
   30–45ml/2–3 tbsp dark soy sauce
   700g/1lb 10oz pork and chicken
    bones
For the soup
   15ml/1 tbsp sugar
   6 rashers (strips) streaky
    (fatty) bacon
   150g/5oz fresh egg noodles
   20 fresh, large prawns (shrimp),
    peeled (add the shells to the stock)
   90g/3½oz beansprouts
   2 spring onions (scallions), trimmed
    and finely sliced
   salt and ground black pepper

1 Put all the stock ingredients into a deep pan along with the prawn shells. Pour in 2 litres/3½ pints/7¾ cups water and bring to the boil. Reduce the heat and simmer gently, uncovered, for about 2 hours, until the stock has reduced by half.

2 Strain the stock into a clean pan and put it over a low heat to keep hot. Season with salt and pepper to taste.

3 In a small pan heat the sugar with 15ml/1 tbsp water. Stir over a low heat until the sugar dissolves, then boil without stirring until it turns a rich brown. Add it to the stock and mix well.

4 Cut the bacon into 1cm/½in slices. In a heavy pan, dry-fry the bacon until it turns crispy and golden. Drain on kitchen paper and set aside.

5 Using a perforated ladle or sieve (strainer), plunge the noodles into the hot stock for 1 minute to heat through, then divide them among four bowls. Add the prawns to the stock, heat for 1 minute, remove with a slotted spoon and add to the bowls. Add the beansprouts to the prawns and noodles and ladle the hot stock into the bowls. Scatter the crispy bacon and spring onions over the top and serve the soup immediately in warmed bowls.

Per Portion Energy 257Kcal/1082kJ; Protein 18.7g; Carbohydrate 27.1g, of which sugars 6.9g; Fat 9g, of which saturates 2.8g; Cholesterol 94mg; Calcium 145mg; Fibre 3g; Sodium 1080mg.

MOOLI AND PRAWN SOUP

THIS VERY SIMPLE SOUP OF CANTONESE ORIGIN IS OFTEN DRUNK AS A COOLING BREW TO COUNTERACT A SURFEIT OF SPICY DISHES. MOOLI IS FULL OF FLAVOUR AND HAS AN IMPORTANT PLACE WITHIN THE RANGE OF CHINESE YIN FOODS PURPORTED TO DISPEL BODY HEAT.

SERVES FOUR

INGREDIENTS
150g/5oz mooli (daikon), peeled
700ml/1¼ pints/2¾ cups water
5ml/1 tsp salt
15ml/1 tbsp sesame oil
115g/4oz prawns (shrimp), shelled
1 spring onion (scallion), trimmed
  and chopped
freshly ground black pepper

COOK'S TIP
Mooli is the Hindi name for the large white radish or daikon.

1 Slice the mooli into thin matchstick pieces. Bring water to the boil, add the mooli, salt and sesame oil and simmer for 15 minutes.

2 Add the prawns and simmer for 5 minutes. Scatter with chopped spring onion, add black pepper to taste and serve immediately.

Per portion Energy 52kcal/215kJ; Protein 5.4g; Carbohydrate 0.8g, of which sugars 0.8g; Fat 3g, of which saturates 0.5g; Cholesterol 56mg; Calcium 31mg; Fibre 0.4g; Sodium 550mg.

HOT AND SOUR PINEAPPLE PRAWN BROTH

THIS SIMPLE NONYA DISH IS SERVED AS AN APPETITE ENHANCER BECAUSE OF ITS HOT AND SOUR FLAVOUR. IT IS ALSO POPULAR AS AN ACCOMPANIMENT TO PLAIN RICE OR NOODLES. IN SOME RESTAURANTS, THE BROTH IS PRESENTED IN A HOLLOWED-OUT PINEAPPLE, HALVED LENGTHWAYS.

SERVES FOUR

INGREDIENTS

30ml/2 tbsp vegetable oil
15–30ml/1–2 tbsp tamarind
  paste
15ml/1 tbsp sugar
450g/1lb raw prawns (shrimp),
  peeled and deveined
4 thick fresh pineapple slices, cored
  and cut into bitesize chunks
salt and ground black pepper
fresh coriander (cilantro) and mint
  leaves, to garnish
steamed rice or plain noodles,
  to serve
For the spice paste
4 shallots, chopped
4 red chillies, chopped
25g/1oz fresh root ginger, peeled
  and chopped
1 lemon grass stalk, trimmed and
  chopped
5ml/1 tsp shrimp paste

1 Grind the shallots, chillies, ginger and lemon grass to a paste. Add the shrimp paste and mix well.

2 Heat the oil in a wok or heavy pan. Stir in the spice paste and fry until fragrant. Stir in the tamarind paste and the sugar, then pour in 1.2 litres/ 2 pints/5 cups water. Mix well and bring to the boil. Reduce the heat and simmer for 10 minutes. Season the broth with salt and pepper.

3 Add the prawns and pineapple to the broth and simmer for 4–5 minutes, or until the prawns are cooked. Using a slotted spoon, lift the prawns and pineapple out of the broth and divide them among four warmed bowls. Ladle over some of the broth and garnish with coriander and mint leaves. The remaining broth can be served separately as a drink, or spooned over steamed rice or plain noodles, if they are accompanying this dish.

Per Portion Energy 192Kcal/808kJ; Protein 20.4g; Carbohydrate 14.2g, of which sugars 13.9g; Fat 6.4g, of which saturates 0.8g; Cholesterol 219mg; Calcium 111mg; Fibre 1.3g; Sodium 216mg.

TAMARIND <u>AND</u> PRAWN SOUP

THIS IS A HYBRID DISH SPANNING INDIAN AND THAI TRADITIONS AND LIBERALLY TWEAKED BY NONYA COOKS, WHO PREFER TO LEAVE PRAWNS IN THEIR SHELLS. TAMARIND PLAYS A KEY ROLE IN ASIAN FOOD, MUCH LIKE LEMON JUICE IN THE WEST. IT USED TO BE SOLD IN NEAR-SOLID BLOCKS FULL OF PIPS AND GRIT, BUT THE MODERN CONCENTRATE NEEDS NO STRAINING AND IS READY TO USE.

SERVES TWO

INGREDIENTS
    6 raw tiger prawns (jumbo shrimp)
    600ml/1 pint/2½ cups water
    30g/2 tbsp tamarind concentrate
    15ml/1 tbsp fish sauce
    5ml/1 tsp sugar
    chopped spring onions (scallions)
      to garnish
For the spice paste
    2 red chillies
    15g/½oz fresh turmeric, peeled
    ½ large onion
    2 garlic cloves
    1 lemon grass stalk, 7.5cm/3in of
      root end only

1 Wash the prawns in cold, fresh water and snip about 1cm/½in of the head and the feelers off with scissors, but leave the shells on. Pat the prawns dry with kitchen towels and set aside in a cool place.

2 Grind the ingredients for the spice paste together until very fine, using a mortar and pestle or a food processor. Blend the water and tamarind concentrate, then bring to the boil in a small pan. Add the spice paste.

3 Simmer for 3 minutes, then add the prawns. Season with the fish sauce and sugar. Cook for about 5 minutes or until the prawns have turned completely pink. Serve immediately, garnished with chopped spring onions.

COOK'S TIP
Leaving the prawns in their shells gives the best flavour, but shelling them makes the soup easier to eat. If you prefer to peel the prawns before cooking, add shells to the pan in step 3, then strain the soup and discard the shells before adding the peeled prawns. This will enrich the flavour of the soup.

Per portion Energy 92kcal/387kJ; Protein 14.2g; Carbohydrate 6.1g, of which sugars 6g; Fat 1.3g, of which saturates 0.3g; Cholesterol 48mg; Calcium 122mg; Fibre 0.8g; Sodium 1627mg.

SINGAPORE LAKSA

THERE ARE AS MANY LAKSA DISHES AS THERE ARE DIVERSE REGIONS IN MALAYSIA AND SINGAPORE. THE BASIC DISH CONSISTS OF NOODLES IN A SPICY COCONUT BROTH. IN THE HOME-COOKED SINGAPORE LAKSA, SLICES OF DEEP-FRIED FISH CAKES ARE OFTEN ADDED AT THE END, WHEREAS THE STALL VERSION IS RICH IN A VARIETY OF SEAFOOD, TOPPED WITH COCKLES.

SERVES FOUR TO SIX

INGREDIENTS
For the spice paste
   8 shallots, chopped
   4 garlic cloves, chopped
   40g/1½oz fresh root ginger, peeled
    and chopped
   2 lemon grass stalks, chopped
   6 candlenuts or macadamia nuts
   4 dried red chillies, soaked until soft
    and seeded
   30ml/2 tbsp dried prawns (shrimp),
    soaked until soft
   5–10ml/1–2 tsp belacan
   5–10ml/1–2 tsp sugar
   15ml/1 tbsp vegetable oil
For the laksa
   vegetable oil, for deep-frying
   6 shallots, finely sliced
   600ml/1 pint/2½ cups coconut milk
   400ml/14fl oz/1⅔ cups chicken
    stock
   90g/3½oz prawns (shrimp), shelled
   90g/3½oz squid, cleaned, trimmed
    and sliced
   6–8 scallops
   75g/3oz cockles, shelled
   225g/8oz fresh rice noodles or dried
    rice vermicelli, soaked in lukewarm
    water until pliable
   90g/3½oz beansprouts
   salt and ground black pepper
   a small bunch of Vietnamese mint or
    fresh garden mint, roughly chopped,
    and chilli oil, to garnish

1 Using a mortar and pestle or food processor, grind all the ingredients for the spice paste mixture, apart from the oil. Add the oil to the paste to bind it and set aside.

2 Heat the oil for deep-frying in a wok. Add the sliced shallots to the oil and deep-fry until crispy and golden. Drain and set aside.

3 Heat 30ml/2 tbsp vegetable oil in a large wok or heavy pan. Stir in the spice paste and cook over a low heat for 3–4 minutes, until fragrant.

4 Add the coconut milk and chicken stock and bring to the boil, stirring all the time. Add the prawns, squid and scallops and simmer gently for 5–10 minutes, until the seafood is cooked. Add the cockles at the last minute and season the broth with salt and pepper.

5 Ladle the noodles into individual bowls. Add the beansprouts and ladle over the broth and seafood, making sure the noodles are submerged in the steaming liquid. Garnish the bowls with the crispy shallots, mint and a drizzle of chilli oil.

Per Portion Energy 300Kcal/1254kJ; Protein 14.2g; Carbohydrate 38g, of which sugars 6.9g; Fat 10.3g, of which saturates 1.4g; Cholesterol 77mg; Calcium 69mg; Fibre 0.7g; Sodium 211mg.

EURASIAN CURRIED SOUP

WITH A CULINARY CULTURE BORN FROM INDIAN, MALAY, CHINESE AND EUROPEAN TRADITIONS, THE EURASIANS HAVE SOME DISTINCT DISHES OF THEIR OWN. BECAUSE THEY TRACE THEIR ROOTS TO MELAKA DURING THE DUTCH AND PORTUGUESE PERIODS, MANY OF THE DISHES ARE LINKED TO THAT REGION AND EMPLOY PORTUGUESE METHODS, SUCH AS COOKING IN EARTHENWARE POTS. CHICKEN FEET ARE SOMETIMES ADDED TO THE STOCK IN THIS RECIPE TO ENRICH IT.

SERVES FOUR TO SIX

INGREDIENTS
    1 chicken, about 1kg/2¼lb
    2 chicken feet (optional)
    2 cinnamon sticks
    5ml/1 tsp black peppercorns
    5ml/1 tsp fennel seeds
    5ml/1 tsp cumin seeds
    15 ml/1 tbsp ghee or vegetable oil
      with a little butter
    15–30ml/1–2 tbsp brown
      mustard seeds
    a handful of fresh curry leaves
    salt and ground black pepper
    2 limes, quartered, to serve
For the curry paste
    40g/1½oz fresh root ginger, peeled
      and chopped
    4 garlic cloves, chopped
    4 shallots, chopped
    2 lemon grass stalks, trimmed and
      chopped
    4 dried red chillies, soaked to soften,
      drained, seeded and the pulp
      scraped out
    15–30ml/1–2 tbsp Indian curry
      powder
    salt and ground black pepper

1 To make the curry paste, grind the ginger with the garlic, shallots and lemon grass, using a mortar and pestle or food processor. Add the chilli pulp and curry powder and set aside.

2 Put the chicken and the chicken feet, if using, in a deep pan with the cinnamon sticks, peppercorns, fennel and cumin seeds. Add enough water to just cover, and bring it to the boil. Reduce the heat and cook gently for about 1 hour, until the chicken is cooked through.

3 Using two forks, remove the chicken from the broth, skin it and shred the meat. Strain the broth through a sieve (strainer).

4 In an earthenware pot or wok, heat the ghee or oil. Stir in the mustard seeds and, once they begin to pop and give off a nutty aroma, add the curry paste. Fry the paste until fragrant, then pour in the strained broth. Bring the broth to the boil and season to taste with salt and pepper.

5 Add the curry leaves and shredded chicken, and ladle the soup into bowls. Serve with wedges of lime to squeeze into the soup.

Per Portion Energy 264Kcal/1093kJ; Protein 20.7g; Carbohydrate 1.6g, of which sugars 1g; Fat 19.4g, of which saturates 6.3g; Cholesterol 112mg; Calcium 19mg; Fibre 0.5g; Sodium 104mg.

SPICY CHICKEN SOUP

THIS FRAGRANT SOUP, SOTO AYAM, IS PARTICULARLY POPULAR IN SINGAPORE. ORIGINALLY FROM JAVA, VARIOUS VERSIONS ARE SERVED AT SOUP AND NOODLE STALLS SPECIALIZING IN INDONESIAN AND MALAY FOOD. AS MANY MALAY SINGAPOREANS CAME FROM INDONESIA, IT IS ALWAYS IN DEMAND. WHEN SERVED AS A MEAL ON ITS OWN, DEEP-FRIED POTATO FRITTERS OR CHIPS, OR THE MALAY COMPRESSED RICE CAKES, KETUPAT, ARE ADDED TO THE SOUP.

SERVES SIX

INGREDIENTS

1 small chicken, about 900g/2lb
2 lemon grass stalks, bruised
25g/1oz fresh root ginger, peeled and sliced
2 fresh kaffir lime leaves
1 dried red chilli
30ml/2 tbsp vegetable oil
50g/2oz mung bean thread noodles, soaked until pliable
3 hard-boiled eggs, peeled and halved
115g/4oz beansprouts
a small bunch of fresh coriander (cilantro), roughly chopped, to garnish
2 limes, quartered, chilli oil and soy sauce, to serve

For the rempah
8 shallots, chopped
8 garlic cloves, chopped
6 candlenuts or macadamia nuts
50g/2oz galangal, chopped
2 lemon grass stalks, chopped
4 fresh kaffir lime leaves
15ml/1 tbsp ground coriander
10ml/2 tsp ground turmeric
15ml/1 tbsp vegetable oil

COOK'S TIP
Use a free-range chicken to produce really well-flavoured stock.

1 Using a mortar and pestle or a food processor, grind all the rempah ingredients to a paste. Set aside.

2 Put the chicken, lemon grass, ginger, lime leaves and chilli in a deep pan and pour in enough water to just cover. Bring to the boil, reduce the heat, cover and simmer for about 1 hour, until the chicken is tender. Remove the chicken from the stock, take off and discard the skin and pull the meat from the bones. Tear the meat into shreds. Strain the stock and reserve.

3 In a wok or heavy pan, heat the oil. Stir in the rempah and cook for 1–2 minutes, until fragrant. Pour in the stock and stir well. Season to taste with salt and pepper.

4 Divide the noodles among six bowls. Add the hard-boiled eggs, beansprouts and shredded chicken. Ladle the steaming broth into each bowl and garnish with coriander. Serve the soup immediately with the lime wedges, chilli oil and soy sauce to squeeze, drizzle and pour over it.

Per Portion Energy 493Kcal/2050kJ; Protein 36g; Carbohydrate 8.5g, of which sugars 1g; Fat 35.1g, of which saturates 9.1g; Cholesterol 258mg; Calcium 47mg; Fibre 0.8g; Sodium 178mg.

INDIAN MUTTON SOUP

SOP KAMBING IS A POPULAR DISH AT THE MUSLIM AND MALAY HAWKER STALLS AS WELL AS IN THE COFFEE SHOPS. IT IS A WARMING, SUBSTANTIAL SOUP THAT COMES INTO ITS OWN LATE AT NIGHT, WHEN IT IS VALUED FOR ITS RESTORATIVE QUALITIES. IT ALSO MAKES A GREAT SUPPER DISH, SERVED WITH CHUNKS OF CRUSTY BREAD OR INDIAN FLATBREAD.

SERVES FOUR TO SIX

INGREDIENTS

25g/1oz fresh root ginger, peeled
   and chopped
4–6 garlic cloves, chopped
1 red chilli, seeded and chopped
15ml/1 tbsp ghee or vegetable oil
5ml/1 tsp coriander seeds
5ml/1 tsp cumin seeds
5ml/1 tsp ground fenugreek
5ml/1 tsp sugar
450g/1lb meaty mutton ribs, cut into
   bitesize pieces
2 litres/3½ pints/7¾ cups lamb stock
   or water
10ml/2 tsp tomato purée (paste)
1 cinnamon stick
4–6 cardamom pods, bruised
2 tomatoes, peeled and quartered
salt and ground black pepper
fresh coriander (cilantro) leaves,
   roughly chopped, to garnish

1 Using a mortar and pestle or a food processor, grind the ginger, garlic and chilli to a paste.

2 Heat the ghee or oil in a wok or heavy pan and stir in the coriander and cumin seeds. Add the ginger, garlic and chilli paste along with the fenugreek and sugar. Stir until the mixture is fragrant and beginning to colour. Add the chopped mutton ribs, searing the meat on both sides.

3 Pour in the stock or water and stir in the tomato purée, cinnamon stick and cardamom pods. Bring to the boil, then reduce the heat, cover the pan and simmer gently for 1½ hours, until the meat is very tender and starting to fall away from the bones.

4 Season to taste with salt and pepper. Stir in the tomatoes, and garnish with coriander. Serve hot with chunks of fresh crusty bread or Indian flatbread.

Per Portion Energy 166Kcal/693kJ; Protein 15.2g; Carbohydrate 2.8g, of which sugars 2.5g; Fat 10.6g, of which saturates 5.2g; Cholesterol 62mg; Calcium 12mg; Fibre 0.5g; Sodium 87mg.

INDIAN SPICY NOODLES

THERE ARE VERY FEW NOODLE DISHES IN INDIAN COOKING, BUT MEE REBUS IS ONE OF THE BETTER KNOWN. IT'S REALLY A HYBRID, AS IT USES CHINESE INGREDIENTS SUCH AS PRESERVED SOY BEANS AND WHEAT NOODLES, LIBERALLY SPICED WITH INDIAN AND MALAY SPICES. REBUS MEANS "BOILED" IN MALAY, AND THE DISH IS ESSENTIALLY BOILED NOODLES WITH A THICK, SWEET, SPICY SAUCE.

SERVES FOUR

INGREDIENTS
400g/14oz fresh egg noodles
150g/5oz beansprouts
For the gravy
10 dried red chillies, soaked until
    soft, squeezed dry and seeded
5 candlenuts
115g/4oz onion, sliced
15g/½oz galangal, peeled
    and chopped
25g/1oz ground coriander
75g/3oz preserved soy (yellow)
    beans, crushed
800ml/28 fl oz/3½ cups water
500g/1¼lb sweet potatoes, boiled
    and mashed
45ml/3 tbsp vegetable oil
1 beef stock cube
5ml/1 tsp salt
For the garnishes
4 hard-boiled eggs, quartered
30ml/2 tbsp fried shallots
5 green chillies, sliced
4 limes
30ml/2 tbsp dark soy sauce
fresh celery leaves

1 To make the gravy, grind the chillies, candlenuts, onion and galangal to a smooth paste. Dry fry the ground coriander in a wok over a low heat for 2 minutes and mix into the paste.

2 Heat the oil in a wok or large pan and fry the mixture for 2 minutes, then stir in the soy beans. Add the water and crumble in the stock cube.

3 Bring the stock to the boil and add the mashed sweet potatoes. Season to taste with salt. Cook for 5 minutes, until the sauce is the consistency of thick cream. Remove from the heat and keep the sauce warm.

COOK'S TIP
Have some extra mashed sweet potato standing by if you like a thick sauce.

4 Bring a pan of water to the boil and blanch the beansprouts for 2 minutes. Drain. Do the same with the noodles. Divide the noodles and beansprouts among serving plates and pour a few spoonfuls of sauce over each portion.

5 Garnish each serving with eggs, shallots, green chillies, lime slices, dark soy sauce and fresh celery leaves.

Per portion Energy 615kcal/2598KJ; Protein 16.5g; Carbohydrate 105.4g, of which sugars 12.1g; Fat 17.3g, of which saturates 3.5g; Cholesterol 30mg; Calcium 87mg; Fibre 8g; Sodium 906mg.

PORK BONE TEA

THE LITERAL TRANSLATION OF BAK KUT TEH, PORK BONE TEA, DOESN'T DO JUSTICE TO THIS AROMATIC, PEPPERY BROTH MADE FROM PORK RIBS AND SOMETIMES THE INTERNAL ORGANS OF THE PIG. IT IS A FAVOURITE AT THE LATE-NIGHT HAWKER STALLS AND IN THE COFFEE SHOPS, WHERE IT IS PARTICULARLY POPULAR WITH THE OLDER FOLK, WHO LIKE TO SIP IT WHEN THEY GATHER FOR A CHAT. THE BROTH IS SERVED WITH BOWLS OF STEAMED WHITE RICE, AND THE PIECES OF TENDER PORK FLESH ARE DIPPED INTO SOY SAUCE INFUSED WITH CHILLIES.

1 To make the dipping sauce, stir the soy sauce and chillies together in a small bowl and set aside.

2 To make the spice bag, lay the piece of muslin flat and place all the spices in the centre. Gather up the edges and tie together to form a bag.

3 Put the pork ribs and loin into a deep pan. Add the garlic, cinnamon sticks, star anise and the spice bag. Pour in 2.5 litres/4½ pints/10 cups water and bring to the boil.

4 Skim off any fat from the surface, then stir in the soy sauces and sugar. Reduce the heat and simmer, partially covered, for about 2 hours, until the pork is almost falling off the bones. Season to taste with salt and lots of black pepper.

5 Remove the loin from the broth and cut it into bitesize pieces. Remove the spice bag and discard. Divide the meat and ribs among four to six bowls and ladle the broth over the meat. Remove the star anise and cinnamon, or retain them for decoration only.

6 Serve with the soy and chilli sauce as a dip for the pieces of pork, and steamed rice. Guests will need a fork or chopsticks to eat and dip the pieces of meat and a spoon for the broth.

SERVES FOUR TO SIX

INGREDIENTS
500g/1¼lb meaty pork ribs, trimmed and cut into 5cm/2in lengths
225g/8oz pork loin
8 garlic cloves, unpeeled and bruised
2 cinnamon sticks
5 star anise
120ml/4fl oz/½ cup light soy sauce
50ml/2fl oz/¼ cup dark soy sauce
15ml/1 tbsp sugar

salt and ground black pepper
steamed rice, to serve
For the dipping sauce
120ml/4fl oz/½ cup light soy sauce
2 red chillies, seeded and finely chopped
For the spice bag
6 cloves
15ml/1 tbsp dried orange peel
5ml/1 tsp black peppercorns
5ml/1 tsp coriander seeds
5ml/1 tsp fennel seeds
a piece of muslin (cheesecloth)

Per Portion Energy 49Kcal/206kJ; Protein 8.1g; Carbohydrate 0.8g, of which sugars 0.8g; Fat 1.5g, of which saturates 0.5g; Cholesterol 24mg; Calcium 3mg; Fibre 0g; Sodium 145mg.

BEEF BALL SOUP

THE MAKING OF BEEF BALLS WAS ORIGINALLY A VIETNAMESE WAY OF USING UP CHEAPER CUTS BUT THIS DISH HAS TRANSCENDED RACIAL GROUPS, AS MANY SOUTH VIETNAMESE WERE OF CANTONESE AND TEOCHEW ORIGIN. BEEF BALL SOUP IS NOW SERVED IN MANY CHINESE RESTAURANTS THROUGHOUT MALAYSIA AND SINGAPORE. READY-MADE BEEF BALLS ARE WIDELY AVAILABLE IN CHINESE AND THAI SUPERMARKETS, BUT THEY ARE EASY TO MAKE YOURSELF. USE A LEAN CUT OF BEEF SUCH AS SIRLOIN AND MAKE SURE IT IS FINELY GROUND FOR AN AUTHENTIC TEXTURE.

SERVES FOUR TO SIX

INGREDIENTS

- 500g/1¼lb lean minced (ground) beef
- 15ml/1 tbsp cornflour (cornstarch)
- 1 litre/1¾ pints/4 cups water
- 5ml/1 tsp salt
- 45ml/3 tbsp fish sauce
- 1 beef stock cube
- 2 cinnamon sticks, each about 10cm/4 in long
- 6 cloves
- 2 star anise
- 1 large onion, sliced
- 6 garlic cloves
- 115g/4oz celery stalks
- fresh celery leaves, to garnish
- freshly ground black pepper

1 Put the beef with the cornflour into a pestle and mortar or a food processor, and grind it until very smooth. Add salt and a little water as you go along.

2 Shape the beef into individual balls, each the size of a small lime. To do this, place a small amount in the palm of your hand, form a tight circle with the thumb and fore finger and squeeze. You will get nicely shaped balls.

COOK'S TIP
The longer you process the beef the more springy the resulting texture will be – a requisite for good beef balls.

3 Bring the water to the boil and add the salt, fish sauce, stock cube, cinnamon, cloves, star anise, sliced onion, garlic cloves and celery. Simmer for 30 minutes then strain the stock.

4 Return the stock to the pan and bring to the boil. Drop in the beef balls and cook for 10 minutes. Serve in individual bowls, garnished with celery leaves and ground black pepper.

Per portion Energy 201kcal/837KJ; Protein 16.7g; Carbohydrate 3.3g, of which sugars 0.7g; Fat 13.6g, of which saturates 5.8g; Cholesterol 50mg; Calcium 19mg; Fibre 0.4g; Sodium 456mg.

STREET FOOD AND SNACKS

The appetizing snacks in this chapter are staples of the vibrant street food scene in Malaysia and Singapore. Often eaten hot and fresh from the grill (broiler), they are ideal finger food — there are savoury pancakes and toasts, neat little parcels securely wrapped in pastry, succulent bitesize morsels of fish cooked in crisp batter, and tender pieces of meat such as the classic chicken and pork satay, threaded on sticks and all ready to dip into a delicious spicy sauce.

FRIED INDIAN BREAD

ROTI STALLS ARE GENERALLY RUN BY INDIANS, WHO EXPERTLY KNEAD AND SLAP THE BREAD DOUGHS AND FLICK THEM IN THE AIR BEFORE FRYING THEM ON A GRIDDLE. THIS RECIPE IS FOR THE PLAIN, FLAKY FLATBREAD CALLED ROTI PARATHA. IT IS SERVED WITH CURRIES FOR BREAKFAST, LUNCH AND SUPPER, OR IS SIMPLY SPRINKLED WITH SUGAR FOR A QUICK, SWEET, MID-MORNING SNACK.

SERVES FOUR (MAKES 8 *PARATHAS*)

INGREDIENTS

225g/8oz/2 cups plain (all-purpose) white flour or rice flour
225g/8oz/2 cups wholemeal (whole-wheat) flour
5ml/1 tsp salt
200g/7oz/scant 1 cup ghee or butter
extra flour, for dusting

1 Sift the flours with the salt into a wide bowl. Make a well in the centre and pour in 300ml/½ pint/1¼ cups water. Incorporate the flour gradually, drawing it in from the sides, to make a soft dough. Knead the dough for about 10 minutes, then cover the bowl with a damp dish towel and set aside for 3 hours. Put the ghee or butter into a small pan and melt it over a low heat.

2 Knead the dough again and divide it into 8 portions, rolling each one into a ball – if the dough is sticky, add a little extra flour. Dust a work surface with flour and, using the palm of your hand, flatten one of the balls of dough on it. Roll the dough into an 18cm/7in circle and brush it with the melted ghee.

3 Dust a little flour over the ghee, then roll the paratha into a tight sausage. Wrap it around itself into a coil and place it on the floured surface.

4 Press down on the coil with the palm of your hand to form a patty and roll it into an 18cm/7in circle again. Repeat with the other balls of dough and keep them moist under a damp dish towel.

5 Heat a cast-iron griddle or heavy frying pan and place one paratha on it. Leave it for 30 seconds, then lift it up and brush some ghee under it. Press down on the paratha, moving it around occasionally, for about 2 minutes, then brush some ghee over the top side and flip it over. Cook the second side for about 3 minutes, pressing down on it and moving it around occasionally – it should be nicely browned in patches.

6 Wrap the cooked paratha in foil or a dry dish towel, and repeat with the other balls of dough. They can be cooked and stacked in foil, then heated in the oven before serving. Serve with Indian and Malay curries and soups, or on their own with sugar or jam.

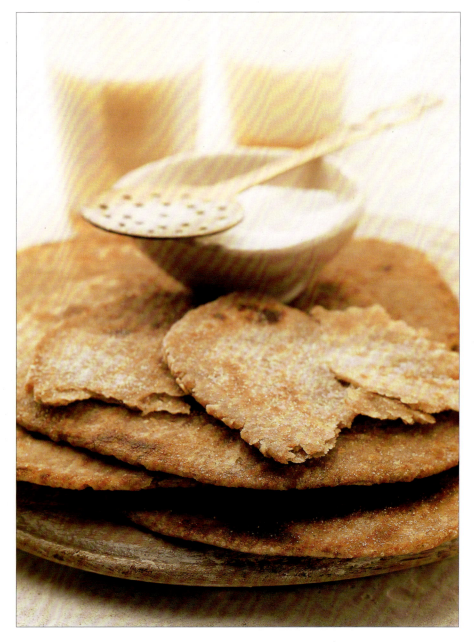

Per Portion Energy 738Kcal/3087kJ; Protein 12.7g; Carbohydrate 80g, of which sugars 2.3g; Fat 43.1g, of which saturates 26.3g; Cholesterol 107mg; Calcium 109mg; Fibre 6.8g; Sodium 798mg.

ONION PANCAKES

A Chinese dim sum staple, these pancakes are now actually made with spring onions although the name is unchanged. You can use onions, but you won't get the same delicate flavour. This recipe makes about 12 pancakes. It is essential to use lard to brush them as oil will not give the same fragrance and smooth texture.

SERVES FOUR

INGREDIENTS
225g/8oz plain (all-purpose) flour
150ml/¼ pint/⅔ cup water
15ml/1 tbsp lard
6 spring onions (scallions), trimmed
  and finely chopped
5ml/1 tsp salt
10ml/2 tsp sesame oil
oil for frying

1 Sift the flour into a large bowl and pour in the water, a little at time, stirring to create a smooth dough.

2 Work the dough until it is soft and pliable. Knead for 5 minutes and set aside, covered with a damp cloth, for 20 minutes.

3 Divide the dough into 12 pieces. Roll out into rectangles 5mm/¼in thick.

4 Toss the spring onions with salt and sesame oil. Brush each pancake with melted lard and scatter with some of the chopped spring onions.

5 Roll up the pancakes lengthways to encase the onions then flatten slightly so that they will not unwrap during cooking.

COOK'S TIP
Eat the pancakes just as they are or with soy sauce or another dipping sauce.

6 Heat a wok with about 15ml/1 tbsp oil and fry the pancakes one or two at a time until light brown along the edges. Add more oil as required.

7 Flip over and cook the other side. Each pancake should take about 3 minutes to cook and puff up slightly.

Per portion Energy 242Kcal/1023kJ; Protein 5.6g; Carbohydrate 44.2g, of which sugars 1.3g; Fat 6g, of which saturates 1.9g; Cholesterol 3mg; Calcium 85mg; Fibre 2g; Sodium

FRIED HARD-BOILED EGGS IN HOT RED SAUCE

A popular snack at Malay stalls, this spicy egg dish originally came from Indonesia. Served wrapped in a banana leaf, the Malays often eat it with plain steamed rice, sliced chillies, onion and coriander — ideal for a quick, tasty snack or light lunch.

SERVES FOUR

INGREDIENTS
    vegetable oil, for deep-frying
    8 eggs, hard-boiled and shelled
    1 lemon grass stalk, trimmed,
       quartered and crushed
    2 large tomatoes, skinned, seeded
       and chopped to a pulp
    5–10ml/1–2 tsp sugar
    30ml/2 tbsp dark soy sauce
    juice of 1 lime
    fresh coriander (cilantro) and mint
       leaves, coarsely chopped, to garnish
For the rempah
    4–6 red chillies, seeded and chopped
    4 shallots, chopped
    2 garlic cloves, chopped
    2.5ml/½ tsp shrimp paste

1 Using a mortar and pestle or food processor, grind the ingredients for the rempah to form a smooth paste. Set aside.

2 Heat enough oil for deep-frying in a wok or heavy pan and deep-fry the whole boiled eggs until golden brown. Lift them out and drain.

3 Reserve 15ml/1 tbsp of the oil and discard the rest. Heat the oil in the wok or heavy pan and stir in the rempah until it becomes fragrant. Add the lemon grass, followed by the tomatoes and sugar. Cook for 2–3 minutes, until it forms a thick paste.

4 Reduce the heat and stir in the soy sauce and lime juice. Add 30ml/2 tbsp water to thin the sauce. Toss in the eggs, making sure they are thoroughly coated, and serve hot, garnished with chopped coriander and mint leaves.

COOK'S TIP
If you don't want to deep-fry the eggs, plain hard-boiled eggs can be heated up in the spicy sauce.

Per Portion Energy 271Kcal/1125kJ; Protein 13.3g; Carbohydrate 5.5g, of which sugars 5g; Fat 22.3g, of which saturates 4.4g; Cholesterol 381mg; Calcium 67mg; Fibre 0.7g; Sodium 679mg.

FRIED DRIED ANCHOVIES
WITH PEANUTS

THE MALAYS AND PERANAKANS LOVE FRIED DRIED ANCHOVIES, IKAN BILIS GORENG. GENERALLY, THEY ARE SERVED AS A SNACK WITH BREAD OR AS AN ACCOMPANIMENT TO NASI LEMAK (COCONUT RICE). THE MALAYS ALSO ENJOY THEM WITH BUBUR (RICE PORRIDGE), FOR BREAKFAST.

SERVES FOUR

INGREDIENTS

    4 shallots, chopped
    2 garlic cloves, chopped
    4 dried red chillies, soaked in warm
      water until soft, then seeded and
      chopped
    30ml/2 tbsp tamarind pulp, soaked
      in 150ml/¼ pint/⅔ cup water
      until soft
    vegetable oil, for deep-frying
    115g/4oz/1 cup peanuts
    200g/7oz dried anchovies, heads
      removed, washed and drained
    30ml/2 tbsp sugar
    bread or rice, to serve

1 Using a mortar and pestle or food processor, grind the shallots, garlic and chillies to a coarse paste. Squeeze the tamarind pulp to help soften it in the water and press it through a sieve (strainer). Measure out 120ml/4fl oz/ ½ cup of the tamarind water.

2 Heat enough oil for deep-frying in a wok. Add the anchovies to the oil and deep-fry until brown and crisp. Drain the anchovies on kitchen paper.

3 Lower the heat and deep-fry the peanuts in a wire basket, until they colour. Drain them on kitchen paper.

4 Pour out most of the oil from the wok, reserving 30ml/2 tbsp. Stir in the spice paste and fry until fragrant. Add the sugar, anchovies and peanuts. Gradually stir in the tamarind water, allowing it to evaporate and be soaked in so that the mixture remains dry.

5 Serve the dish hot or cold with bread or blended with steamed rice.

Per Portion Energy 338Kcal/1400kJ; Protein 17g; Carbohydrate 4.8g, of which sugars 2.6g; Fat 28g, of which saturates 4.4g; Cholesterol 24mg; Calcium 134mg; Fibre 2g; Sodium 1475mg.

CRISPY PEPPERY SQUID

This is an often-seen dish at seafood stalls in most coastal towns. All along the east coast of Singapore, where seafood stalls predominate, peppery squid is sold together with the much-loved chilli crab. Cantonese chefs make excellent use of fresh baby squid cooked whole in their ink. They are so small you can eat them whole.

SERVES FOUR

INGREDIENTS
    24 small whole squid
    10ml/2 tsp cornflour (cornstarch)
    10ml/2 tsp freshly ground black
      pepper
    5ml/1 tsp salt
    oil for deep-frying
    sweet chilli sauce, to serve

COOK'S TIP
If baby squid are not available you can use squid rings for this dish, although the flavour will not be quite as good.

1 Wash the squid but leave them whole. Dry them thoroughly and place them in a plastic bag. Add the cornflour and toss well to coat the squid.

2 Shake off the excess cornflour and season the squid liberally with salt and freshly ground pepper, pressing them in firmly.

3 Heat the oil in a wok or heavy pan and fry the squid until crispy, a few at a time so that they do not stick together.

4 Reserve the fried squid on crumpled paper on a warm plate until they are all ready, and serve immediately with a sweet chilli sauce and wedges of lemon to squeeze over.

Per portion Energy 346kcal/1462kJ; Protein 31.2g; Carbohydrate 31.3g, of which sugars 2.6g; Fat 11.6g, of which saturates 1.8g; Cholesterol 422mg; Calcium 32mg; Fibre 0g; Sodium 1741mg.

SWEET AND SOUR DEEP-FRIED SQUID

A FAVOURITE AT THE HAWKER STALLS OF SINGAPORE, DEEP-FRIED SQUID SERVED WITH A SWEET AND SOUR SAUCE IS POPULAR WITH MALAYS, CHINESE, PERANAKANS AND EURASIANS. THIS IS AN EXAMPLE OF A DISH WHERE THE WESTERN INFLUENCE COMES INTO PLAY — THE DIPPING SAUCE IS MADE USING TOMATO KETCHUP AND WORCESTERSHIRE SAUCE.

SERVES FOUR

INGREDIENTS
    900g/2lb fresh young, tender squid
    vegetable oil, for deep-frying
For the marinade
    60ml/4 tbsp light soy sauce
    15ml/1 tbsp sugar
For the dipping sauce
    30ml/2 tbsp tomato ketchup
    15ml/1 tbsp Worcestershire sauce
    15ml/1 tbsp light soy sauce
    15ml/1 tbsp vegetable or sesame oil
    sugar or honey, to sweeten
    chilli oil, to taste

COOK'S TIP
To avoid the spitting fat, lightly coat the squid in flour before deep-frying. Alternatively, fry in a deep-fat fryer with a lid or use a spatterproof cover on the wok or pan.

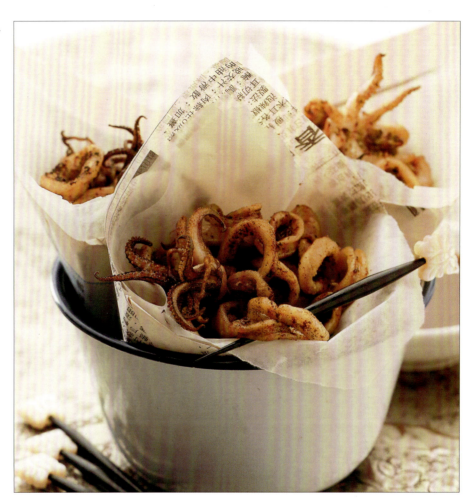

1 First prepare the squid. Hold the body in one hand and pull off the head with the other. Sever the tentacles and discard the rest. Remove the backbone and clean the body sac inside and out. Pat dry using kitchen paper and cut into rings.

2 In a bowl, mix the soy sauce with the sugar until it dissolves. Toss in the squid rings and tentacles and leave to marinate for 1 hour.

3 Meanwhile prepare the sauce. Mix together the tomato ketchup, soy sauce, Worcestershire sauce and oil. Sweeten with sugar or honey to taste and add as much chilli oil as you like. Set aside until ready to serve.

4 Heat enough oil for deep-frying in a wok or heavy pan. Thoroughly drain the squid of any marinade, pat well with kitchen paper to avoid spitting, and fry the squid rings until they are golden and crispy. Drain on kitchen paper and serve immediately, accompanied by the dipping sauce.

Per Portion Energy 315Kcal/1320kJ; Protein 35.2g; Carbohydrate 4.5g, of which sugars 1.7g; Fat 17.6g, of which saturates 2.5g; Cholesterol 506mg; Calcium 39mg; Fibre 0g; Sodium 1361mg.

GRILLED TAMARIND PRAWNS

THE AROMA EMANATING FROM THE MALAY GRILL STALLS AS LARGE, MARINATED PRAWNS ARE GRILLED OVER CHARCOAL MAKES YOU FEEL VERY HUNGRY. RATHER EXPERTLY, THE MALAYSIANS CRUNCH THE WHOLE PRAWN, SUCKING IN ALL THE TAMARIND FLAVOURING WHILE SPITTING OUT THE BITS OF SHELL. THE MARINADE IS SEASONED AND SWEETENED WITH KECAP MANIS, AN INDONESIAN-STYLE CONDIMENT OF SOY SAUCE SWEETENED WITH PALM SUGAR, BUT YOU COULD REPLACE IT WITH THE SAME QUANTITY OF DARK SOY SAUCE BLENDED WITH A LITTLE PALM OR MUSCOVADO SUGAR.

3 In a bowl, mix together the strained tamarind juice with the kecap manis, sugar and black pepper. Pour the mixture over the prawns, rubbing it over the shells and into the incisions in the tails. Cover the bowl and leave to marinate for 1 hour.

4 Prepare the charcoal, or heat a conventional grill (broiler) to a high heat, and place the prawns on the rack. Grill (broil) the prawns for about 3 minutes on each side until they are cooked through, brushing them with the marinade as they cook.

5 Serve immediately, garnished with coriander and chillies.

VARIATION

The seasonings and method of cooking in this recipe works well with other shellfish, as well as with chicken wings and drumsticks. The dish makes a tangy addition to a barbecue – cook it on a clean griddle to keep the flavours pure.

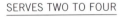
SERVES TWO TO FOUR

INGREDIENTS
  500g/1¼ lb fresh, large prawns
    (shrimp)
  45ml/3 tbsp tamarind pulp
  30ml/2 tbsp kecap manis
  15ml/1 tbsp sugar
  ground black pepper
  fresh coriander (cilantro) leaves and
    2–4 green chillies, seeded and
    quartered lengthways, to garnish

1 Devein the prawns and remove the feelers and legs. Rinse well, pat dry with kitchen paper and, using a sharp knife, make an incision along the curve of the tail.

2 Put the tamarind pulp in a bowl and add 250ml/8fl oz/1 cup warm water. Soak the pulp until soft, squeezing it with your fingers to help it dissolve in the water. Strain the liquid and discard any fibre.

Per Portion Energy 74Kcal/309kJ; Protein 11.4g; Carbohydrate 4.9g, of which sugars 4.8g; Fat 1.1g, of which saturates 0.3g; Cholesterol 39mg; Calcium 97mg; Fibre 0.6g; Sodium 1301mg.

DEEP-FRIED OYSTERS

EATING OYSTERS ON THE HALF SHELL IS NOT A COMMON MALAYSIAN PRACTICE — APART FROM SOPHISTICATES USED TO WESTERN FARE — AS THE BEST ONES ARE IMPORTED, AND CONSEQUENTLY EXPENSIVE. THE LOCAL OYSTERS ARE NOT AS GOOD, BUT LEND THEMSELVES TO COOKING IN INVENTIVE WAYS, ESPECIALLY AMONG THE TEOCHEWS IN MALAYSIA AND SINGAPORE. THESE OYSTERS FRIED IN A LIGHT BATTER ARE CRISPY AND LIGHT AS AIR ON THE OUTSIDE AND SUCCULENT ON THE INSIDE. CANNED OYSTERS ARE ALSO GOOD COOKED THIS WAY.

SERVES FOUR

INGREDIENTS
16 large fresh oysters, shelled
oil for deep-frying
sweet chilli sauce or lime wedges,
   to serve
For the batter
50g/2oz rice flour
25g/1oz self-raising (self-rising) flour
100ml/3½ fl oz cold water
1 egg white

1 Wash and drain the oysters thoroughly. Blend the flours and stir in the cold water until well mixed.

2 Beat the egg white in a clean, dry bowl with an electric whisk until stiff peaks form, then fold it lightly into the batter. Stir thoroughly but gently until the batter is smooth.

3 Heat the oil in a wok or heavy pan. Dip each oyster in the batter and deep-fry for 1–2 minutes until brown and crispy. Serve with a sweet chilli sauce or a good squeeze of lime juice.

Per portion Energy 244kcal/1012kJ; Protein 6.4g; Carbohydrate 15.8g, of which sugars 0.1g; Fat 17.2g, of which saturates 2g; Cholesterol 23mg; Calcium 81mg; Fibre 0.5g; Sodium 242mg.

OYSTER OMELETTE

OFTEN DEVOURED AS A LATE-NIGHT TREAT, OYSTER OMELETTE, OR LUAH, IS A FAVOURITE HAWKER STALL SNACK IN SINGAPORE. ALMOST DECADENT IN ITS LAVISH USE OF OYSTERS, THIS IS A TASTY AND SATISFYING DISH, INSPIRED BY THE CHINESE.

SERVES TWO

INGREDIENTS
   30ml/2 tbsp vegetable oil
   2 garlic cloves, finely chopped
   1 red chilli, finely chopped
   8 large fresh oysters, shelled
      and rinsed
   15ml/1 tbsp light soy sauce
   15ml/1 tbsp Chinese wine
   4 eggs, lightly beaten with
      30ml/2 tbsp milk
   8 small fresh oysters, shelled
      and rinsed
   chilli oil
   salt and ground black pepper
   fresh coriander (cilantro) leaves,
      finely chopped, to garnish

COOK'S TIP
In Penang a generous splash of oyster sauce is added with the small oysters.

1 Heat the oil in a heavy frying pan. Stir in the garlic and chilli until they become fragrant. Add the large oysters and cook for 1 minute, then stir in the soy sauce and Chinese wine. Season with salt and black pepper.

2 Pour in the beaten egg mixture and, using a wooden spatula, pull it back from the edge of the pan until it begins to solidify.

3 Reduce the heat. Scatter the small oysters over the top of the egg and drizzle with chilli oil. Cover the pan and leave to steam for 5–10 minutes until firm. Sprinkle the omelette with chopped coriander, cut it into wedges and serve it from the pan.

Per Portion Energy 370Kcal/1543kJ; Protein 32.2g; Carbohydrate 6.1g, of which sugars 1.3g; Fat 24.6g, of which saturates 4.9g; Cholesterol 481mg; Calcium 322mg; Fibre 0g; Sodium 1573mg.

POPIAH

THIS NONYA CREATION IS A GREAT DO-IT-YOURSELF DISH. ITS CLOSEST RELATIVE IS PERHAPS THE VIETNAMESE RICE PAPER ROLL, WHERE THE WRAPS AND ALL THE INDIVIDUAL INGREDIENTS ARE PREPARED AND SELF-ASSEMBLED AT THE DINNER TABLE.

SERVES FOUR TO SIX

INGREDIENTS
    45ml/3 tbsp vegetable oil
    225g/8oz firm tofu, rinsed, drained
        and diced
    4 garlic cloves, finely chopped
    4 rashers (strips) streaky (fatty)
        bacon, finely sliced
    45ml/3 tbsp fermented soya beans
        (tau cheo), mashed to a paste
    450g/1lb fresh prawns (shrimp),
        peeled and deveined
    225g/8oz jicama (sweet turnip),
        peeled and shredded
    450g/1lb bamboo shoots, rinsed
        and grated
    15ml/1 tbsp dark soy sauce
    10ml/2 tsp sugar
    4–6 red chillies, seeded and pounded
        to a paste
    6–8 garlic cloves, pounded to
        a paste
    kecap manis, to serve
    12 cos or romaine lettuce leaves,
        washed and patted dry
    1 small cucumber, peeled, seeded
        and finely shredded
    225g/8oz beansprouts, washed and
        drained
    2 Chinese sausages, fried
        and sliced
    225g/8oz cooked prawns (shrimp),
        peeled
    225g/8oz cooked crab meat
    3 eggs, beaten and fried to form
        a plain omelette, sliced into
        thin ribbons
    fresh coriander (cilantro) leaves,
        roughly chopped
    12 popiah wraps or Mexican
        corn tortillas

1 Heat the oil in a wok or heavy pan. Fry the tofu until golden. Remove from the oil and pat dry on kitchen paper.

2 Fry the garlic and bacon in the oil, stirring constantly, until they begin to colour. Stir in the fermented soya beans and fresh prawns.

3 Add the jicama, bamboo shoots, soy sauce and sugar. Fry over a high heat to reduce the water released from the jicama. Toss in the fried tofu and cook the mixture gently until almost dry. Transfer to a serving dish.

4 Assemble the remaining ingredients in separate bowls and place them on the table. Place the wraps on a plate.

5 To serve, everyone should help themselves to a wrap and smear it with the chilli and garlic pastes, followed by the kecap manis. A lettuce leaf goes on top followed by cucumber, beansprouts, and the cooked filling. Add Chinese sausage, prawns and crab, a few strips of omelette and a little coriander, then roll up the wrap, tucking in the ends, to make a tight package.

Per Portion Energy 457Kcal/1916kJ; Protein 32.3g; Carbohydrate 39.2g, of which sugars 5.8g; Fat 20.1g, of which saturates 4.9g; Cholesterol 213mg; Calcium 396mg; Fibre 4.5g; Sodium 989mg.

CRAB TOFU PARCELS

THIS IS AN INNOVATIVE WAY TO USE CRAB MEAT AND IS A STAPLE DISH IN CHINESE RESTAURANTS. USE ONLY THE FRESHEST CRAB MEAT OR TOP-QUALITY CANNED CRAB MEAT. MOST LONG-LIFE TOFU COMES IN TWO TYPES, SOFT AND FIRM. USE THE FIRM VARIETY FOR THESE PARCELS.

SERVES FOUR

INGREDIENTS
    150g/5oz fresh or canned
      crab meat
    5ml/1 tsp cornflour (cornstarch)
    1 egg, lightly beaten
    15 ml/1 tbsp sesame oil
    2 packets firm tofu, about
      500g/1¼lb
    2 spring onions (scallions), trimmed
      and finely chopped
    salt and ground black pepper

1 Lightly crush the crab meat and mix to a paste with the cornflour and beaten egg.

2 Add salt, pepper and sesame oil and mix thoroughly.

3 Divide the tofu into 4 square pieces. With a melon baller, gently scoop out a hollow in each piece.

4 Fill each hollow with the crab meat mixture and place in a deep plate. Sprinkle each piece with finely chopped spring onion.

5 Steam the parcels for 5 minutes and serve as a warm appetizer.

Per portion Energy 170Kcal/706kJ; Protein 18.6g; Carbohydrate 2g, of which sugars 0.5g; Fat 9.8g, of which saturates 1.5g; Cholesterol 75mg; Calcium 692mg; Fibre 0.1g; Sodium 230mg.

PRAWN AND SESAME TOASTS

THESE IRRESISTIBLE LITTLE TOAST TRIANGLES ARE A POPULAR HOT SNACK PREPARED BY CHINESE COOKS, MAKING USE OF THE WHITE BREAD INTRODUCED TO SOUTH-EAST ASIA BY EUROPEAN SETTLERS. THEY ARE SURPRISINGLY EASY TO PREPARE AND YOU CAN COOK THEM IN A FEW MINUTES.

SERVES FOUR

INGREDIENTS

225g/8oz peeled raw prawns (shrimp)
15ml/1 tbsp sherry
15ml/1 tbsp soy sauce
30ml/2 tbsp cornflour (cornstarch)
2 egg whites, whisked until stiff
4 slices white bread
115g/4oz/½ cup sesame seeds
oil, for deep-frying
sweet chilli sauce, to serve

1 Process the prawns, sherry and soy sauce in a food processor. Add the whisked egg whites with the cornflour and lightly but thoroughly fold them together until well blended.

2 Cut each slice of bread into four triangular quarters. Spread out the sesame seeds on a large plate.

3 Spread the prawn paste over one side of each bread triangle, then press the coated sides into the sesame seeds so that they stick and cover the prawn paste.

COOK'S TIPS
• Always use a very clean, dry bowl and whisk to prepare egg whites, otherwise they will fail to stiffen.
• Prepare the toasts a few hours ahead and chill them until you are ready to fry and serve them.
• The spicy, sweet dipping sauce on page 89 goes very well with these prawn toasts, but you can buy bottles of sauce for convenience.

4 Heat the oil in a wok or deep-fryer, to 190°C/375°F or until a cube of bread, added to the oil, browns in about 45 seconds. Add the toasts, a few at a time, prawn side down, and deep-fry for 2–3 minutes, then turn and fry on the other side until golden.

5 Drain on kitchen paper and serve hot with sweet chilli sauce.

Per portion Energy 433Kcal/1806kJ; Protein 19.1g; Carbohydrate 27.7g, of which sugars 1.2g; Fat 27.6g, of which saturates 3.6g; Cholesterol 110mg; Calcium 271mg; Fibre 2.7g; Sodium 559mg.

SAMOSAS

These tasty vegetarian parcels travelled to Malaysia and Singapore with migrant Indian workers in the 19th century. They are an ideal street snack, eaten at any time of day. Filo pastry can be used instead of spring roll wrappers if you prefer.

MAKES ABOUT 20

INGREDIENTS
  1 packet 25cm/10in square spring
    roll wrappers, thawed if frozen
  30ml/2 tbsp plain (all-purpose) flour,
    mixed to a paste with water
  vegetable oil, for deep frying
  coriander (cilantro) leaves, to garnish
  cucumber, carrot and celery, cut into
    matchsticks, to serve (optional)
For the filling
  25g/1oz/2 tbsp ghee or unsalted
    butter
  1 small onion, finely chopped
  1cm/½in piece fresh root ginger,
    peeled and chopped
  1 garlic clove, crushed
  2.5ml/½ tsp chilli powder
  1 large potato, about 225g/8oz,
    cooked until just tender and
    finely diced
  50g/2oz/½ cup cauliflower florets,
    lightly cooked, chopped into
    small pieces
  50g/2oz/½ cup frozen peas, thawed
  5–10ml/1–2 tsp garam masala
  15ml/1 tbsp chopped fresh coriander
    (leaves and stems)
  squeeze of lemon juice
  salt

1 Heat the ghee or butter in a large wok and fry the onion, ginger and garlic for 5 minutes until the onion has softened. Add the chilli powder, cook for 1 minute, then stir in the cauliflower, potato and peas. Sprinkle with garam masala and set aside to cool. Stir in the coriander, lemon juice and salt.

2 Cut the spring roll wrappers into three strips (or two for larger samosas). Brush the edges with a little of the flour paste. Place a small spoonful of filling about 2cm/¾in in from the edge of one strip.

3 Fold one corner over the filling to make a triangle and continue this folding until the entire strip has been used and a triangular pastry packet has been formed.

4 Seal any open edges with more flour and water paste, if necessary adding more water if the paste is very thick.

5 In a wok or heavy pan heat the oil to 190°C/375°F and deep fry the samosas, a few at a time, until golden and crisp. Drain well on kitchen paper and serve hot garnished with coriander leaves and accompanied by crunchy cucumber, carrot and celery matchsticks, if liked.

Per portion Energy 56Kcal/2351kJ; Protein 1.4g; Carbohydrate 10.4g, of which sugars 0.6g; Fat 1.3g, of which saturates 0.7g; Cholesterol 3mg; Calcium 17mg; Fibre 0.6g; Sodium 9mg.

CHARGRILLED SPICY CHICKEN WINGS

SPICY GRILLED CHICKEN JOINTS ARE VERY POPULAR AS A QUICK SNACK, WHICH CAN EVEN BE ENJOYED ON THE MOVE. THEY ARE OFTEN SERVED ON THEIR OWN, OR FORM PART OF THE SELECTION OF DISHES ON DISPLAY AT THE TZE CHAR STALLS, WHERE PEOPLE FILL THEIR BOWLS WITH WHATEVER THEY WANT.

SERVES FOUR

INGREDIENTS

    12 chicken wings
    fresh coriander (cilantro) leaves,
      roughly chopped, and 2–3 green
      chillies, seeded and quartered
      lengthways, to garnish
For the spice paste
    4 shallots, chopped
    4 garlic cloves, chopped
    25g/1oz fresh root ginger, chopped
    8 red chillies, seeded and chopped
    1 lemon grass stalk, trimmed
      and chopped
    30ml/2 tbsp sesame or groundnut
      (peanut) oil
    15ml/1 tbsp tomato purée (paste)
    10ml/2 tsp sugar
    juice of 2 limes
    salt and ground black pepper

VARIATION
If you prefer boneless chicken, use 6 halved breast fillets instead of the wings and cook them in the same way.

1 First make the spice paste. Using a mortar and pestle or food processor, grind the shallots, garlic, ginger, chillies and lemon grass to a paste. Bind with the oil and stir in the tomato purée, sugar and lime juice. Season with salt and pepper.

2 Rub the spice paste into the chicken wings and leave to marinate for 2 hours.

3 Prepare the charcoal grill. Lift the chicken wings out of the marinade and place them on the rack. Cook them for about 5 minutes each side until cooked through, brushing with the remaining marinade while they cook.

4 Serve the chicken wings immediately, garnished with chopped coriander and slivers of chilli.

Per Portion Energy 350Kcal/1455kJ; Protein 30.7g; Carbohydrate 2.6g, of which sugars 2.6g; Fat 24.1g, of which saturates 5.9g; Cholesterol 134mg; Calcium 11mg; Fibre 0.1g; Sodium 99mg.

CHICKEN SATAY

THIS POPULAR DISH IS A DELICACY THAT EVERY SOUTH-EAST ASIAN COUNTRY CLAIMS AS THEIR OWN. HOWEVER, MALAYSIA CAN BOAST SOME OF THE BEST AVAILABLE, ESPECIALLY IN RURAL AREAS, AND IN SINGAPORE THE MANY SATAY STALLS ALONG BEACH ROAD IN THE 1950s CAME TO BE KNOWN AS THE SATAY CLUB. LEMON GRASS, BRUISED AT THE ROOT END, MAKES A FEATHERY BASTING BRUSH.

1 Blend together all the ingredients for the marinade in a non-metallic dish. Add the chicken and marinate for several hours or overnight.

2 To make the sauce, grind the onions, garlic, shrimp paste, galangal, lemon grass and chillies to make a fine paste. Heat the oil and fry the paste over medium heat for 15 minutes, stirring constantly. When the oil separates, add the tamarind blended with the water and bring to the boil. Season to taste with salt and sugar and simmer for 10 minutes.

3 Thread 3–4 pieces of chicken on to each stick, pressing them together. Grill (broil) over hot coals or under a hot grill (broiler) for 8 minutes, turning once.

4 Dip the lemon grass in oil and baste them to impart a delicious lemony tang.

5 Heat the sauce through, add the ground nuts and stir well. Remove from the heat immediately and serve with the satay sticks.

MAKES ABOUT 20–24 STICKS

INGREDIENTS
  500g/1¼lb chicken breast, cut into pieces 4 x 2.5 x 1cm/1½ x 1 x ½in
  20–24 bamboo or wooden skewers, soaked in water
For the marinade
  15ml/1 tbsp ground coriander
  15ml/1 tbsp ground cumin
  5ml/1 tsp ground turmeric
  5ml/1 tsp chilli powder
  150ml/5 fl oz/¾ cup coconut milk
  5ml/1 tsp salt
  10ml/2 tsp sugar
  45ml/3 tbsp oil
  1 stalk lemon grass, bruised at the root end to make a brush
For the sauce (makes about 1 litre/ 1¾ pints/4 cups)
  2 large onions, roughly chopped

4 cloves garlic, roughly chopped
25g/1oz shrimp paste
15g/½oz galangal, roughly chopped
2 stalks lemon grass, 7.5cm/3in of root end
10 dried chillies, soaked until soft and seeds removed (optional for milder flavour)
300g/11oz peanuts, finely ground
45ml/3 tbsp tamarind concentrate
400ml/14 fl oz/1⅔ cups water
10ml/2 tsp salt
25g/1oz sugar
150ml/5 fl oz/⅔ cup vegetable oil

COOK'S TIP
Add the ground peanuts to the sauce just before serving the satay, otherwise they tend to settle down and make the sauce too stiff. If this happens, warm it in a microwave oven for 1–2 minutes.

Per portion Energy 33Kcal/139kJ; Protein 7.1g; Carbohydrate 0.4g, of which sugars 0.3g; Fat 0.3g, of which saturates 0.1g; Cholesterol 20mg; Calcium 2mg; Fibre 0.1g; Sodium 107mg.

SPICY LENTIL AND MEAT PATTIES

OTHERWISE KNOWN AS SHAMI KEBABS, THESE LENTIL AND LAMB PATTIES ARE POPULAR ON THE MALAY AND MUSLIM STALLS, WHICH ARE OFTEN GROUPED TOGETHER. OF INDIAN ORIGIN, THE SHAMI KEBABS OF MALAYSIA AND SINGAPORE HAVE BEEN ADAPTED TO SUIT THE LOCAL TASTES, OFTEN SERVED WITH RICE AND A SAMBAL, OR EVEN BETWEEN CHUNKS OF BREAD WITH TOMATO KETCHUP, LIKE A BURGER.

SERVES FOUR

INGREDIENTS
- 150g/5oz/generous ½ cup red, brown, yellow or green lentils, rinsed
- 30ml/2 tbsp vegetable oil
- 2 onions, finely chopped
- 2 garlic cloves, finely chopped
- 1 green chilli, seeded and finely chopped
- 25g/1oz fresh root ginger, finely chopped
- 250g/9oz lean minced (ground) lamb
- 10ml/2 tsp Indian curry powder
- 5ml/1 tsp ground turmeric
- 4 eggs
- vegetable oil, for shallow frying
- salt and ground black pepper
- fresh coriander (cilantro) leaves, roughly chopped, to garnish
- 1 lemon, quartered, to serve

COOK'S TIP
These patties are delicious served in a baguette, halved lengthways, layered with lettuce leaves, coriander (cilantro), mint, yogurt and a hot chutney or a chilli sauce.

1 Put the lentils in a pan and cover with plenty of cold water. Bring the water to the boil and cook gently until the lentils have softened but still have a little bite to them – this may take 20–40 minutes depending on the type of lentil you are using. Drain well.

2 Heat the oil in a heavy pan and stir in the onions, garlic, chilli and ginger. Fry until they begin to colour, then add the lentils and minced lamb. Cook for a few minutes, then add the curry powder and turmeric. Season with salt and pepper and cook the mixture over a high heat until the moisture has evaporated. The mixture needs to be dry for the patties.

3 Leave the meat mixture aside until it is cool enough to handle. Beat one of the eggs lightly and stir it into the meat.

4 Using your fingers, take small portions of the mixture and roll them into balls about the size of a plum or apricot. Press each ball in the palm of your hand to a form a thick, flat patty – if the mixture sticks to your hands, wet your palms with a little water.

5 Beat the remaining eggs in a bowl. Heat enough oil in a heavy pan for shallow frying. Dip each patty in turn in beaten egg and place them all in the hot oil. Fry for about 3–4 minutes each side, until golden. Garnish with fresh coriander and serve with lemon wedges to squeeze over.

Per Portion Energy 488Kcal/2033kJ; Protein 28g; Carbohydrate 25.7g, of which sugars 3.7g; Fat 31.2g, of which saturates 7.4g; Cholesterol 238mg; Calcium 87mg; Fibre 3.1g; Sodium 140mg.

MINCED PORK AND TARO PUFFS

A DIM SUM FAVOURITE, THESE ARE CALLED WU KOK IN CANTONESE AND THEY MAKE VERY SAVOURY SNACKS. TARO, OTHERWISE KNOWN AS YAM, IS SOLD IN MOST CHINESE SUPERMARKETS. LOOK FOR THE TYPE THAT HAS LIGHT PURPLE FLESH WITH DARK SPECKS, AS IT HAS THE BEST FLAVOUR AND IS STARCHY ENOUGH TO MAKE A STIFF DOUGH.

SERVES FOUR

INGREDIENTS
   cornflour (cornstarch), for dusting
   oil, for deep-frying
For the pastry
   500g/1¼lb taro
   30ml/2 tbsp plain (all-purpose) flour
   15ml/1 tbsp lard
   pinch of bicarbonate of soda
    (baking soda)
   15ml/1 tbsp sesame oil
   5ml/1 tsp sugar
   salt and ground black pepper
For the filling
   150g/5oz minced (ground) pork
   5ml/1 tsp cornflour (cornstarch)
   30ml/2 tbsp vegetable oil
   30ml/2 tbsp frozen peas
   5g/1 tsp sugar
   15ml/1 tbsp sesame oil
   salt and ground black pepper

1 To make the pastry, peel the taro and cut it into chunks. Steam for about 15 minutes until soft. Mash while still warm and mix with the remaining pastry ingredients to form a dough.

2 Turn out on to a lightly floured board and knead until the dough is soft and pliable. Set it aside while you make the filling, covered with a damp dish towel to prevent it drying out.

3 Mix the pork with the cornflour and moisten the mixture with a little water. Heat the vegetable oil in a pan and fry the pork until nearly cooked. Stir in all other filling ingredients.

4 Remove from the heat and leave to cool a little. Meanwhile, divide the dough into four portions and roll out into flat rounds.

5 Fill each round with 15ml/1 tbsp of the pork mixture. Shape into an oval pasty, sealing the pastry well around the filling. Dust with cornflour and deep-fry until golden brown.

Per portion Energy 367Kcal/1541kJ; Protein 11.2g; Carbohydrate 45.7g, of which sugars 3.8g; Fat 16.8g, of which saturates 3.7g; Cholesterol 27mg; Calcium 36mg; Fibre 2.2g; Sodium 30mg.

PORK SATAY WITH SPICY PINEAPPLE SAUCE

A popular dish at Malay food stalls, satay is the Malay and Indonesian answer to Middle Eastern kebabs. It may be made with beef (not for Hindus), chicken, goat, lamb, duck, seafood or pork (not for Muslims). In this Nonya version, pork is marinated before being threaded on to skewers, grilled over charcoal and served with pineapple sauce.

SERVES FOUR

INGREDIENTS

   500g/1¼ lb pork fillet, cut into
     bitesize strips or cubes
   salt and ground black pepper
   bamboo or wooden skewers
   fresh coriander (cilantro) leaves,
     roughly chopped, to garnish
For the marinade
   4 shallots, chopped
   4 garlic cloves, chopped
   5ml/1 tsp ground coriander
   5ml/1 tsp ground cumin
   2.5ml/½ tsp ground turmeric
   30ml/2 tbsp dark soy sauce
   30ml/2 tbsp sesame or groundnut
     (peanut) oil
For the sauce
   4 shallots, chopped
   2 garlic cloves, chopped
   4 dried red chillies, soaked in warm
     water until soft, seeded and
     chopped
   1 lemon grass stalk, trimmed
     and chopped
   25g/1oz fresh root ginger, chopped
   30ml/2 tbsp sesame or groundnut
     (peanut) oil
   200ml/7fl oz/scant 1 cup
     coconut milk
   10ml/2 tsp tamarind paste
   10ml/2 tsp palm sugar (jaggery)
   1 fresh pineapple, peeled, cored and
     cut into slices

1 First make the marinade. Using a mortar and pestle or food processor, grind the shallots and garlic to form a paste. Stir in the spices and soy sauce and bind with the oil. Rub the marinade into the meat. Cover and set aside for 2 hours at room temperature, or in the refrigerator if leaving for longer than 2 hours.

2 Meanwhile, prepare the sauce. Using a mortar and pestle or food processor, pound the shallots, garlic, chillies, lemon grass and ginger to form a paste.

3 Heat the oil in a heavy pan and stir in the paste. Cook for 2–3 minutes until fragrant and beginning to colour, then stir in the coconut milk, tamarind paste and sugar. Bring the mixture to the boil, then reduce the heat and leave to simmer for 5 minutes. Season to taste and leave to cool.

4 Using a mortar and pestle or a food processor, crush three pineapple slices and beat them into the sauce. Soak the skewers in cold water.

5 Prepare the charcoal grill and thread the marinated meat on to the skewers. Arrange the skewers over the hot charcoal and place the remaining slices of pineapple beside them. Char the pineapple slices and chop them into chunks. Grill the meat until just cooked, about 2–3 minutes each side, and serve immediately with the pineapple chunks and the sauce.

Per Portion Energy 294Kcal/1233kJ; Protein 27.5g; Carbohydrate 16.4g, of which sugars 16g; Fat 13.6g, of which saturates 3g; Cholesterol 79mg; Calcium 47mg; Fibre 1.4g; Sodium 145mg.

RICE AND NOODLES

*Either rice or noodles are eaten with every meal in Malaysia
and Singapore, from breakfast to late-night snacks; many
noodles are themselves made of rice. A bowl of simple steamed
or boiled rice is filling and nourishing, and provides the
background for vibrantly spiced meat, fish and vegetable
accompaniments. Soft, comforting noodles go into fragrant
broths with meat or fish balls, and are tossed into countless
stir-fries to make satisfying and speedy meals.*

MALAY YELLOW RICE

COLOURED A VIBRANT YELLOW WITH TURMERIC, NASI KUNING IS A DELICATELY FLAVOURED RICE DISH THAT IS OFTEN SERVED AT MALAY FESTIVALS. IT IS ALSO ONE OF THE POPULAR ITEMS AT MALAY NASI CAMPUR STALLS, WHERE IT IS SERVED WITH A VARIETY OF MEAT AND VEGETABLE DISHES. LONG GRAIN, SUCH AS JASMINE RICE, OR SHORT GRAIN OR STICKY RICE CAN BE USED FOR THIS DISH, WHICH IS COOKED IN THE SAME WAY AS PLAIN STEAMED RICE, USING THE ABSORPTION METHOD.

SERVES FOUR

INGREDIENTS

30ml/2 tbsp vegetable or sesame oil
3 shallots, finely chopped
2 garlic cloves, finely chopped
450g/1lb/generous 2 cups long grain
  rice, thoroughly washed and drained
400ml/14fl oz/1⅔ cups coconut milk
10ml/2 tsp ground turmeric
4 fresh curry leaves
2.5ml/½ tsp salt
ground black pepper
2 red chillies, seeded and finely
  sliced, to garnish

1 Heat the oil in a heavy pan and stir in the shallots and garlic. Just as they begin to colour, stir in the rice until it is coated in the oil.

2 Add 450ml/¾ pint/scant 2 cups water, the coconut milk, turmeric, curry leaves, salt and pepper. Bring to the boil, then turn down the heat and cover. Cook gently for 15–20 minutes, until all the liquid has been absorbed.

3 Turn off the heat and leave the rice to steam in the pan for 10 minutes. Fluff up the rice with a fork and serve garnished with red chillies.

COOK'S TIP
To serve neat individual portions of rice, pack it into ramekin dishes and unmould the rice onto each diner's plate.

Per Portion Energy 481Kcal/2011kJ; Protein 8.8g; Carbohydrate 95.9g, of which sugars 5.8g; Fat 6.4g, of which saturates 0.9g; Cholesterol 0mg; Calcium 54mg; Fibre 0.2g; Sodium 356mg.

GHEE RICE <u>WITH</u> TURMERIC

A cousin of Malay yellow rice, this is a Malaysian/Indian version that uses ghee instead of oil. Traditionally served with rich lamb curries, it is often cooked with glutinous rice, whose starchy texture makes it easier to scoop up when eaten with the fingers. Basmati will do as well if you use a little more water than is needed with normal rice. The addition of rose water gives it a lovely perfume.

SERVES FOUR

INGREDIENTS

250g/9oz/1¼ cups basmati rice
400ml/14fl oz/1¾ cups water
10ml/2 tsp ground turmeric
30ml/2 tbsp ghee
15ml/1 tbsp rose water
red chillies, to garnish

1 Soak the rice in water for half an hour then place in a pan with the water, turmeric, ghee and rose water.

2 Bring the rice to the boil and simmer, tightly covered, for 10–15 minutes, until the water is absorbed. Remove from the heat and leave to steam, still covered, for 5–10 more minutes.

3 To make chilli flowers, cut four deep slits from tip to stalk, leaving the stalk end intact. Remove the seeds and soak the chillies in ice-cold water, where they will curl up. Wash your hands thoroughly after handling the chillies and be careful not to touch your eyes.

4 Transfer the rice to a bowl and turn it out to form a little mound. Serve on a banana leaf, garnished with the decorative chilli flowers.

Per portion Energy 299Kcal/1246kJ; Protein 5g; Carbohydrate 50.8g, of which sugars 0g; Fat 8.1g, of which saturates 3.6g; Cholesterol 0mg; Calcium 17mg; Fibre 0g; Sodium 1mg.

FRAGRANT COCONUT RICE

Nasi lemak, fragrant coconut rice, is particularly favoured by Malays and Peranakans. In rice stalls and coffee shops, it is often served wrapped in banana leaves for breakfast or with a variety of dishes on one plate. A typical meal might include a curry, fried chicken or fish, rendang, hard-boiled quail's eggs, strips of cucumber, roasted peanuts and vegetable pickle. The Malays are particularly fond of eating nasi lemak with sambal ikan bilis, a sauce made with dried anchovies, chillies and spices, whereas the Peranakans tend to top theirs with sambal belacan, the chilli and shrimp paste.

SERVES FOUR

INGREDIENTS

   1 litre/1¾ pints/4 cups coconut milk
   450g/1lb/2¼ cups short grain rice,
     thoroughly washed and drained
   1 pandan (screwpine) leaf, tied in a
     loose knot
   salt

1 Heat the coconut milk in a heavy pan and stir in the rice with a little salt. Add the knotted pandan leaf and bring the liquid to the boil. Reduce the heat and simmer until the liquid has been absorbed by the rice.

2 Turn off the heat. Remove the lid and cover the pan with a clean dish towel, then replace the lid to keep the towel in place. Leave to steam for a further 15–20 minutes, then remove the pandan leaf and fluff up the rice with a fork before serving.

Per Portion Energy 459Kcal/1927kJ; Protein 9.1g; Carbohydrate 102g, of which sugars 12.3g; Fat 1.3g, of which saturates 0.5g; Cholesterol 0mg; Calcium 94mg; Fibre 0g; Sodium 275mg.

PANDAN LEAF RICE

Almost every kitchen garden in South-east Asia has a pandan or screwpine plant, and the long leaves are used to perfume both sweet and savoury dishes. While they are widely used in Malaysia and Singapore, they are put to the most ingenious use in northern Malaysia. This rice dish, although simple, is notable for its subtle perfume. In Kedah it is sometimes made with glutinous rice and topped with strips of omelette. Because the rice is steamed, less water is required than when cooking by the absorption method. The long soaking also helps to shorten the steaming time.

SERVES FOUR

INGREDIENTS

    250g/9oz/1¼ cups glutinous rice
    10g/2 tsp salt
    4 pandan (screwpine) leaves, cut into
       10cm/4in lengths

1 Wash the rice and put in a bowl with cold water to cover. Leave to soak for at least 2 hours, then drain.

2 Place the soaked rice in a steaming tray and add 400ml/14fl oz/1⅔ cups water. Add the salt, stirring it into the rice to distribute well.

3 Arrange the lengths of pandan leaves all over the rice, pressing a few into the surface.

4 Steam for 20 minutes, until the grains are tender. Discard the pandan leaves and serve with curries and sambals.

Per portion Energy 238Kcal/995kJ; Protein 6g; Carbohydrate 49.3g, of which sugars 2.5g; Fat 1.1g, of which saturates 0g; Cholesterol 0mg; Calcium 35mg; Fibre 1.1g; Sodium 988mg.

AROMATIC INDIAN PILAFF WITH PEAS

THIS FRAGRANT, VERSATILE RICE DISH IS OFTEN SERVED AS PART OF AN ELABORATE MEAL AT INDIAN FESTIVALS AND CELEBRATORY FEASTS, WHICH INCLUDE SEVERAL MEAT AND VEGETABLE CURRIES, A YOGURT DISH, AND CHUTNEYS. ON OCCASION, GROUND TURMERIC OR GRATED CARROT IS ADDED FOR AN EXTRA SPLASH OF COLOUR. SPRINKLE THE PILAFF WITH CHOPPED FRESH MINT AND CORIANDER, IF YOU LIKE, OR WITH ROASTED CHILLI AND COCONUT.

SERVES FOUR

INGREDIENTS

    350g/12oz/1¾ cups basmati rice
    45ml/3 tbsp ghee or 30ml/2 tbsp
      vegetable oil and a little butter
    1 cinnamon stick
    6–8 cardamom pods, crushed
    4 cloves
    1 onion, halved lengthways and
      sliced
    25g/1oz fresh root ginger, peeled
      and grated
    5ml/1 tsp sugar
    130g/4½oz fresh peas, shelled
    5ml/1 tsp salt

1 Rinse the rice in several changes of water, until the water runs clear. Put the rice in a bowl, cover with plenty of water and leave to soak for about 30 minutes. Drain thoroughly.

2 Heat the ghee, or oil and butter, in a heavy pan. Stir in the cinnamon stick, cardamom and cloves. Add the onion, ginger and sugar, and fry until golden.

3 Add the peas, followed by the rice, and stir for 1 minute to coat the grains in ghee.

4 Pour in 600ml/1 pint/2½ cups water with the salt, stir once and bring the liquid to the boil.

5 Reduce the heat and allow to simmer gently for 15–20 minutes, until all the liquid has been absorbed. Stir the rice occasionally just to check that it is not sticking to the bottom of the pan.

6 Turn off the heat. Remove the lid and cover the pan with a clean dish towel, then replace the lid to keep the towel in place. Leave to steam for a further 10 minutes. Spoon the rice on to a serving dish.

VARIATION
This Indian pilaff can be made using diced carrot or beetroot (beet), or chickpeas instead of peas. Instead of turmeric, you can add a little tomato paste to give the rice a red tinge.

Per Portion Energy 451Kcal/1880kJ; Protein 8.9g; Carbohydrate 75.7g, of which sugars 2.6g; Fat 12.2g, of which saturates 5.4g; Cholesterol 0mg; Calcium 28mg; Fibre 1.8g; Sodium 328mg.

CANTONESE FRIED RICE

THERE ARE MANY RECIPES FOR FRIED RICE, BUT THE CANTONESE, WHEREVER THEY MAY LIVE, ARE PAST MASTERS AT TRANSFORMING WHAT IS BASICALLY A HUMBLE DISH DEVISED TO USE UP YESTERDAY'S LEFTOVER RICE INTO ONE FIT FOR EMPERORS. IT IS ALSO A VERY ADAPTABLE CREATION, AS YOU CAN ADD EXTRA INGREDIENTS OF YOUR CHOICE, FROM CHICKEN TO KING PRAWNS OR SCALLOPS. TRADITIONALLY, A SPECIAL CHINESE HAM CALLED KING HUA HAM IS USED TO ADD EXTRA FLAVOUR, BUT ANY GOOD-QUALITY HAM CAN BE USED.

SERVES FOUR

INGREDIENTS

600g/1lb 6oz cooked cold rice
60ml/4 tbsp oil
½ large onion, chopped
3 eggs
100g/3¾oz lean cooked ham, cubed
100g/3¾oz raw, shelled prawns (shrimp)
50g/2oz canned crab meat
50g/2oz frozen peas
2 spring onions (scallions), trimmed and finely sliced
30ml/2 tbsp light soy sauce
½ tsp sugar
freshly ground black pepper
sliced cucumber and chilli sauce, to serve

1 If the rice has been refrigerated, rake it with a fork to loosen the grains.

2 Heat the oil in a wok or heavy pan and fry the onion until soft, but not brown. Push to one side and crack in the eggs. Cook until set, cutting them up roughly with a spatula.

3 Push the eggs to one side and add the ham, prawns and crab meat.

4 Stir-fry for 2 minutes, then add the rice and stir vigorously until heated through. Add the peas, spring onions, soy sauce and sugar and black pepper. Serve with cucumber and chilli sauce.

Per portion Energy 437Kcal/1837kJ; Protein 20.4g; Carbohydrate 51g, of which sugars 2.3g; Fat 18.4g, of which saturates 3.3g; Cholesterol 211mg; Calcium 84mg; Fibre 1.1g; Sodium 1025mg.

COMPRESSED RICE CAKES

In Malaysia, these compressed rice cakes, ketupat, are cooked in little woven packages made from strips of palm fronds and served with satay. The packages containing the uncooked rice are tied in bundles and lowered into a deep pan of boiling water, where they are left to simmer over a very low heat for about 3 hours. To make ketupat in a Western home, it's easier to pre-cook the rice and then steam it in foil or banana leaves, which are available fresh or preserved from Asian markets.

SERVES FOUR

INGREDIENTS
   225g/8oz/generous 1 cup short
     grain rice, thoroughly washed
     and drained
   2.5ml/½ tsp salt
   dipping sauce, to serve
   4 sheets of aluminium foil, each
     measuring 20 x 30cm/8 x 12in

1 In a heavy pan, bring 600ml/1 pint/ 2½ cups water to the boil. Stir in the rice and salt. When the water starts to bubble again, reduce the heat and cover the pan. Allow to simmer for about 20 minutes, until all the water has been absorbed.

2 Spoon one-quarter of the rice about 2.5cm/1in in from the shorter edge of each foil sheet, then roll up loosely, leaving room for the rice to expand. Twist the ends to seal. Place the parcels in a bamboo steamer set in a wok, or a conventional steamer.

3 Steam for 40 minutes, then leave the parcels to cool, twisting the ends more tightly if necessary, before unwrapping. Slice the compressed rice into bitesize rounds and serve with a Malay curry dish, satay or simply with soy sauce or a sambal for dipping.

Per Portion Energy 202Kcal/845kJ; Protein 4.2g; Carbohydrate 44.9g, of which sugars 0g; Fat 0.3g, of which saturates 0g; Cholesterol 0mg; Calcium 11mg; Fibre 0g; Sodium 164mg.

LOTUS LEAF RICE

THIS DISH IS EATEN ON FESTIVE OCCASIONS BUT IS ALSO A TASTY DIM SUM ITEM IN RESTAURANTS. LOTUS SEEDS ARE ADDED FOR FLAVOUR AND TEXTURE AS WELL AS FOR SYMBOLIC REASONS, AS THEY REPRESENT FERTILITY. THE LEAVES ARE AVAILABLE IN ALL CHINESE STORES AND NEED ONLY BE WIPED BEFORE USE. THEY IMPART A DISTINCTIVE FLAVOUR AND MAKE AN IMPRESSIVE DISPLAY WHEN OPENED.

SERVES FOUR

INGREDIENTS
  250g/9oz/1¼ cups sticky (glutinous)
    rice, soaked for at least 2 hours,
    then drained
  250ml/8fl oz/1 cup water
  10ml/2 tsp salt
  2 large lotus leaves
For the filling
  150g/5oz chicken breast
  4 dried Chinese (shiitake)
    mushrooms, soaked until soft, or
    canned mushrooms
  30ml/2 tbsp vegetable oil
  3 garlic cloves, crushed
  30ml/2 tbsp oyster sauce
  5ml/1 tsp ground black pepper
  15ml/1 tbsp sesame oil
  45ml/3 tbsp water
  20 canned lotus seeds

1 Put the soaked rice in a steamer, add the water and salt and steam for 20 minutes. Set aside to cool.

2 To make the filling, slice the chicken into small dice and cut each mushroom into quarters. Heat the vegetable oil and fry the garlic until golden brown. Add the pieces of chicken and stir-fry for 2 minutes.

3 Add the mushrooms, oyster sauce, lotus seeds, pepper, sesame oil and water and continue to stir until the chicken is completely cooked.

4 Spread out the lotus leaves, laying one on top of the other to insure against splitting or leaking.

5 Spread the steamed rice on top, flattening it with a spatula. Spread the chicken and mushrooms evenly over it.

6 Make a firm parcel with the lotus leaves, tucking the ends under to secure. Steam for 5 minutes or microwave for 2 minutes before serving.

Per portion Energy 377Kcal/1581kJ; Protein 20.7g; Carbohydrate 63.7g, of which sugars 2.4g; Fat 4g, of which saturates 1.2g; Cholesterol 43mg; Calcium 31mg; Fibre 0.8g; Sodium 1082mg.

BUBUR

ORIGINATING FROM CHINA, THIS THICK RICE PORRIDGE OR CONGEE HAS BECOME POPULAR ALL OVER SOUTH-EAST ASIA. BUBUR IS THE MALAY NAME OF THE DISH. IT IS DESIGNED TO BE NOURISHING AND BLAND, AND THE MAIN INTEREST OF THE MEAL IS DERIVED FROM THE ADDITIONAL INGREDIENTS, OR OTHER DISHES, THAT ARE EATEN ALONGSIDE THE BUBUR.

SERVES FOUR TO SIX

INGREDIENTS
- 25g/1oz fresh root ginger, peeled and sliced
- 1 cinnamon stick
- 2 star anise
- 2.5ml/½ tsp salt
- 115g/4oz/½ cup short grain rice, thoroughly washed and drained

1 Bring 1.2 litres/2 pints/5 cups water to the boil in a heavy pan. Stir in the spices, the salt and the rice.

2 Reduce the heat, cover the pan, and simmer gently for 1 hour, or longer if you prefer a smoother, thicker and more porridge-like consistency.

3 Serve steaming hot as an accompaniment to highly-flavoured or spicy meat, fish or vegetable dishes. You may prefer to remove the woody cinnamon sticks and star anise as they are inedible, but they make an attractive presentation.

COOK'S TIP
The Teochew version of bubur is called muay. With its addition of pickles and strips of omelette, it is popular for supper in Singapore. Bubur is enjoyed by Malays for breakfast with fried or grilled fish, chicken and beef, as well as pickles. Often flavoured with ginger, cinnamon and star anise, bubur is usually cooked until it is thick but the grains are still visible, whereas some of the Chinese versions are cooked for longer so that the rice breaks down completely. The consistency varies from family to family.

Per Portion Energy 69Kcal/288kJ; Protein 1.4g; Carbohydrate 15.3g, of which sugars 0g; Fat 0.1g, of which saturates 0g; Cholesterol 0mg; Calcium 4mg; Fibre 0g; Sodium 164mg.

MUSHROOM CLAY POT RICE

CLAY POTS ARE OFTEN REFERRED TO IN THE CANTONESE DIALECT AS "SAND POTS" OR SAR PO. THESE ARE VERY HANDY AS, IF PROPERLY SEASONED, THEY CAN GO STRAIGHT FROM THE FIRE TO THE TABLE, WHICH MAKES LIFE EASY AND LOOKS GOOD. HOWEVER, IF YOU ARE WORRIED THAT YOUR POT MAY CRACK OVER DIRECT HEAT, A SAFER METHOD IS TO COOK THE RICE IN A WOK OR PAN AND TRANSFER IT TO AN OVEN-WARMED CLAY POT TO SERVE.

SERVES FOUR

INGREDIENTS
    250g/9oz/1¼ cups jasmine rice
    400ml/14fl oz/1⅔ cups water
    30ml/2 tbsp vegetable oil
    15ml/1 tbsp sesame oil
    8 dried Chinese black (shiitake)
      mushrooms, soaked until soft, or 8
      canned mushrooms
    3 garlic cloves, crushed
    30g/2 tbsp oyster sauce
    5ml/1 tsp freshly ground black
      pepper

5 About 5 minutes before the rice is done, pile the mushrooms on top and cover the pan to finish cooking.

6 Remove the warmed claypot from the oven and transfer the rice and mushroom mixture to it to serve.

1 Place the rice in a pan with the water, bring to the boil and simmer, tightly covered, for about 20 minutes, until the water is absorbed. Remove from the heat and leave to steam for 10 minutes. Alternatively, cook the rice in the normal way in a microwave or rice cooker.

2 While the rice is cooking, prepare the topping. Slice the Chinese mushrooms into strips. Heat the oil in a wok or pan and fry the garlic until golden brown. Add the sliced mushrooms and stir-fry for 2 minutes.

3 Add the oyster sauce and the black pepper. Pour in 100ml/3½fl oz/scant ½ cup water and stir for 2 minutes.

4 Pre-heat a clay pot in a hot oven for 10 minutes.

Per portion Energy 315Kcal/1312kJ; Protein 5.3g; Carbohydrate 53.2g, of which sugars 3.2g; Fat 8.7g, of which saturates 1.1g; Cholesterol 0mg; Calcium 15mg; Fibre 0.4g; Sodium 185mg.

FISH CONGEE

What the Western world knows as congee, to the Chinese is sustenance, coming as it did from the kitchens of humble families who had to eke out their ration of rice during lean months. Today, this peasant dish has been elevated to five-star restaurant status but it still retains its humble character. It was traditionally cooked with broken rice, but jasmine rice, when cooked for a long period, has the right porridge-like consistency.

SERVES FOUR

INGREDIENTS

115g/4oz jasmine rice
1 litre/1¾ pints/4 cups water
200g/7oz fillets of meaty fish such
  as snapper, grouper or cod
30ml/2 tbsp light soy sauce
1 fish stock (bouillon) cube
30ml/2 tbsp sesame oil

For the garnish

15ml/1 tbsp preserved winter
  vegetable (dung choy)
25g/1oz fresh root ginger, finely
  shredded
2 spring onions (scallions), chopped

1 Put the rice in a pan with the water. Bring to the boil and simmer for 1 hour. You may have to add more hot water if the congee becomes too thick.

2 Slice the fish into small pieces and add in the last 10 minutes, with the soy sauce, stock cube and sesame oil. Cook for 5 minutes and serve hot in individual bowls with the garnishes.

Per portion Energy 330Kcal/1384kJ; Protein 10.9g; Carbohydrate 56.2g, of which sugars 2.8g; Fat 7g, of which saturates 0.8g; Cholesterol 0mg; Calcium 56mg; Fibre 2.1g; Sodium 64mg.

CHINESE CLAY POT RICE
WITH CHICKEN

THIS CANTONESE DISH IS A GREAT FAMILY ONE-POT MEAL. IT CAN ALSO BE FOUND ON CHINESE STALLS AND IN SOME COFFEE SHOPS. THE TRADITIONAL CLAY POT ENSURES THAT THE INGREDIENTS REMAIN MOIST, WHILE ALLOWING THE FLAVOURS TO MINGLE.

SERVES FOUR

INGREDIENTS
  500g/1¼ lb chicken breast fillets,
    cut into thin strips
  5 dried Chinese (shiitake)
    mushrooms, soaked in hot water for
    30 minutes, until soft
  1 Chinese sausage, sliced
  750ml/1¼pints/3 cups chicken stock
  225g/8oz/generous 1 cup long grain
    rice, thoroughly washed and drained
  fresh coriander (cilantro) leaves,
    finely chopped, to garnish
For the marinade
  30ml/2 tbsp sesame oil
  45ml/3 tbsp oyster sauce
  30ml/2 tbsp soy sauce
  25g/1oz fresh root ginger, finely
    grated (shredded)
  2 spring onions (scallions), trimmed
    and finely sliced
  1 red chilli, seeded and finely sliced
  5ml/1 tsp sugar
  ground black pepper

3 Using a sharp knife, remove any hard stems from the mushrooms and cut the caps in half. Add the caps and the Chinese sausage to the chicken.

4 Bring the stock to the boil in the clay pot. Stir in the rice and bring it back to the boil. Reduce the heat, cover the pot, and leave to simmer on a low heat for 15–20 minutes, until almost all the liquid has been absorbed.

5 Spread the marinated mixture over the top of the rice and cover the pot again. Leave to steam for about 10–15 minutes, until all the liquid is absorbed and the chicken is cooked. Garnish the rice with chopped coriander and serve at once.

COOK'S TIP
Remember, if you are using a newly bought clay pot, you need to season it first to stop it cracking. Fill it with water and slowly bring it to the boil. Simmer for 5–10 minutes, then leave it to cool. Pour out the water and wipe the pot dry. Now it is ready to use.

1 In a bowl, mix together the ingredients for the marinade. Toss in the chicken, making sure it is well coated. Set aside.

2 Check that the shiitake mushrooms are soft (leave them to soak for longer, if necessary). Squeeze them to get rid of any excess water.

Per Portion Energy 371Kcal/1560kJ; Protein 36.2g; Carbohydrate 46.8g, of which sugars 1g; Fat 4g, of which saturates 1.2g; Cholesterol 93mg; Calcium 54mg; Fibre 0.7g; Sodium 721mg.

LENTILS WITH GINGER AND COCONUT MILK

THOUGH NOT A RICE OR NOODLE DISH, DHAL (MEANING EITHER LENTILS OR THE COOKED DISH) IS SO POPULAR — EITHER EATEN SIMPLY WITH RICE OR INDIAN BREAD, OR AS PART OF A MORE ELABORATE MEAL — THAT IT COULD NOT BE LEFT OUT. FOR THE LARGELY VEGETARIAN SOUTH INDIAN IMMIGRANTS WHO INTRODUCED IT, DHAL IS AN IMPORTANT SOURCE OF PROTEIN. IT MAKES A FABULOUS VEGETARIAN ADDITION TO A MALAYSIAN FEAST, OR A SIMPLE AND SATISFYING DISH FOR AN EVERYDAY SUPPER.

1 Heat the ghee, or the oil and butter, in a heavy pan. Stir in the onion, garlic, chillies and ginger and fry until they are fragrant and beginning to colour. Add the sugar, cumin seeds, turmeric and garam masala, taking care not to burn the spices.

2 Stir in the lentils and coat in the spices and ghee. Pour in 600ml/ 1 pint/2½ cups water, mix thoroughly, and bring to the boil. Reduce the heat to a gentle simmer for 35–40 minutes until the mixture is thick.

3 Stir in the coconut milk and continue to simmer for a further 30 minutes until thick and mushy – if at any time the dhal seems too dry, add more water or coconut milk. Season to taste with salt.

4 In a small pan, heat the mustard seeds. As soon as they begin to pop, add the curry leaves and chillies. When the chillies begin to darken, stir in the ghee until it melts.

5 Spoon the mixture over the dhal, or fold it in until well mixed. Serve the dhal with yogurt or as part of an Indian-style meal, with curry, rice and chutney.

COOK'S TIP
Ghee is made by simmering unsalted butter until the liquid has evaporated and the solids settle at the bottom of the pan. The clarified oil is then skimmed off. It is usually sold in jars.

SERVES FOUR

INGREDIENTS
  30ml/2 tbsp ghee, or 15ml/1 tbsp
    vegetable oil and 15g/½oz/1 tbsp
    butter
  1 onion, chopped
  4 garlic cloves, chopped
  2 red chillies, seeded and chopped
  50g/2oz fresh root ginger, peeled
    and chopped
  10ml/2 tsp sugar
  7.5ml/1½ tsp cumin seeds
  5ml/1 tsp ground turmeric

  15ml/1 tbsp garam masala
  225g/8oz/generous 1 cup brown
    lentils, washed thoroughly
    and drained
  600ml/1 pint/2½ cups
    coconut milk
  salt
  yogurt or curry, rice and chutney,
    to serve
For the garnish
  10ml/2 tsp mustard seeds
  a small handful dried curry leaves
  1–2 dried red chillies
  15ml/1 tbsp ghee

Per Portion Energy 322Kcal/1358kJ; Protein 14g; Carbohydrate 41.3g, of which sugars 10.6g; Fat 12.4g, of which saturates 5.7g; Cholesterol 0mg; Calcium 77mg; Fibre 3g; Sodium 186mg.

SINGAPORE VEGETARIAN BEE HOON

DURING BUDDHIST FESTIVALS THIS DISH IS SERVED AT MOST TEMPLES, WHERE IT IS DISPENSED FREE TO ALL DEVOTEES. THE CLASSIC INGREDIENTS ARE RICE VERMICELLI (BEE HOON), SLICED CABBAGE, FRIED BEAN CURD WAFERS AND MUSHROOMS. THESE CAN BE BULKED UP WITH BEANSPROUTS AND SLICED FRENCH BEANS. STRICT BUDDHIST VEGETARIANS DO NOT EAT GARLIC BUT ITS INCLUSION ADDS A DELICIOUS FLAVOUR AND SMELLS WONDERFUL.

SERVES FOUR

INGREDIENTS
oil for deep-frying
6 bean curd wafers
4 garlic cloves, crushed
100g/3½oz thinly sliced cabbage
10 canned Chinese black
  mushrooms, thinly sliced
100g/3½oz beansprouts
200ml/7 fl oz/scant 1 cup water
175g/6oz bee hoon, soaked
  until soft
30ml/2 tbsp light soy sauce
freshly ground black pepper

COOK'S TIP
If you are using dried Chinese mushrooms, soak them in warm water for 30 minutes before slicing.

1 Heat the oil in a wok and fry the bean curd wafers until they are crisp. Remove and drain on kitchen paper.

2 Put 30ml/2 tbsp fresh oil in the wok and fry the garlic until golden brown. Add the cabbage, mushrooms and beansprouts and stir-fry for 5 minutes. Add the water and stir for 1 minute.

3 Add the bee hoon and continue to stir until it is heated through and well blended with the other ingredients. Add the light soy sauce and season to taste with black pepper.

4 Cut the fried bean curd wafers into strips and use them to garnish the fried bee hoon. Serve immediately.

Per portion Energy 330Kcal/1377kJ; Protein 17.5g; Carbohydrate 49.9g, of which sugars 4.5g; Fat 6.6g, of which saturates 0.8g; Cholesterol 110mg; Calcium 125mg; Fibre 1.9g; Sodium 960mg.

SPICY FRIED NOODLES

BOTH INDIAN AND MALAY HAWKERS OFTEN SELL MEE GORENG *TOGETHER WITH* MEE REBUS *BUT ITS INVENTION IS GENERALLY ATTRIBUTED TO THE CULINARY INGENUITY OF THE EARLY INDIAN MIGRANTS. IN MOST MALAYSIAN TOWNS YOU WILL FIND IT SOLD IN ESTABLISHMENTS KNOWN AS MAMAK SHOPS, A TERM THAT REFERS TO SOUTH INDIANS. THERE IS NO OTHER NOODLE DISH IN THE INDIAN CULINARY TRADITION, AND THIS VERSION IS PECULIAR TO MALAYSIA AND SINGAPORE.*

SERVES FOUR

INGREDIENTS
90ml/6 tbsp vegetable oil
15–30ml/1–2 tbsp tamarind
  concentrate
45ml/3 tbsp water
2 eggs
450g/1lb fresh yellow noodles
100g/3¾oz beansprouts
2 tomatoes, peeled and quartered
salt
lime or lemon wedges, to serve
For the spice paste
4 dried chillies
½ large onion
3 garlic cloves

COOK'S TIP
As a time-saving substitute for the spice paste, you can use a bottled chilli and garlic sauce in this recipe.

1 Grind the spice paste ingredients in a mortar and pestle or food processor until fine. Heat 60ml/4 tbsp oil in a wok and fry the paste over low heat for about 8 minutes, then add the tamarind concentrate and water. Stir for 2 minutes and remove from the heat.

2 Heat the remaining oil in a wok and fry the eggs until set. Cut up roughly and add the noodles and beansprouts.

3 Mix the eggs and vegetables vigorously, then add 30ml/2 tbsp of the spice paste. Stir fry for 1 minute.

4 Add the tomatoes and continue to cook, stirring constantly, until the tomatoes are soft and everything is well mixed. Season to taste with salt.

5 Serve immediately with a squeeze of lime or lemon juice.

Per portion Energy 421kcal/1771kJ; Protein 13.7g; Carbohydrate 58.9g, of which sugars 4.2g; Fat 16.2g, of which saturates 3.2g; Cholesterol 85mg; Calcium 165mg; Fibre 2.7g; Sodium 416mg.

PERAK SOUR LAKSA

A LAKSA IS ANY SPICY NOODLE DISH, OF WHICH THERE ARE MANY DIFFERENT KINDS. SINGAPORE LAKSA IS RICH IN COCONUT MILK AND PENANG LAKSA IS TART WITH TAMARIND. IN SINGAPORE THERE ARE STREETS WHERE THREE, FOUR OR MORE STALLS SELL LAKSA, EACH CLAIMING TO HAVE BEEN THE ORIGINATOR. THIS GENTLE VERSION ORIGINATED IN THE NORTH MALAYSIAN PROVINCE OF PERAK. UNUSUALLY, IT USES NEITHER COCONUT MILK NOR TAMARIND BUT IS MADE WITH LIME JUICE.

SERVES TWO TO THREE

INGREDIENTS
  45ml/3 tbsp oil
  2 whole mackerel, gutted and
    cleaned
  1 large onion, sliced
  45ml/3 tbsp lime juice
  5ml/1 tsp salt
  5ml/1 tsp sugar
  ½ cucumber
  200g/7oz bee hoon (rice vermicelli),
    soaked until soft
  6–8 laksa leaves
For the spice paste
  5 red chillies
  6 shallots
  15g/½oz shrimp paste
  15g/½oz fresh turmeric
  3 garlic cloves
  1 stalk lemon grass, trimmed to
    7.5cm/3in at the root end

1 To make the spice paste, grind all the ingredients using a mortar and pestle or in a food processor to a smooth paste.

2 Heat the oil in a wok and fry the spice paste for 3 minutes until fragrant. Set aside.

3 Put the mackerel and the sliced onion in a pan with 600ml/1 pint/2½ cups water. Bring to the boil and simmer for 10 minutes. Remove the mackerel, debone and flake the flesh. Set aside.

4 Continue to simmer the stock for about 15 minutes, or until the onion is completely soft. Strain the stock and discard the onion. Add the stock to the wok and stir it into the fried spice paste. Simmer for 5 minutes.

5 Add the lime juice, salt and sugar to the stock, adjusting the seasoning to taste. Return the flaked mackerel to the wok and bring to a gentle simmer. Cook for 3 minutes, then remove from the heat and keep warm.

6 Peel and de-seed the cucumber and shred very finely. To serve, divide the bee hoon into two or three portions and top with some of the mackerel. Ladle the stock over the top and garnish with laksa leaves and cucumber.

COOK'S TIP
Have extra lime juice to hand to add to the stock at the last minute if you prefer the laksa to be quite sour. The tangy flavour goes well with the mellow richness of the fish.

Per portion Energy 593Kcal/2468kJ; Protein 28.3g; Carbohydrate 56.8g, of which sugars 3g; Fat 28g, of which saturates 4.7g; Cholesterol 79mg; Calcium 104mg; Fibre 0.5g; Sodium 943mg.

MIXED SEAFOOD HOR FUN

HOR FUN IS THE CANTONESE NAME FOR STIR-FRIED RICE NOODLES, A POPULAR HAWKER STAPLE AS WELL AS A RESTAURANT DISH WHEN ENRICHED WITH CHOICE INGREDIENTS SUCH AS BEEF AND PRAWNS. IN MALAYSIA, IN THE TOWN OF IPOH ESPECIALLY, FRESH RICE NOODLES ARE REPUTED TO BE MADE TO A SECRET RECIPE THAT HAS FOUND LEGIONS OF FANS. AS A RESULT, IPOH HOR FUN HAS COME TO MEAN THE SUPERLATIVE VERSION OF THIS DISH.

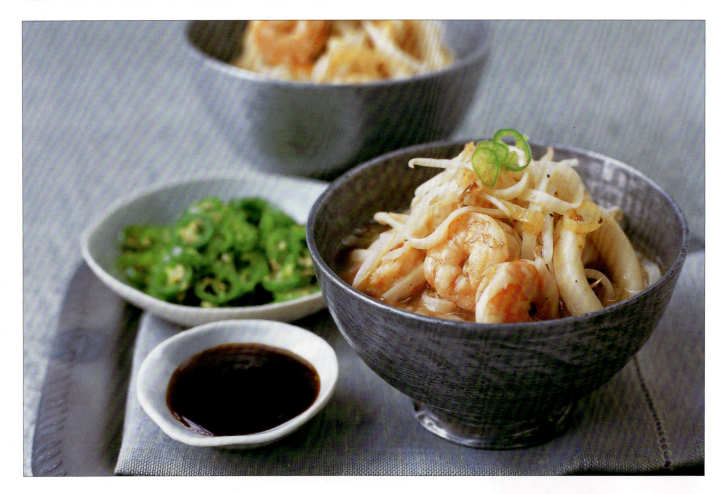

SERVES FOUR

INGREDIENTS
- 150g/5oz rice sticks
- 8 raw tiger prawns (jumbo shrimp)
- 30ml/2 tbsp vegetable oil
- ½ large onion, sliced
- 100g/3¾oz squid rings
- 100g/3¾oz beansprouts
- 30ml/2 tbsp oyster sauce
- 2.5ml/½ tsp black pepper
- 150ml/¼ pint/⅔ cup water or fish stock
- fresh or pickled chillies, to serve

COOK'S TIP
Rice sticks, or dried rice noodles, double in bulk when reconstituted. They are available in various thicknesses.

1 Bring a pan of water to the boil and cook the rice sticks according to the packet instructions or until soft. Taste a strand to check. Drain and set aside.

2 Shell and de-vein the prawns by making a deep slit down the back. This will also make them curl up nicely.

3 Heat the oil and fry the onion until soft. Add the prawns and squid and stir-fry for 2 minutes. Add the beansprouts, noodles, oyster sauce and pepper and stir to toss well. Add the water or stock and let it bubble and reduce. As soon as the sauce is thick, serve the noodles with sliced or pickled chillies.

Per portion Energy 259Kcal/1084kJ; Protein 15.3g; Carbohydrate 34g, of which sugars 2.6g; Fat 6.4g, of which saturates 0.8g; Cholesterol 154mg; Calcium 53mg; Fibre 0.5g; Sodium 251mg.

CHINESE STIR-FRIED NOODLES

THIS CHINESE DISH OF STIR-FRIED RICE NOODLES AND SEAFOOD, CHAR KWAY TEOW, IS ONE OF THE MOST POPULAR AT THE HAWKER STALLS OF MALAYSIA AND SINGAPORE. BREAKFAST, LUNCH, SUPPER, MID-MORNING, MID-AFTERNOON OR LATE EVENING, THERE'S ALWAYS CHAR KWAY TEOW ON THE GO. VARIATIONS INCLUDE RED SNAPPER, CLAMS AND PORK. KWAY TEOW IS IN FACT THE NAME FOR THE BROAD, FRESH RICE NOODLES THAT ARE SOLD IN CHINESE MARKETS.

SERVES THREE TO FOUR

INGREDIENTS

2 small squid, trimmed, cleaned and skinned
12 fresh prawns (shrimp), peeled
45ml/3 tbsp vegetable oil
2 garlic cloves, finely chopped
2 red chillies, seeded and finely sliced
1 Chinese sausage, finely sliced
500g/1¼lb fresh rice noodles
30ml/2 tbsp light soy sauce
45ml/3 tbsp kecap manis
2–3 mustard greens, chopped
a handful of beansprouts
2 eggs, lightly beaten
ground black pepper
fresh coriander (cilantro) leaves, finely chopped, to serve, plus a few reserved sprigs for decoration

COOK'S TIP
If you are unable to find it in you local Asian market or supermarket, you can replace kecap manis with the same quantity of dark soy sauce mixed with a little sugar.

1 Slice the squid into strips or rings about 1cm/⅓ in wide. Check that the prawns have all their shells and veins removed, or do so with a sharp knife.

2 Heat a wok and add the oil. Stir in the garlic and chillies and fry until fragrant.

3 Add the Chinese sausage, then the prawns and squid, mixing them well.

4 Toss in the noodles and mix thoroughly. Add the soy sauce and kecap manis, then the mustard leaves and beansprouts.

5 Pour in the beaten eggs and stir them rapidly into the noodles until set, which will take only a few seconds.

6 Season with black pepper, garnish with coriander and serve immediately.

Per Portion Energy 618Kcal/2582kJ; Protein 24.8g; Carbohydrate 100g, of which sugars 1.1g; Fat 12.9g, of which saturates 2.1g; Cholesterol 217mg; Calcium 96mg; Fibre 0.5g; Sodium 717mg.

MALAY BEE HOON

IN MALAYSIA AND SINGAPORE THERE ARE ENDLESS STIR-FRIED NOODLE DISHES. SOME OF THESE STILL FOLLOW CLASSIC CHINESE RECIPES; OTHERS HAVE BEEN INFLUENCED BY THE CHINESE BUT ADAPTED TO SUIT THE TASTES OF THE DIFFERENT COMMUNITIES. BEE HOON IS THE MALAY NAME FOR THE RICE VERMICELLI WHICH, IN THIS POPULAR SNACK, IS STIR-FRIED WITH PRAWNS AND LOTS OF CHILLI.

SERVES FOUR

INGREDIENTS
    30ml/2 tbsp vegetable oil
    1 carrot, cut into matchsticks
    225g/8oz fresh prawns
      (shrimp), peeled
    120ml/4fl oz/½ cup chicken stock
      or water
    30ml/2 tbsp light soy sauce
    15ml/1 tbsp dark soy sauce
    175g/6oz beansprouts
    115g/4oz mustard greens or pak choi
      (bok choy), shredded
    225g/8oz dried rice vermicelli,
      soaked in lukewarm water until
      pliable, and drained
    1–2 fresh red chillies, seeded and
      finely sliced, and fresh coriander
      (cilantro) leaves, roughly chopped,
      to garnish

For the rempah
    4 dried red chillies, soaked until
      soft and seeded
    4 garlic cloves, chopped
    4 shallots, chopped
    25g/1oz fresh root ginger, peeled
      and chopped
    5ml/1 tsp ground turmeric

1 Using a mortar and pestle or a food processor, grind the ingredients for the rempah to a paste.

2 Heat the oil in a wok or heavy pan, and stir in the rempah until it begins to colour and become fragrant.

3 Toss in the carrots for a minute, followed by the prawns. Pour in the stock or water and soy sauces and cook for 1 minute.

4 Add the beansprouts and the shredded mustard greens or pak choi, followed by the rice vermicelli. Toss well to make sure the vegetables and noodles are all well coated and heated through.

5 Transfer the noodles to a serving plate and garnish with sliced chillies and chopped coriander. Serve immediately.

Per Portion Energy 330Kcal/1377kJ; Protein 17.5g; Carbohydrate 49.9g, of which sugars 4.5g; Fat 6.6g, of which saturates 0.8g; Cholesterol 110mg; Calcium 125mg; Fibre 1.9g; Sodium 960mg.

SINGAPORE EGG NOODLES

OTHERWISE KNOWN AS HOKKEIN MEE, THIS IS A VERY POPULAR STIR-FRIED DISH IN SINGAPORE, WHERE MOST OF THE CHINESE POPULATION IS HOKKEIN. IT TAKES ITS NAME FROM THE PEOPLE, AS WELL AS FROM THE THICK NOODLES, CALLED HOKKEIN NOODLES, WHICH ARE ALSO USED IN MALAY AND INDIAN DISHES. FILLED WITH SQUID, PRAWNS, FISH AND PORK, THIS MAKES A SATISFYING MEAL.

SERVES FOUR

INGREDIENTS
  30ml/2 tbsp vegetable oil
  3 garlic cloves, finely chopped
  115g/4oz pork fillet, cut into
    thin strips
  115g/4oz fresh fish fillets
    (such as red snapper, grouper
    or trout), cut into bitesize
    pieces
  115g/4oz fresh prawns (shrimp),
    shelled and deveined
  2 small squid, with innards and
    quill removed, trimmed, cleaned,
    skinned and sliced
    (reserve tentacles)

  300ml/½ pint/1¼ cups
    chicken stock
  450g/1lb fresh egg noodles
  1 carrot, shredded
  6 long white Chinese cabbage
    leaves, shredded
  30ml/2 tbsp dark soy sauce
  30ml/2 tbsp light soy sauce
  ground black pepper
  a small bunch of fresh coriander
    (cilantro), roughly chopped

1 Heat the oil in a wok and stir in the garlic. When it becomes fragrant, stir in the pork, fish, prawns and squid, tossing them around the pan for 1 minute. Pour in the stock and bubble it up to reduce it.

2 Add the noodles and toss them around the wok for 1 minute. Stir in the shredded carrot and cabbage, add the soy sauces and cook until most of the liquid has evaporated. Season with pepper, sprinkle with coriander, divide the noodles among four bowls and eat while steaming hot.

Per Portion Energy 609Kcal/2571kJ; Protein 35.2g; Carbohydrate 84.4g, of which sugars 5.3g; Fat 16.9g, of which saturates 3.8g; Cholesterol 186mg; Calcium 81mg; Fibre 4.2g; Sodium 867mg.

FISH AND SHELLFISH

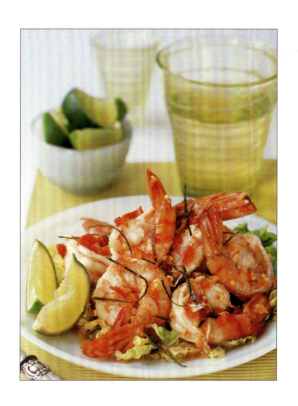

Seafood is one of the greatest glories of the cuisines of Malaysia and Singapore, as a huge variety of tropical fish and shellfish are daily hauled from the seas and rivers and sold in the wet markets set up in every town and village. A myriad inventive dishes range from elegantly steamed whole fish, scented with ginger and other aromatics in the Chinese style, to Singapore's famous specialities, fish head curry and chilli crab.

SPICED FISH CAKES WRAPPED IN BANANA LEAVES

THE OILY FLESH OF MACKEREL IS GENERALLY USED FOR THIS NONYA DISH, IKAN OTAK-OTAK. BAKED, STEAMED OR GRILLED OVER CHARCOAL, THESE FISH CAKES MAKE A TASTY ADDITION TO A SUMMER DINNER, OR A PICNIC SNACK. THEY CAN BE EATEN HOT OR COLD AS FISH CAKES, OR USED AS LITTLE PACKAGES OF FISH PASTE TO SPREAD ON TOAST OR COCKTAIL CANAPÉS. BANANA LEAVES ARE SOLD IN ASIAN MARKETS, BUT YOU COULD USE PREPARED VINE LEAVES OR ALUMINIUM FOIL.

2 Put the mackerel and lime leaves in a bowl. Pour in the spiced coconut cream and the beaten eggs. Season with salt and pepper. Gently, using a fork or your hand, toss the fish in the coconut cream and eggs until it is well coated.

3 Place 30ml/2 tbsp of the fish mixture just off centre on a square of banana leaf and fold the sides of the leaf over the top, leaving a little room for expansion.

4 Secure the package with a cocktail stick threaded through each end, and repeat with the rest of the mixture.

5 Preheat the oven to 200°C/400°F/Gas 6 or prepare a charcoal grill. Bake the fish cakes in the oven for 30 minutes, or grill them for 15 minutes each side.

6 Serve the fish cakes in the banana leaves for everyone to unwrap, with lime quarters for squeezing over and chilli or peanut sambal for dipping.

SERVES FOUR TO SIX

INGREDIENTS
4 shallots, chopped
1 lemon grass stalk, trimmed
  and chopped
25g/1oz galangal, chopped
4 candlenuts or macadamia
  nuts, roasted
4 dried red chillies,
  soaked in warm water
  until soft, squeezed dry
  and seeded
5ml/1 tsp shrimp paste
5–10ml/1–2 tsp ground turmeric
250ml/8fl oz/1 cup coconut cream
15ml/1 tbsp dark soy sauce
10ml/2 tsp palm sugar (jaggery)

450g/1lb fresh mackerel, cleaned,
  skinned and flaked
4–6 lime leaves, finely shredded
2 eggs, lightly beaten
salt and ground black pepper
12 banana leaves, cut into pieces
  about 20cm/8in square
cocktail sticks (toothpicks)
2 limes, quartered lengthways, and
  chilli or peanut sambal, to serve

1 Using a mortar and pestle or food processor, grind the shallots, lemon grass, galangal, candlenuts or macadamia nuts and chillies to a paste. Beat in the shrimp paste and turmeric. Stir in the coconut cream, soy sauce and sugar until blended.

Per Portion Energy 396Kcal/1642kJ; Protein 19.5g; Carbohydrate 4.5g, of which sugars 4.2g; Fat 33.5g, of which saturates 16.1g; Cholesterol 117mg; Calcium 60mg; Fibre 0.5g; Sodium 382mg.

GRILLED STINGRAY WINGS
WITH CHILLI SAMBAL

CHARGRILLED STINGRAY IS A VERY POPULAR STREET SNACK IN SINGAPORE. THE STALLS SELLING GRILLED CHICKEN WINGS AND SATAY OFTEN SERVE STINGRAY WINGS ON A BANANA LEAF WITH A GENEROUS SPOONFUL OF CHILLI SAMBAL. THE COOKED FISH IS EATEN WITH FINGERS, OR CHOPSTICKS, BY TEARING OFF PIECES AND DIPPING THEM IN THE SAMBAL. IF YOU CAN'T FIND STINGRAY WINGS, YOU COULD SUBSTITUTE A FLAT FISH, SUCH AS PLAICE.

SERVES FOUR

INGREDIENTS

4 medium-sized stingray wings, about
    200g/7oz, rinsed and patted dry
salt
4 banana leaves, about 30cm/
    12in square
2 fresh limes, halved
For the chilli sambal
    6–8 red chillies, seeded and chopped
    4 garlic cloves, chopped
    5ml/1 tsp shrimp paste
    15ml/1 tbsp tomato purée (paste)
    15ml/1 tbsp palm sugar (jaggery)
    juice of 2 limes
    30ml/2 tbsp vegetable or groundnut
        (peanut) oil

1 First make the chilli sambal. Using a mortar and pestle or food processor, grind the chillies with the garlic to form a paste. Beat in the shrimp paste, tomato purée and sugar. Add the lime juice and bind with the oil.

2 Prepare a charcoal grill. Rub each stingray wing with a little chilli sambal and place them on the rack. Cook for 3–4 minutes on each side, until tender. Sprinkle with salt and serve on banana leaves with the remaining chilli sambal and the limes.

Per Portion Energy 195Kcal/823kJ; Protein 30.4g; Carbohydrate 4.5g, of which sugars 4.5g; Fat 6.3g, of which saturates 0.7g; Cholesterol 0mg; Calcium 83mg; Fibre 0.1g; Sodium 249mg.

GRILLED MACKEREL <u>WITH</u> SOY SAUCE, CHILLI <u>AND</u> LIME SAMBAL

MACKEREL, WHEN IT IS REALLY FRESH, IS ABSOLUTELY DELICIOUS GRILLED AND EATEN WITH A SHARP CHILLI DIP. WHEN CHOOSING MACKEREL, LOOK FOR CLEAR, SILVERY SKIN AND BRIGHT EYES. WHEN YOU PRESS DOWN ON THE FLESH, IT SHOULD BE FIRM AND SPRING BACK A LITTLE. IF IT'S SOFT TO THE TOUCH, THE MACKEREL IS NOT FRESH ENOUGH AND NOT WORTH BUYING.

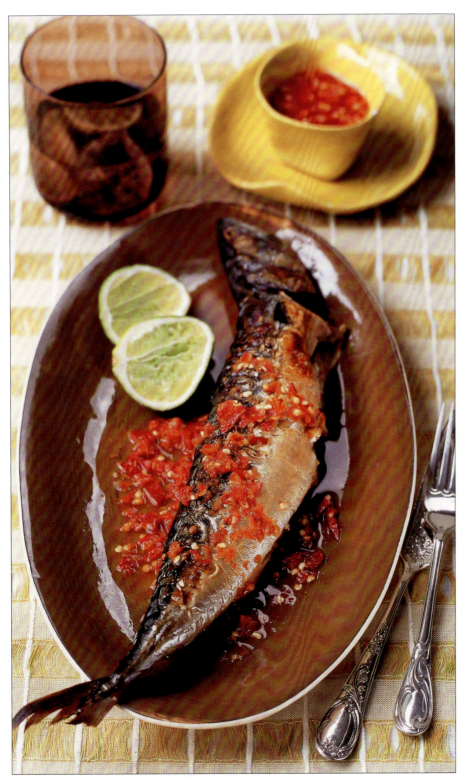

<u>SERVES FOUR</u>

INGREDIENTS
   2 whole mackerel, gutted and
   cleaned
   5ml/1 tsp salt
   15ml/1 tbsp light fish sauce
   15ml/1 tbsp lime juice
   30ml/2 tbsp vegetable oil
For the chilli and lime sambal
   2–3 red chillies, seeded and chopped
   juice of 2 limes
   5ml/1 tsp salt
   pinch of sugar

1 Preheat the grill (broiler) to high. Grind the chillies for the sambal and stir in the other ingredients. Set aside.

2 Rub the fish inside and outside with salt. Place on a sheet of aluminium foil on a rack over a roasting pan.

3 Brush with fish sauce, lime juice and oil and grill for 10–15 minutes, turning once. Serve with the sambal.

Per portion Energy 216kcal/895kJ; Protein 14.1g; Carbohydrate 0.3g, of which sugars 0.3g; Fat 17.6g, of which saturates 3.1g; Cholesterol 41mg; Calcium 9mg; Fibre 0g; Sodium 788mg.

STEAMED WHOLE FISH NONYA-STYLE

IN MALAY AND INDIAN COOKING, WHOLE FISH IS OFTEN GRILLED OR FRIED, WHEREAS THE CHINESE AND PERANAKANS PREFER TO STEAM IT. PLUMP POMFRET RANKS AS ONE OF THE FAVOURITES TO STEAM WHOLE, OFTEN WITH SUBTLE FLAVOURINGS SO AS NOT TO SPOIL THE FRESH TASTE OF THE FISH. THIS NONYA DISH IS PARTICULARLY POPULAR IN PENANG, MELAKA AND SINGAPORE.

SERVES FOUR

INGREDIENTS

3 spring onions (scallions), trimmed into 2.5cm/1in pieces and cut into strips
25g/1oz fresh root ginger, peeled and cut into 2.5cm/1in strips
4 dried shiitake mushrooms, soaked in hot water until soft and squeezed dry
1 whole fresh fish, such as pomfret (porgy) or sea bass, weighing about 900g/2lb, gutted and cleaned
30ml/2 tbsp vegetable or sesame oil
30ml/2 tbsp light soy sauce
salt and ground black pepper
1 red chilli, seeded and cut into thin strips and fresh coriander (cilantro) leaves, to garnish
steamed rice and chilli sambal, to serve

1 Put the spring onions and ginger in a bowl. Trim the shiitake mushrooms, discarding the hard stems, and cut them into thin strips. Add them to the spring onions and ginger and mix well.

2 Fill a wok one-third of the way up with water. Place a metal steaming rack in the wok, cover with a lid and put the wok over the heat. Score the fish diagonally three or four times on each side and season with salt and pepper. Place it on a heatproof plate and scatter the spring onion, ginger and shitake mushrooms over it. Place the plate on the rack, cover and steam the fish for 15–20 minutes, until cooked.

COOK'S TIP
To check that the fish is done insert the point of a kitchen knife into the thickest part of the flesh: it should be just opaque and lift away from the bone.

3 When the fish is cooked, heat the oil in a small pan. Stir in the soy sauce and pour it over the fish. Garnish the dish with the chillies and coriander leaves and serve with steamed rice and chilli sambal.

Per Portion Energy 278Kcal/1165kJ; Protein 43.7g; Carbohydrate 0.5g, of which sugars 0.5g; Fat 11.2g, of which saturates 1.6g; Cholesterol 180mg; Calcium 296mg; Fibre 0.1g; Sodium 423mg.

BRAISED GROUPER IN BLACK BEAN SAUCE

GROUPER IS ONE OF THE MOST DESIRABLE FISH ON ACCOUNT OF ITS RICH FLAVOUR AND MEATY TEXTURE. TRADITIONALLY, BRAISED FISH IS COOKED WHOLE, HEAD AND ALL, AND ONLY THE MOST INEDIBLE FINS ARE REMOVED. SOME RESTAURANT CHEFS DEEP-FRY THE FISH BEFORE BRAISING IT AS IT LOOKS MORE IMPRESSIVE AND, WHEN COOKED, STAYS IN SHAPE BETTER.

SERVES FOUR

INGREDIENTS
  1 grouper, about 450g/1lb
  oil for deep-frying (optional)
  30ml/2 tbsp chopped spring onions
    (scallions)
  fresh coriander (cilantro) sprigs, to
    garnish
For the sauce
  30ml/2 tbsp black bean sauce
  15ml/1 tbsp oyster sauce
  10ml/2 tsp garlic purée
  10g/2 tsp ginger purée
  5ml/1 tsp sugar
  2.5ml/½ tsp ground black pepper
  30ml/2 tbsp sesame oil
  60ml/4 tbsp Chinese wine
  15ml/1 tbsp cornflour (cornstarch),
    to thicken (optional)

1 Gut and clean the fish but leave the head on. Trim off the fins with scissors and cut off half the tail if it protrudes too much from the pan you are going to cook it in.

2 Heat enough oil for deep-frying in a wok or large pan and fry the grouper until golden brown if you wish.

3 Blend all the sauce ingredients with 400ml/14fl oz/1$\frac{2}{3}$ cups water and mix well. Bring to the boil in a wok or deep pan and cook for 2 minutes. Add the whole fish and simmer, uncovered, for 10 minutes.

4 Spoon the sauce over the fish from time to time as it cooks, but do not turn the fish over as it might break.

5 Serve the fish hot, garnished with fresh coriander. If you wish to thicken the sauce a little, mix 15ml/1 tbsp cornflour with a little water and stir it into the sauce for the last 2 minutes of cooking.

COOK'S TIP
Don't worry if you don't like the thought of gutting the fish – just ask your fishmonger to do it for you. You could also use fillets rather than a whole fish if you prefer it without the head and tail.

Per portion Energy 173Kcal/727kJ; Protein 14.5g; Carbohydrate 8.8g, of which sugars 5.2g; Fat 7.4g, of which saturates 1.2g; Cholesterol 26mg; Calcium 38mg; Fibre 0.2g; Sodium 274mg.

SWEET AND SOUR SNAPPER

THERE MUST BE MORE SWEET AND SOUR RECIPES THAN ANYONE COULD COUNT; VARIATIONS OF THIS IDEA HAVE SPREAD ALL OVER THE WORLD. ESSENTIALLY, THE SWEET AND SOUR TAG REFERS TO THE YIN-YANG BALANCE OF CONTRASTING AND BALANCING FLAVOURS THAT UNDERSCORES MUCH OF CHINESE CUISINE. THIS IS A TROPICAL VERSION, WHICH IS FLAVOURED WITH LIBERAL DASHES OF GARLIC, CHILLIES AND GINGER — BEAUTIFUL, CLEAN FLAVOURS THAT COMPLEMENT THE SNAPPER.

SERVES FOUR

INGREDIENTS

    1 snapper, about 500g/1¼lb
    50g/2oz/¼ cup cornflour
      (cornstarch)
    oil for deep-frying
    2 spring onions (scallions)
For the sauce
    2 garlic cloves
    50g/2oz fresh root ginger, peeled
    45ml/3 tbsp plum sauce
    15ml/1 tbsp tomato sauce
    15ml/1 tbsp hoisin sauce
    100ml/3½fl oz/scant ½ cup water
    15ml/1 tbsp vegetable oil
    2 red chillies, seeded

1 Clean and gut the snapper and trim off the fins, but leave the head on. Spread the cornflour on a plate and dip the fish in it to coat. Heat the oil in a wok or large pan and deep-fry the fish for 7–8 minutes, until it is golden brown and crisp and the flesh is cooked.

2 Slice the garlic and ginger into fine strips. Trim the chillies and spring onions and cut into 5cm/2in lengths.

3 For the sauce, mix the plum, tomato and hoi sin sauces with the water.

4 Heat the oil and fry the garlic and ginger until golden. Add the sauce mixture and bring to the boil. Add the sliced chillies and simmer for 1 minute.

5 Arrange the fried fish on a serving plate and pour over the sweet and sour sauce. Garnish with the spring onions and serve immediately.

Per portion Energy 121Kcal/508kJ; Protein 16g; Carbohydrate 3.9g, of which sugars 3.7g; Fat 4.8g, of which saturates 0.7g; Cholesterol 29mg; Calcium 36mg; Fibre 0.1g; Sodium 545mg.

FISH HEAD CURRY

THE ORIGINS OF THIS SINGAPORE STREET DISH HAVE BECOME BLURRED WITH TIME. SOME SAY IT CAME WITH IMMIGRANTS FROM KERALA IN SOUTH INDIA; OTHERS CLAIM AN INDIAN CHEF CREATED IT IN SINGAPORE IN THE 1950S OR '60S. WHATEVER ITS ORIGINS, KA LI YU TOU IS IN DEMAND AT INDIAN AND MALAY FOOD STALLS, WHERE THERE ARE NUMEROUS VERSIONS. IT IS SAID THAT THE BEST FISH HEAD CURRY, PRIZED FOR THE SUCCULENT CHEEKS, IS STILL FOUND AT COFFEE SHOPS IN SINGAPORE.

SERVES TWO

INGREDIENTS
  30ml/2 tbsp ghee or vegetable oil
  10ml/2 tsp brown mustard seeds
  5ml/1 tsp fenugreek seeds
  5ml/1 tsp cumin seeds
  a handful of curry leaves
  15ml/1 tbsp palm sugar (jaggery)
  30ml/2 tbsp tamarind pulp, soaked
    in 150ml/¼ pint/⅔ cup water and
    strained for juice
  600ml/1 pint/2½ cups coconut milk
  1 large fresh fish head, such as red
    snapper (about 900g/2lb), cleaned
  5 okra, halved diagonally
  2 large tomatoes, skinned, seeded
    and quartered
  salt and ground black pepper
  steamed rice and pickles, to serve
For the spice paste
  8 shallots, chopped
  6 garlic cloves, chopped
  4 red chillies, seeded and chopped
  50g/2oz fresh root ginger, peeled
    and chopped
  25g/1oz fresh turmeric, chopped
  1 lemon grass stalk, trimmed and
    chopped
  30ml/2 tbsp fish curry powder

COOK'S TIP
Any large fish head, such as salmon, grouper or tuna, can be used.

1 To make the spice paste, grind all the ingredients together using a mortar and pestle or food processor.

2 Heat the ghee or oil in a wok or heavy pan. Stir in the mustard seeds, fenugreek and cumin seeds along with the curry leaves. Fry until the mustard seeds begin to pop and then stir in the spice paste.

3 Fry the spice paste until fragrant, then stir in the sugar, followed by the tamarind juice and coconut milk.

4 Bring to the boil, reduce the heat and add the fish head. Simmer gently for 10 minutes, then add the okra and tomatoes. Simmer for another 10 minutes or until the fish head is cooked. Season the sauce to taste and serve the fish head curry with steamed rice and pickles.

Per Portion Energy 417Kcal/1760kJ; Protein 42.2g; Carbohydrate 30.4g, of which sugars 29.1g; Fat 15.2g, of which saturates 2.7g; Cholesterol 74mg; Calcium 231mg; Fibre 2.7g; Sodium 497mg.

SOUR RAY FISH CURRY

RAYS AND BABY SHARK ARE FAVOURITE FOODS IN MALAYSIA AND SINGAPORE, ESPECIALLY IN NONYA COOKING. BOTH FISH ARE CARTILAGINOUS, SO THEY DON'T HAVE THE FINE BONES THAT CHARACTERIZE OTHER FISH, AND LEND THEMSELVES TO SOUR CURRIES VERY WELL. THE RAYS BROUGHT TO MARKET TEND TO BE FAIRLY SMALL. SKATE COMES FROM THE SAME FAMILY, AND SKATE WINGS COULD ALSO BE USED IN THIS DISH VERY SUCCESSFULLY.

SERVES FOUR

INGREDIENTS
500g/1¼lb ray steaks
6 sour star fruit
30ml/2 tbsp tamarind
  concentrate
350ml/12floz/1½ cups water
juice of 1 lime
5ml/1 tsp sugar
salt
sweet basil leaves, to garnish
For the spice paste
2 red chillies, seeded and
  chopped
8 shallots, chopped
15g/½oz fresh turmeric
15g/½oz galangal
15g/½oz shrimp paste

1 Cut the fish into large pieces and rub them with about 5ml/1 tsp salt. Slice the sour star fruit in half lengthways and discard the pith.

2 Grind the ingredients for the spice paste together with a mortar and pestle, until fine and well blended.

3 In a pan, blend the tamarind with water and lime juice, add the paste and bring to the boil. Simmer for 3 minutes then add the fish and the star fruit and cook for a further 10 minutes.

4 Add salt and sugar to taste and garnish with basil leaves before serving.

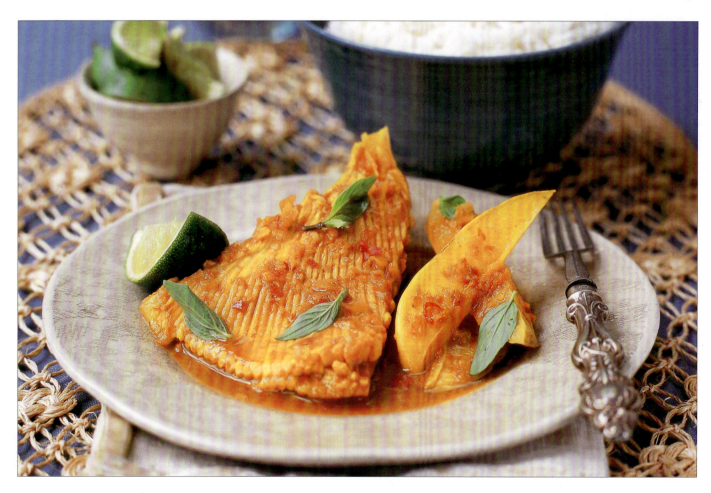

Per portion Energy 168Kcal/710kJ; Protein 31.6g; Carbohydrate 6.4g, of which sugars 4.8g; Fat 2g, of which saturates 0.3g; Cholesterol 74mg; Calcium 80mg; Fibre 0.2g; Sodium 339mg.

SOUR FISH CURRY

ALTHOUGH THIS DISH IS SIMILAR IN ESSENCE TO SOUR RAY FISH CURRY, THE SPICE PASTE IS QUITE DIFFERENT, AND IS FRIED FIRST BEFORE IT IS ADDED TO THE SAUCE. A LITTLE COCONUT MILK IS ALSO ADDED TO TEMPER THE TARTNESS OF THE TAMARIND, GIVING THE DISH A MUCH RICHER FLAVOUR. CHOOSE A FISH WITH FIRM, MEATY FLESH, SUCH AS POMFRET, BABY SHARK OR EVEN SALMON. THE VEGETABLES TRADITIONALLY ADDED ARE AUBERGINE AND TOMATOES.

SERVES FOUR

INGREDIENTS

500g/1¼lb thick fish cutlets
1 aubergine (eggplant)
2 tomatoes
30ml/2 tbsp tamarind concentrate
350ml/12 floz/1½ cups water
45ml/3 tbsp coconut milk
5ml/1 tsp sugar
30ml/2 tbsp vegetable oil
15ml/1 tbsp chilli oil (optional)
salt

For the spice paste
2 dried red chillies, softened in warm water, seeded and chopped
½ large onion, chopped
15g/½oz fresh turmeric
15g/½oz shrimp paste
3 garlic cloves, chopped

1 Cut the fish into large pieces and rub with about 5ml/1 tsp salt. Slice the aubergine lengthways and cut into half moon shapes. Quarter the tomatoes.

2 To make the spice paste, grind all the ingredients together using a mortar and pestle or a food processor. Heat the oil and fry the paste until it is fragrant.

3 Blend the tamarind concentrate with the water and stir it into the fried spice paste. Add the coconut milk, fish, aubergine and tomato.

4 Simmer for 8 minutes until the fish is done. Season to taste with salt and sugar. If you wish, add a swirl of chilli oil to give the dish a rich colour.

Per portion Energy 205Kcal/860kJ; Protein 26.5g; Carbohydrate 9.4g, of which sugars 8.9g; Fat 7.1g, of which saturates 1g; Cholesterol 76mg; Calcium 79mg; Fibre 2.7g; Sodium 257mg.

MALAY FISH CURRY

THE FISH CURRIES OF MALAYSIA DIFFER SLIGHTLY FROM REGION TO REGION, BUT MOST OF THEM INCLUDE A VARIETY OF INDIAN SPICES AND MANY ARE ENRICHED WITH COCONUT MILK. THE MALAY FOOD STALLS OFTEN FEATURE A FISH, CHICKEN OR BEEF CURRY, WHICH IS USUALLY SERVED WITH BREAD OR RICE, PICKLES AND EXTRA CHILLIES.

1 To make the curry paste, use a mortar and pestle or food processor to grind the shallots, garlic, ginger, turmeric and chillies to a paste, transfer to a bowl and set aside.

2 Again, using the mortar and pestle or food processor, grind the roasted coriander and cumin seeds, the fish curry powder, fennel seeds and peppercorns to a powder. Add this mixture to the paste in the bowl. Bind with 15ml/1 tbsp water and thoroughly mix together.

3 Heat the oil in a wok or heavy pan. Stir in the curry paste and fry until fragrant. Stir in the tamarind concentrate. Add the fish and cook for 1 minute on each side.

4 Pour in the coconut milk, mix well and bring to the boil. Reduce the heat and simmer for 8–10 minutes until the fish is cooked.

5 Season to taste with salt. Scatter the coriander over the top and serve with plain or yellow rice, or with chunks of crusty bread to mop up the sauce.

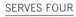
SERVES FOUR

INGREDIENTS
  30ml/2 tbsp vegetable oil
  7.5ml/1½ tsp tamarind concentrate
  8 thick fish cutlets, about 90g/3½oz
    each, such as grouper, red snapper,
    trout or mackerel
  800ml/1½ pints coconut milk
  salt
  fresh coriander (cilantro) leaves,
    roughly chopped, to garnish
  rice or crusty bread, to serve

For the curry paste
  4 shallots, chopped
  4 garlic cloves, chopped
  50g/2oz fresh root ginger, peeled
    and chopped
  25g/1oz fresh turmeric, chopped
  4–6 dried red chillies, softened in
    warm water, seeded and chopped
  15ml/1 tbsp coriander seeds, roasted
  15ml/1 tbsp cumin seeds, roasted
  10ml/2 tsp fish curry powder
  5ml/1 tsp fennel seeds
  2.5ml/½ tsp black peppercorns

COOK'S TIP
To roast the spices, heat them gently in a dry, heavy pan until they begin to colour and develop a nutty aroma. Take care not to burn them.

Per Portion Energy 264Kcal/1109kJ; Protein 36.6g; Carbohydrate 12.7g, of which sugars 12.1g; Fat 7.7g, of which saturates 1.3g; Cholesterol 89mg; Calcium 110mg; Fibre 1g; Sodium 354mg.

NEW YEAR RAW FISH SALAD

To celebrate the lunar New Year, Chinese families in Malaysia and Singapore get together to eat special dishes such as this salad, yu sheng, which all the diners must help to mix with their chopsticks, while they shout "lo hei" ("toss the fish") for good luck. Many Chinese restaurants offer this festive dish with the addition of sliced jellyfish.

SERVES FOUR TO SIX

INGREDIENTS

 175g/6oz fresh tuna or salmon,
  finely sliced
 115g/4oz white fish fillet, finely
  sliced
 25g/1oz fresh root ginger,
  peeled and finely
  chopped
 2 garlic cloves, crushed
 juice of 2 limes
 225g/8oz mooli (daikon),
  cut into julienne strips
 2 carrots, cut into julienne
  strips
 1 small cucumber, peeled,
  seeded and cut into
  julienne strips
 4 spring onions (scallions),
  trimmed and cut into
  julienne strips
 1 pomelo, segmented
  and sliced
 4 fresh kaffir lime leaves, cut into
  fine ribbons
 50g/2oz preserved sweet melon,
  finely sliced
 50g/2oz preserved sweet red
  ginger, finely sliced
 ground black pepper
 30ml/2 tbsp roasted peanuts,
  coarsely crushed,
  to garnish
For the dressing
 30ml/2 tbsp sesame oil
 15ml/1 tbsp light soy sauce
 15ml/1 tbsp red vinegar
 30ml/2 tbsp sour plum sauce
 2 garlic cloves, crushed
 10ml/2 tsp caster (superfine)
  sugar

COOK'S TIP
The Chinese add jellyfish to this salad
for the texture rather than the taste.
If you would like to add a different
ingredient for its texture, you could try
50g/2oz cubes of steamed or stir-fried
firm tofu.

1 In a shallow, non-metallic, dish, toss
the slices of fish with the ginger, garlic
and lime juice. Season with black
pepper and set aside for at least
30 minutes to marinate.

2 Place the mooli, carrots, cucumber,
spring onions, pomelo and lime leaves
in a large bowl. Add the pieces of
preserved melon and ginger. Toss well
for an even distribution of ingredients.

3 Mix together the ingredients for the
dressing, adjusting the sweet and sour
balance to taste.

4 Just before serving, place the
marinated fish on top of the vegetables
in the bowl. Pour the dressing over the
top and sprinkle with the roasted
peanuts. Place the bowl in the middle
of the table and get everyone to toss the
salad with their chopsticks.

Per Portion Energy 126Kcal/528kJ; Protein 13.2g; Carbohydrate 6.5g, of which sugars 6.4g; Fat 5.4g, of which saturates 1g; Cholesterol 22mg; Calcium 36mg; Fibre 1.3g; Sodium 222mg.

SPICED LOBSTER IN BANANA LEAF

ANY FOOD THAT IS SPICED AND WRAPPED IN BANANA LEAF BEFORE BEING GRILLED OR STEAMED IS GENERALLY CALLED OTAK OTAK IN MALAYSIA AND SINGAPORE, REGARDLESS OF THE INGREDIENTS THAT GO INTO IT. OTAK OTAK IS OFTEN MADE WITH FISH, ESPECIALLY ON THE HAWKER STALLS IN COASTAL AREAS. THIS LUXURIOUS VERSION OF THE RECIPE USES LOBSTER FOR A SPECTACULAR AND DELICIOUS PARTY PIECE, BUT YOU COULD USE THE SAME METHOD TO COOK ANY FIRM FISH.

SERVES FOUR

INGREDIENTS
  2 lobster tails, shelled and minced
    (ground) coarsely
  4 lime leaves, cut into fine ribbons
  5ml/1 tsp salt
  5ml/1 tsp sugar
  2 eggs, lightly beaten
  30ml/2 tbsp vegetable oil
  175ml/6fl oz/¾ cup coconut cream
  8 pieces banana leaf, each measuring
    25cm/10in square
For the spice paste
  200g/7oz onion, chopped
  6 candlenuts
  15ml/1 tbsp ground coriander
  10ml/2 tsp chilli powder
  15g/½oz shrimp paste
  15g/½oz galangal, peeled and
    chopped
  5ml/1 tsp ground turmeric

1 To make the spice paste, grind all the ingredients together until fine using a mortar and pestle or a food processor. Mix with the lime leaves, salt and sugar and transfer to a bowl.

2 Add the lobster to the bowl and mix well with the spices. Add the eggs, oil and coconut cream and stir thoroughly. The consistency should be like that of softened butter.

3 Scald the banana leaves in boiling water to soften them, and drain. Lay each piece of leaf out on a flat surface and place 30–45ml/2–3 tbsp of the spiced lobster mixture in the centre, spreading it out until it is about 6mm/¼in thick.

4 Fold the opposite edges of the leaf over the filling and tuck in the sides to make a firm parcel.

5 Prepare a charcoal grill or preheat a grill (broiler) to high. Grill the banana leaf parcels for 8–10 minutes, turning once halfway through cooking. Serve immediately, to be unwrapped at the table.

COOK'S TIP
The coconut cream used in this recipe gives the fish mixture a luscious consistency. Coconut cream can be taken from the top of a can of coconut milk or may be the first squeeze from freshly reconstituted desiccated coconut.

Per portion Energy 369Kcal/1531kJ; Protein 18.5g; Carbohydrate 8g, of which sugars 4.6g; Fat 29.7g, of which saturates 16.5g; Cholesterol 168mg; Calcium 119mg; Fibre 0.8g; Sodium 359mg.

SINGAPORE CHILLI CRAB

THIS COULD PERHAPS BE DESCRIBED AS SINGAPORE'S SIGNATURE DISH. IT IS AN ALL-TIME FAVOURITE AT HAWKER STALLS AND COFFEE SHOPS, WHERE STEAMING WOKS OF CRAB DEEP-FRYING ARE A COMMON SIGHT. THE CRABS ARE PLACED IN THE MIDDLE OF THE TABLE WITH A BOWL FOR THE DISCARDED PIECES OF SHELL, AND SMALL BOWLS OF WATER FOR CLEANING YOUR FINGERS. CRACK THE SHELLS, DIP THE MEAT INTO THE COOKING SAUCE, THEN MOP UP THE SAUCE WITH LOTS OF CRUSTY BREAD.

SERVES FOUR

INGREDIENTS

 vegetable oil, for deep-frying
 4 fresh crabs, about 250g/9oz each,
  halved and cleaned
 30ml/2 tbsp sesame oil
 30–45ml/2–3 tbsp chilli sauce
 45ml/3 tbsp tomato ketchup
 15ml/1 tbsp soy sauce
 15ml/1 tbsp sugar
 250ml/8fl oz/1 cup chicken stock
  or water
 2 eggs, beaten
 salt and ground black pepper
 2 spring onions (scallions), finely
  sliced, and fresh coriander
  (cilantro) leaves, finely chopped,
  to garnish
For the spice paste
 4 garlic cloves, chopped
 25g/1oz fresh root ginger, chopped
 4 red chillies, seeded and chopped

COOK'S TIP
To chop a crab in half, killing it instantly, lay it on its back and position a cleaver down the centre line, then strike the back of the cleaver with a mallet.

1 Using a mortar and pestle or food processor, grind the ingredients for the spice paste and set aside.

2 Heat enough oil for deep-frying in a wok or heavy pan. Drop in the crabs and fry until the shells turn bright red. Remove from the oil and drain.

3 Heat the sesame oil in a wok and stir in the spice paste. Fry the paste until fragrant then stir in the chilli sauce, ketchup, soy sauce and sugar.

4 Toss in the fried crab and coat well in the sauce. Pour in the chicken stock or water and bring to the boil. Reduce the heat and simmer for 5 minutes. Season the sauce to taste.

5 Pour in the eggs, stirring gently, to let them set in the sauce.

6 Serve immediately, garnished with spring onions and coriander.

Per Portion Energy 276Kcal/1144kJ; Protein 12.1g; Carbohydrate 8.6g, of which sugars 8.1g; Fat 21.7g, of which saturates 3.1g; Cholesterol 126mg; Calcium 23mg; Fibre 0.3g; Sodium 674mg.

SABAHAN SQUID IN HOT YELLOW SAUCE

Simple fishermen's dishes such as this one are cooked the length and breadth of Malaysia's coastline. This recipe comes from Sabah, the northernmost state in Malaysian Borneo, and includes enough chillies to set your tongue on fire. Serve it with rice or bread to temper the heat. In Sabah the dish is often served with the local staple, sago porridge, and finely shredded green mango tossed in lime juice.

1 First prepare the squid. Hold the body sac in one hand and pull off the head with the other. Sever the tentacles just above the eyes, and discard the rest of the head and innards. Clean the body sac inside and out and remove the skin.

2 Pat the squid dry, cut it into thick slices and put them in a bowl, along with the tentacles. Mix the lime juice with the salt and rub it into the squid. Set aside for 30 minutes.

3 Meanwhile, using a mortar and pestle or food processor, grind the shallots, garlic, galangal, turmeric and chillies to a coarse paste.

4 Heat the oil in a wok or heavy pan, and stir in the coarse paste. Cook the paste until fragrant, then stir in the palm sugar, lemon grass and whole kaffir lime leaves.

5 Drain the squid of any juice and toss it around the wok, coating it in the flavourings. Pour in the coconut milk and bring it to the boil. Reduce the heat and simmer for 5–10 minutes, until the squid is tender.

6 Season with salt and pepper and serve with chunks of fresh, crusty bread or steamed rice.

SERVES FOUR

INGREDIENTS
500g/1¼lb fresh squid
juice of 2 limes
5ml/1 tsp salt
4 shallots, chopped
4 garlic cloves, chopped
25g/1oz galangal, chopped
25g/1oz fresh turmeric, chopped
6–8 red chillies, seeded and chopped
30ml/2 tbsp vegetable or groundnut (peanut) oil
7.5ml/1½ tsp palm sugar (jaggery)
2 lemon grass stalks, crushed
4 kaffir lime leaves
400ml/14fl oz/1⅔ cups coconut milk
salt and ground black pepper
crusty bread or steamed rice,
 to serve

Per Portion Energy 185Kcal/780kJ; Protein 19.8g; Carbohydrate 9.4g, of which sugars 7.6g; Fat 8g, of which saturates 1.4g; Cholesterol 281mg; Calcium 50mg; Fibre 0.2g; Sodium 739mg.

CRAB CURRY

SINGAPORE HAS BEEN THE HOME OF MANY MIGRANT SRI LANKANS FOR OVER A CENTURY, AND THEY ARE THE SOURCE OF ONE OF THE ISLAND'S MOST CAPTIVATING DISHES, SRI LANKAN CRAB CURRY, WHICH IS MADE WITH MOTTLED BLUE CRABS. IN MALAYSIA AND SINGAPORE THERE IS ANOTHER VARIETY OF CRAB CALLED THE THUNDER CRAB. LEGEND HAS IT THAT WHEN ONE NIPS YOU WITH ITS CLAWS, ONLY A THUNDERCLAP WILL MAKE IT RELEASE ITS HOLD.

SERVES FOUR

INGREDIENTS
    8 mottled blue crabs
    60ml/4 tbsp oil
    500m/16 fl oz/2 cups coconut milk
    30ml/2 tbsp lime juice
    5ml/1 tsp salt
    30ml/2 tbsp seafood curry powder,
      blended with a little water to
      make a paste
For the spice paste
    ½ large onion, chopped
    5 garlic cloves, chopped
    15ml/1 tbsp grated fresh root ginger

4 Heat the oil in a wok or large pan and fry the spice paste for about 3 minutes. Add the coconut milk, lime juice and salt and simmer for 2 minutes.

5 Add the crabs to the sauce and cook for about 8 minutes, turning constantly, until the shells have turned completely pink. Serve with rice or bread.

1 Remove the shells of the crabs and discard the spongy fibrous tissues.

2 Separate the claws from the bodies if they are large. The smaller legs have very little meat in them, but leave them attached to the bodies as they make good handles for eating with the fingers.

3 Grind the ingredients for the spice paste together using a mortar and pestle or a food processor. Mix the curry powder, blended with water, into the paste.

COOK'S TIP
Blue crabs are available frozen from some Indian stores. If you cannot find them, use any other large, meaty variety that is available from your fishmonger.

Per portion Energy 288Kcal/1205kJ; Protein 22.5g; Carbohydrate 11.6g, of which sugars 7.1g; Fat 17.4g, of which saturates 2.2g; Cholesterol 55mg; Calcium 86mg; Fibre 0.6g; Sodium 506mg.

SARAWAK SAMBAL UDANG

THIS VERSION OF THE MALAYSIAN DISH SAMBAL UDANG IS SIMPLE AND FIERY. TO ACCOMPANY THE DISH IN SARAWAK, YOU MIGHT BE OFFERED THE LOCAL, THICK SAGO PASTE, A BOWL OF STIR-FRIED FERN SHOOTS AND A LITTLE TUAK, THE HEADY, HOME-BREWED RICE WINE. THE DAYAKS, IBANS AND MELANAU ALSO COOK THE GRUBS FOUND IN SAGO PALMS IN THIS WAY.

SERVES FOUR

INGREDIENTS

8 shallots, chopped
4 garlic cloves, chopped
8–10 dried red chillies, soaked in
  warm water until soft, squeezed dry,
  seeded and chopped
5ml/1 tsp shrimp paste
30ml/2 tbsp vegetable or groundnut
  (peanut) oil
250ml/8fl oz/1 cup coconut cream
500g/1¼lb raw prawns (shrimp),
  peeled and deveined
10ml/2 tsp tamarind concentrate
15ml/1 tbsp palm sugar (jaggery)
salt and ground black pepper
2 red chillies, seeded and finely
  chopped, and fresh coriander
  (cilantro) leaves, finely chopped,
  to garnish
crusty bread or steamed rice and
  pickles, to serve

1 Using a mortar and pestle or food processor, grind the shallots, garlic and dried chillies to a coarse paste. Beat in the shrimp paste.

2 Heat the oil in a wok or heavy pan and stir in the paste until fragrant. Add the coconut cream and bubble it up until it separates. Toss in the prawns, reduce the heat and simmer for 3 minutes until the prawns have changed colour.

3 Stir in the tamarind concentrate and the sugar and cook for a further 2 minutes until the sauce is very thick. Season with salt and pepper and scatter the chopped chillies and coriander over the top. Serve immediately with chunks of fresh, crusty bread to mop up the sauce, or with steamed rice and pickles.

Per Portion Energy 330Kcal/1371kJ; Protein 25.9g; Carbohydrate 3.7g, of which sugars 3.2g; Fat 23.6g, of which saturates 15.6g; Cholesterol 263mg; Calcium 156mg; Fibre 0.4g; Sodium 408mg.

TOMATO AND CHILLI PRAWNS

IN SINGAPORE THIS IS A SUPREME RESTAURANT DISH CALLED HAR LOKE, WHICH USES PRAWNS IN THEIR SHELLS, COOKED IN A STICKY, SPICY SAUCE. IT IS NEVER MADE WITH SHELLED PRAWNS AS THE SHELLS ACTUALLY SEAL IN THE FULL FLAVOURS OF THE SEAFOOD. IT MAY BE FIDDLY TO PEEL THE PRAWNS WHEN EATING THEM BUT IT IS WELL WORTH THE EFFORT.

SERVES FOUR

INGREDIENTS

   16 raw tiger prawns (jumbo shrimp)
   45ml/3 tbsp vegetable or groundnut
     (peanut) oil
   1 large onion, finely sliced
   2 tomatoes, quartered
For the sauce
   30ml/2 tbsp tomato sauce
   15ml/1 tbsp oyster sauce
   15ml/1 tbsp plum sauce
   15ml/1 tbsp chilli sauce
   90ml/6 tbsp water

1 Snip off about 1cm/½in from the head of each prawn, removing the feelers. Wash and pat dry.

2 In a dry wok, fry the prawns over a high heat for 3 minutes, until they are nearly cooked. Remove and set aside.

3 Add the oil to the wok and fry the onions until soft but not brown. Add the tomatoes and stir-fry for 2 minutes.

4 Mix all the ingredients for the sauce until well blended. Stir the mixture into the vegetables. Return the prawns to the wok and stir constantly until well incorporated and bubbling. The prawns should be completely cooked after about 2 minutes. Serve immediately.

Per portion Energy 166Kcal/693kJ; Protein 10.2g; Carbohydrate 12.2g, of which sugars 10.4g; Fat 8.9g, of which saturates 1.1g; Cholesterol 98mg; Calcium 63mg; Fibre 1.6g; Sodium 225mg.

PRAWNS <u>IN</u> LIME JUICE

THIS DISH HAS ECHOES OF A DELICIOUS TRADITIONAL BURMESE SALAD IN WHICH THE PRAWNS ARE NOT COOKED BUT ARE STEEPED IN LIME JUICE UNTIL THEY ARE PRACTICALLY PICKLED, IN A TECHNIQUE REMINISCENT OF THE SOUTH AMERICAN CEVICHE. IF YOUR TASTE DOES NOT RUN TO RAW SHELLFISH, BLANCH THE PRAWNS BRIEFLY IN BOILING WATER UNTIL JUST COOKED.

SERVES FOUR

INGREDIENTS

    16 raw tiger prawns (jumbo shrimp)
    4 limes
    3 fresh red chillies, seeded and
      chopped
    3 cloves garlic
    15ml/1 tbsp ginger purée
    15ml/1 tbsp caster (superfine) sugar
    5ml/1 tsp salt
    3 lime leaves, finely shredded

COOK'S TIP

If you can only find ready prepared and cooked tiger prawns in your local supermarket or fishmonger, simply miss out step 1.

1 Shell and devein the prawns. Bring a pan of water to the boil. Drop in the prawns and cook briefly, until they turn pink. Lift them out quickly with a slotted spoon and and drain them thoroughly. Do not overcook.

2 Squeeze the limes and grind the chillies until fine. Blend with the lime juice, ginger purée, sugar, salt and shredded lime leaves.

3 Toss the prawns in the sauce and steep for 10 minutes. Chill for an hour and serve on a bed of crisp, shredded lettuce with wedges of lime.

Per portion Energy 55Kcal/234kJ; Protein 9.2g; Carbohydrate 4g, of which sugars 4g; Fat 0.4g, of which saturates 0.1g; Cholesterol 98mg; Calcium 45mg; Fibre 0g; Sodium 587mg.

INDIAN DRY PRAWN AND POTATO CURRY

THIS IS ONE OF THE MOST POPULAR CURRIES AT THE INDIAN STALLS IN SINGAPORE. IN AN INDIAN HOME IT WOULD PROBABLY BE SERVED WITH FLATBREAD, A YOGURT DISH AND CHUTNEY, BUT AT THE NASI KANDAR STALLS IT IS OFTEN ONE OF SEVERAL CURRIED DISHES SERVED WITH RICE. IT'S EQUALLY DELICIOUS MADE WITH PRE-COOKED SWEET POTATOES INSTEAD OF ORDINARY ONES.

SERVES FOUR

INGREDIENTS
   30ml/2 tbsp ghee, or 15ml/1 tbsp
      vegetable oil and 15g/½oz/
      1 tbsp butter
   1 onion, halved lengthways and
      sliced along the grain
   a handful of fresh or dried
      curry leaves
   1 cinnamon stick
   2–3 medium-size waxy potatoes,
      lightly steamed, peeled and diced
   500g/1¼ lb large raw prawns
      (shrimp), peeled and deveined
   200ml/7fl oz/scant 1 cup
      coconut milk
   10ml/2 tsp fennel seeds
   10ml/2 tsp brown mustard seeds
   salt and ground black pepper
   fresh coriander (cilantro) leaves,
      roughly chopped, to garnish
For the spice paste
   4 garlic cloves, chopped
   25g/1oz fresh root ginger, peeled
      and chopped
   2 red chillies, seeded and chopped
   5ml/1 tsp ground turmeric
   15ml/1 tbsp fish curry powder

1 Grind the garlic, ginger and chillies to a coarse paste with a mortar and pestle. Stir in the turmeric and curry powder.

2 Heat the ghee in a heavy pan or earthenware pot. Stir in the onion and fry until golden. Stir in the curry leaves, then the cinnamon stick and the spice paste. Fry until fragrant, then add the potatoes, coating them in the spices. Toss in the prawns and cook for 12 minutes. Stir in the coconut milk and bubble it up to thicken and reduce it. Season with salt and pepper to taste.

3 Roast the fennel and mustard seeds in a small heavy pan until they begin to pop and give off a nutty aroma. Stir them into the curry and serve immediately, sprinkled with coriander.

Per Portion Energy 204Kcal/857kJ; Protein 23.5g; Carbohydrate 13.5g, of which sugars 5.2g; Fat 6.6g, of which saturates 0.9g; Cholesterol 244mg; Calcium 126mg; Fibre 1g; Sodium 299mg.

MALAY COCKLE CURRY

THIS SEAFOOD CURRY IS QUITE FIERY, THE WAY THE MALAYS LIKE IT. IN THE TOWN OF KOTA BARU ON THE EAST COAST OF THE MALAY PENINSULA, THE HAWKER STALLS SELL A RANGE OF SPICY CURRIES AND, AS SEAFOOD IS VARIED AND ABUNDANT HERE, SHELLFISH TURN UP IN MANY OF THE DISHES. YOU CAN USE MUSSELS, COCKLES OR CLAMS IN THIS RECIPE.

SERVES FOUR

INGREDIENTS
    500g/1¼lb cockles
    45ml/3 tbsp vegetable oil
    300m/½ pint/1¼ cups coconut milk
    30ml/2 tbsp lime juice
    5ml/1 tsp salt
    2 tomatoes, quartered
    small sprig sweet basil, plus extra to
        garnish
For the spice paste
    ½ large onion, chopped
    5 garlic cloves, chopped
    15ml/1 tbsp fresh root ginger, peeled
    5 red chillies, seeded and chopped
    15ml/1 tbsp ground coriander
    10ml/2 tsp ground cumin
    15g/½oz shrimp paste

1 Wash and shell the cockles.

2 Grate the ginger and grind all the ingredients for the spice paste using a pestle and mortar or a food processor.

3 Heat the oil in a wok or pan and fry the paste for 2–3 minutes until fragrant. Add the coconut milk, lime juice and salt and simmer for 5 minutes.

4 Add the cockles, tomatoes and basil and cook over a medium heat for 3 more minutes.

5 Serve hot in warmed bowls, garnished with more sweet basil sprigs.

COOK'S TIP
To this basic curry can be added extra ingredients such as diced pineapple, cucumber or sour star fruit (carambola).

Per portion Energy 198Kcal/832kJ; Protein 18.8g; Carbohydrate 8.6g, of which sugars 6.1g; Fat 10.3g, of which saturates 1.6g; Cholesterol 85mg; Calcium 199mg; Fibre 0.7g; Sodium 865mg.

POULTRY

Chicken is a staple part of the Malaysian diet. The familiar domestic birds are descended from the red junglefowl, whose native habitat includes the Malay Peninsula, so they have no doubt been eaten in this region from the most ancient times. Today's free-range "kampung chickens", which wander around Malay villages, are thought to be especially nutritious. Duck and geese are also popular, but the universally loved chicken satay is considered Malaysia's national dish.

MALAYSIAN FRIED CHICKEN

YOU SHOULD NOT VISIT MALAYSIA OR SINGAPORE WITHOUT TRYING THE FAMOUS FRIED CHICKEN. INDONESIAN IN ORIGIN, AYAM GORENG PUTS WESTERN FRIED CHICKEN TO SHAME. FIRST THE CHICKEN IS COOKED IN SPICES AND FLAVOURINGS TO ENSURE A DEPTH OF FLAVOUR, THEN IT IS SIMPLY DEEP-FRIED TO FORM A CRISP, GOLDEN SKIN.

SERVES FOUR

INGREDIENTS

2 shallots, chopped
4 garlic cloves, chopped
50g/2oz fresh root ginger or
    galangal, chopped
25g/1oz fresh turmeric, chopped
2 lemon grass stalks, chopped
12 chicken thighs or drumsticks or
    6 whole chicken legs, separated
    into drumsticks and thighs
30ml/2 tbsp kecap manis
salt and ground black pepper
vegetable oil, for deep-frying

1 Using a mortar and pestle or food processor, grind the shallots, garlic, ginger or galangal, turmeric and lemon grass to a paste.

COOK'S TIP
Served with a sambal, or pickle, ayam goreng makes a delicious snack, but for a main course serve it with yellow or fragrant coconut rice and a salad. If you cannot find kecap manis, use soy sauce sweetened with palm sugar, available in Chinese and Asian markets, or substitute the same quantity of dark soy sauce and 15ml/1 tbsp sugar.

2 Place the chicken pieces in a heavy pan or earthenware pot and smear with the spice paste. Add the kecap manis and 150ml/¼ pint/⅔ cup water. Bring to the boil, reduce the heat and cook the chicken for about 25 minutes, turning it from time to time, until the liquid has evaporated. The chicken should be dry before deep-frying, but the spices should be sticking to it. Season with salt and pepper.

3 Heat enough oil for deep-frying in a wok. Fry the chicken pieces in batches until golden brown and crisp. Drain them on kitchen paper and serve hot.

Per Portion Energy 396Kcal/1639kJ; Protein 27g; Carbohydrate 1.5g, of which sugars 1.1g; Fat 31.3g, of which saturates 6.8g; Cholesterol 150mg; Calcium 38mg; Fibre 0.2g; Sodium 358mg.

CHICKEN OPOR

OPOR IS OF INDONESIAN ORIGIN AND IS A MILDER KIND OF CURRY. TRADITIONALLY, THE SPICE BLEND IS BOILED RATHER THAN BEING PRE-FRIED IN OIL. IT HAS A SUBTLE TASTE OF COCONUT MILK WITH HINTS OF TARTNESS FROM THE SOUR STAR FRUIT AND TAMARIND. AN INTERESTING TOUCH COMES FROM THE FINAL ADDITION OF FRIED GRATED OR DESICCATED COCONUT.

SERVES FOUR

INGREDIENTS

    4 chicken legs
    500ml/16fl oz/2 cups coconut milk
    2 lime leaves
    2 stalks lemon grass
    5ml/1 tsp salt
    30ml/2 tbsp tamarind concentrate
    5ml/1 tsp sugar
    4 sour star fruit (carambola)
    30ml/2 tbsp desiccated (dry
    unsweetened shredded) coconut

For the spice paste

    2 red chillies, seeded and chopped
    5 candlenuts
    ½ large onion, chopped
    3 garlic cloves, chopped
    30ml/2 tbsp ground coriander
    5ml/1 tsp ground fennel
    2 thin slices galangal
    25g/1oz shrimp paste

1 Separate each chicken leg into a thigh and a drumstick, and remove the skin if desired. Put the coconut milk in a large pan, add the pieces of chicken and bring to the boil.

2 Grind the spice paste ingredients until fine and add to the pan with the lime leaves, bruised 5cm/2.5in root ends of the lemon grass, salt, tamarind and sugar. Simmer for 20 minutes.

3 Slice each sour star fruit into two lengthways, remove the pith and add to the pan. Simmer for a further 10 minutes.

4 While the chicken is cooking, dry fry the desiccated coconut in another pan until it is light brown. When the chicken is cooked, sprinkle the coconut over the dish and serve immediately.

Per portion Energy 292Kcal/1225kJ; Protein 30.6g; Carbohydrate 13.9g, of which sugars 11.4g; Fat 13.2g, of which saturates 6.4g; Cholesterol 118mg; Calcium 136mg; Fibre 1.3g; Sodium 479mg.

HAINANESE CHICKEN RICE

THIS HAINANESE-DERIVED RECIPE FOCUSES ON AN UNUSUAL STEEPING PROCESS TO ENSURE SMOOTH, SILKY CHICKEN, WHICH IS ACCOMPANIED BY AROMATIC RICE, A BOWL OF CHICKEN BROTH, SOY SAUCE FOR DIPPING AND A GARNISH OF CRUNCHY SPRING ONIONS AND CUCUMBER. WITH THEIR PREFERENCE FOR HOT TASTES, THE MALAYS ADD A PUNGENT GINGER AND CHILLI DIPPING SAUCE.

SERVES FOUR TO SIX

INGREDIENTS
    1 chicken (1.25kg/2½lb), cleaned
    30ml/2 tbsp light soy sauce
    15ml/1 tbsp Chinese rice wine
    50g/2oz fresh root ginger, peeled,
        thickly sliced and crushed
    4 garlic cloves, lightly crushed
    2 spring onions (scallions), crushed
    1.5 litres/2½ pints/
        6¼ cups chicken stock
    10ml/2 tsp sesame oil
    225g/8oz/generous 1 cup jasmine
        rice, rinsed and drained
    salt and ground black pepper
For the sambal
    10 red chillies, seeded and chopped
    6 garlic cloves, chopped
    25g/1oz fresh root ginger, peeled
        and chopped
    15ml/1 tbsp sesame or groundnut
        (peanut) oil
    15–30ml/1–2 tbsp fresh lime juice
    10ml/2 tsp sugar
    2.5ml/½ tsp salt
For the garnish
    fresh coriander (cilantro) leaves
    dark soy sauce
    1 small cucumber, halved lengthways
        and finely sliced
    3 spring onions, trimmed and sliced

1 Rub the chicken, inside and out, with 15ml/1 tbsp soy sauce and the rice wine. Place the ginger, garlic and spring onions in the cavity. Leave to stand for 30 minutes.

COOK'S TIP
Adopted from the Hainan communities that settled in Malaysia and Singapore, this dish has become a classic in both regions. It is cooked in the home, and served at hawker stalls, coffee shops and restaurants, but the best places to sample this dish are the chicken rice shops, where it is cooked daily following age-old methods.

2 Immerse the chicken in boiling stock in a deep pan. Bring back to the boil, cover the pan and turn off the heat.

3 Leave the chicken to steep for 15 minutes. Lift the chicken to drain the cavity, reheat the stock to boiling point, cover the pan and steep the chicken in the stock, off the heat, for a further 15 minutes. Repeat the process every 15 minutes, until the chicken has steeped for a total of 1 hour.

4 Lift the chicken out of the stock, allowing the juices to drip back into the pan, and plunge it into a bowl of iced water. Bring the stock back to the boil. Drain the chicken, trim off the wings, neck and legs, and add to the stock. Rub the remaining 15ml/1 tbsp soy sauce and the sesame oil over the chicken and set aside.

5 Keep the stock simmering, skim off any fat from the top and season. Measure 550ml/18fl oz/2½ cups of the stock and pour into a separate pan (cover the remaining stock and keep it barely simmering).

6 Bring the measured stock to the boil and add the rice. Stir once, reduce the heat and simmer until the stock is absorbed. Turn off the heat, cover the pan with a dish towel, then the lid, and leave to stand for 15 minutes.

7 Meanwhile, prepare the sambal. Using a mortar and pestle or food processor, grind the chillies, garlic and ginger to a smooth paste. Bind with the oil and lime juice, and stir in the sugar and salt. Spoon the sambal into individual dipping bowls.

8 To serve, first joint the chicken. Remove the skin and separate the meat from the bones. Slice the thighs and breasts into bitesize pieces. Place the chicken on a platter and garnish with a few coriander leaves.

9 Pack spoonfuls of the rice into a small bowl and invert one on to each plate, so that each person is given a mound of rice. Place the bowls of sambal on each plate, along with individual bowls of dark soy sauce, slices of cucumber and a few coriander leaves.

10 Ladle the hot chicken broth into warmed serving bowls and sprinkle spring onions over the top. Place a plate of rice and sauces, and bowl of broth, in front of each person, and set the chicken in the middle of the table.

11 Use chopsticks to eat, dipping a piece of chicken with some rice into one of the sauces. The broth is sipped or spooned over the rice.

Per Portion Energy 460Kcal/1913kJ; Protein 28.6g; Carbohydrate 30.4g, of which sugars 0.4g; Fat 24.6g, of which saturates 6.7g; Cholesterol 133mg; Calcium 37mg; Fibre 0.5g; Sodium 108mg.

LEMON CHICKEN

A star dish of Chinese restaurants in Malaysia and Singapore, this is a perfect balance of flavours between the richness of the battered fried chicken and the sweet-sour lemon sauce. There are many brands of lemon sauce in the market but nothing beats making your own. Never use a wet batter for the chicken; dry cornflour gives a crisp texture that is unique in Chinese cooking. The trick in giving the sauce an intense yellow colour is simply to use a little ground turmeric.

SERVES FOUR

INGREDIENTS
   2 chicken breasts, skinned
   1 egg, lightly beaten
   30ml/2 tbsp cornflour (cornstarch)
   vegetable or groundnut (peanut) oil
    for deep-frying
   salt
For the sauce
   45ml/3 tbsp lemon juice
   5ml/1 tsp ground turmeric
   15ml/1 tbsp sugar or to taste
   15ml/1 tbsp plum sauce
   175ml/6fl oz water
   5ml/1 tbsp cornflour (cornstarch)

1 Slice each chicken breast across the thickest part to give two thin escalopes. Dip the chicken breasts lightly in beaten egg and coat with cornflour. Heat the oil in a wok or large pan and deep-fry the chicken until golden brown. Keep warm.

2 Mix together all the sauce ingredients, stirring well to avoid lumps. Bring the sauce to a slow simmer in a small pan and cook for 2 minutes. Blend the cornflour with a little water and add, a little at a time, until the sauce is the consistency of pouring (half-and-half) cream. Season to taste with salt.

3 Slice the chicken into 2.5cm/1in strips and place on a serving plate. Pour the sauce over and serve garnished with lemon wedges.

Per portion Energy 231kcal/975kJ; Protein 30.1g; Carbohydrate 13.1g, of which sugars 13.1g; Fat 6.9g, of which saturates 1.2g; Cholesterol 88mg; Calcium 13mg; Fibre 0g; Sodium 76mg.

FUCHOW CHICKEN RICE

THIS IS A REGIONAL VERSION OF HAINANESE CHICKEN RICE, SOUSED WITH PLENTY OF CHINESE WINE. IT IS TRADITIONALLY SERVED COLD WITH FRESHLY COOKED JASMINE RICE BUT IT IS JUST AS GOOD WARM. IN SINGAPORE THERE ARE A FEW RESTAURANTS THAT FEATURE DISHES FROM THIS SUB-PROVINCE OF SOUTH CHINA. FUCHOW COOKS USE AN INGREDIENT THAT GIVES THE DISH A SPECIAL DIMENSION — THE THICK RESIDUE OR "LEES" FROM FUCHOW RED RICE WINE, KNOWN AS ANG CHOW — BUT ORDINARY CHINESE RICE WINE ALSO WORKS WELL.

SERVES FOUR TO SIX

INGREDIENTS

    1 whole chicken (about 1.3kg/3lb)
    60ml/4 tbsp Fuchow rice wine lees or
      Chinese Shao Hsing wine
    30ml/2 tbsp sesame oil
    30ml/2 tbsp ginger purée
    15ml/1 tbsp garlic purée
    5ml/1 tsp salt
    2 spring onions (scallions), trimmed
      and finely sliced

COOK'S TIP

Chinese rice wine is sold in Asian markets, and is similar to Japanese sake. Dry sherry or dry vermouth can be substituted if it is not available.

1 Remove any excess fat from the chicken and place in a deep dish. Blend the wine, sesame oil, ginger, garlic and salt and rub the mixture all over the chicken, including inside the body cavity. Leave to stand for at least 30 minutes to absorb the flavours.

2 Steam for 40–50 minutes until the chicken is tender. Add the spring onions for the last 5 minutes.

3 Allow the chicken to cool. Chop into serving pieces and serve cold or warm with normal jasmine rice.

Per portion Energy 355Kcal/1470kJ; Protein 26.8g; Carbohydrate 0.3g, of which sugars 0.3g; Fat 26g, of which saturates 7g; Cholesterol 139mg; Calcium 16mg; Fibre 0.1g; Sodium 438mg.

NONYA CHICKEN CURRY

THE INCLUSION OF POTATOES IN NONYA CHICKEN CURRY PROBABLY GOES BACK TO COLONIAL TIMES, WHEN BRITISH PLANTATION OWNERS INSISTED THAT THEIR COOKS SERVED POTATOES WITH EVERY MEAL. NOT UNDERSTANDING THE CONCEPT, THE CHINESE OR NONYA COOKS THEY EMPLOYED WOULD SIMPLY ADD THE POTATOES DIRECTLY INTO THE CURRY.

SERVES FOUR TO SIX

INGREDIENTS
   1 whole chicken (about 1.3kg/3lb)
   2 large potatoes
   30ml/2 tbsp curry powder
   475ml/16fl oz/2 cups coconut milk
   30ml/2 tbsp vegetable oil
   25g/1oz ginger purée
   25g/1oz garlic purée
   4 lime leaves
   5ml/1 tsp salt
   5ml/1 tsp sugar
   15ml/1 tbsp lime juice
   30ml/2 tbsp chilli oil
   plain rice, noodles or bread, to serve

3 In the oil remaining in the wok, fry the ginger and garlic purée for 2 minutes, until fragrant.

1 Cut the chicken into serving pieces, removing any excess fat. Wash and pat dry. Peel the potatoes and cut them into chunks.

2 Blend the curry powder with a little of the coconut milk to make a thick paste. Heat the oil in a wok or large pan and fry the potatoes until browned. Lift out and set aside.

4 Add the curry paste and cook gently until the sauce splits. Add the chicken pieces and sauté until browned. Add the potatoes, coconut milk, lime leaves, salt and sugar. Simmer for 30 minutes.

COOK'S TIPS
• You could use left over boiled or roast potatoes in this recipe.
• If you cannot buy ginger and garlic purées simply pound the root or cloves to a pulp with a mortar and pestle.

5 Add the lime juice and chilli oil and simmer for another 10–15 minutes until the chicken is tender. Serve with plain rice, noodles or bread.

Per portion Energy 455kcal/1896kJ; Protein 28.6g; Carbohydrate 17.2g, of which sugars 5.6g; Fat 30.7g, of which saturates 7.7g; Cholesterol 139mg; Calcium 47mg; Fibre 0.7g; Sodium 205mg.

EURASIAN CHICKEN STEW WITH POTATOES

THIS RECIPE IS BELIEVED TO HAVE COME TO THE MALAY PENINSULA WITH THE PORTUGUESE WHO SETTLED IN MELAKA IN THE 16TH CENTURY. IT BECAME A SIGNATURE DISH AMONG THE EURASIAN COMMUNITY, WHO ARE OF MIXED PORTUGUESE, ENGLISH, INDIAN AND CHINESE DESCENT. IT IS NOT FOUND ON RESTAURANT MENUS, ONLY AS A HOME-COOKED DISH.

SERVES FOUR TO SIX

INGREDIENTS
    4 chicken legs
    2 large potatoes
    45ml/3 tbsp vegetable oil
    5 cloves
    7.5cm/3in cinnamon stick
    30ml/2 tbsp Worcestershire sauce
    30ml/2 tbsp dark soy sauce
    475ml/16 fl oz/2 cups water
    15ml/1 tbsp cornflour (cornstarch)
    salt
    crusty bread, to serve

COOK'S TIP
Worcestershire sauce is obviously a British contribution to the dish, added during the 19th century, but the Lea & Perrins recipe was itself derived from flavourings used in Asian cooking.

1 Cut the chicken into serving pieces, removing any excess fat. Peel and quarter the potatoes.

2 Heat the oil in a wok or large pan and sauté the potatoes briefly until browned on all sides. Remove from the pan using a slotted spoon and set aside. Sauté the chicken in the remaining oil until the skin is well browned.

3 Return the potatoes to the pan and stir in the spices, Worcestershire and soy sauces and the water. Season with salt and simmer, covered, for about 35 minutes, until tender.

4 Mix the cornflour with a little water and stir it into the gravy to thicken it. Cook briefly until glossy. Remove the whole spices and serve with bread.

Per portion Energy 238Kcal/1000kJ; Protein 22.2g; Carbohydrate 14.2g, of which sugars 2g; Fat 10.7g, of which saturates 2.1g; Cholesterol 70mg; Calcium 20mg; Fibre 0.7g; Sodium 479mg.

DEVIL'S CURRY

THIS EURASIAN DISH, KNOWN AS CURRY DEBAL, REALLY IS DEVILISHLY HOT. EVERY EURASIAN HOUSEHOLD HAS ITS OWN VERSION OF THIS CHICKEN AND VEGETABLE HOTPOT IN A FIERY, SOUR SAUCE. SERVED AS A MEAL ON ITS OWN, WITH BREAD TO MOP UP THE SAUCE, IT IS OFTEN COOKED FOR FAMILY CELEBRATIONS. YOU CAN LESSEN THE CHILLI CONTENT IF YOU WISH.

SERVES SIX

INGREDIENTS

4–6 chicken breasts or 12 boned chicken thighs, cut into bitesize chunks
60ml/4 tbsp vegetable oil
1 onion, halved lengthways, and sliced along the grain
25g/1oz fresh root ginger, peeled and cut into julienne strips
4 garlic cloves, cut into strips
30–45ml/2–3 tbsp vinegar
10ml/2 tsp sugar
3 medium potatoes, cut into bitesize chunks
2 courgettes (zucchini), partially peeled, halved lengthways, seeded and cut into bitesize chunks
8 Chinese leaves (Chinese cabbage), cut into bitesize squares
10ml/2 tsp brown mustard seeds, ground and mixed to a paste with a little water
salt
crusty bread, to serve
For the spice paste
10 dried chillies, soaked in warm water until soft, squeezed dry and seeded
6 fresh red chillies, seeded and chopped
8 shallots, chopped
6 garlic cloves, chopped
25g/1oz fresh root ginger, peeled and chopped
6 candlenuts or macadamia nuts
10ml/2 tsp ground turmeric
For the marinade
15ml/1 tbsp light soy sauce
15ml/1 tbsp dark soy sauce
10ml/2 tsp rice or white wine vinegar
10ml/2 tsp sugar

COOK'S TIP
The flavour of this curry improves if it is made a day in advance. Cool it quickly then store in the refrigerator overnight to allow the flavours to mingle. Reheat the following day.

1 For the spice paste, grind the chillies, shallots, garlic, ginger and nuts. Stir in the turmeric and set aside.

2 Mix together the marinade ingredients and rub it into the chicken pieces. Leave to marinate for 30 minutes.

3 Heat the oil in a wok or heavy pan. Stir in the onion, ginger and garlic and fry until golden. Add the spice paste and stir until fragrant. Toss in the marinated chicken and stir until it begins to brown, then pour in enough water to cover.

4 Bring to the boil and add the vinegar, sugar and potatoes. Reduce the heat and cook gently until the potatoes are tender when tested with a sharp knife.

5 Add the courgettes and cook for 2 minutes, then stir in the cabbage. Stir in the mustard paste and season with salt. Serve hot with bread.

Per Portion Energy 270Kcal/1136kJ; Protein 32.5g; Carbohydrate 15.4g, of which sugars 4.6g; Fat 9.1g, of which saturates 1.3g; Cholesterol 88mg; Calcium 36mg; Fibre 1.8g; Sodium 441mg.

CURRY KAPITAN WITH COCONUT AND CHILLI RELISH

CURRY KAPITAN RECALLS THE TRADITIONAL ROLE OF THE CHINESE KAPITAN, A MAN OF CONSIDERABLE SOCIAL STANDING AMONG THE MALAY AND CHINESE PEOPLE IN OLD MELAKA. IT IS SAID TO BE A DISH INVENTED BY THE PERANAKANS, PERHAPS TO PRESENT TO THE KAPITAN OR TO CELEBRATE HIS ROLE. A CHICKEN CURRY, MADE WITH COCONUT MILK, IT OWES ITS FLAVOUR TO ALL THE INHABITANTS OF OLD MELAKA THROUGH ITS USE OF SPICES AND FLAVOURINGS – CHINESE, MALAY, PORTUGUESE AND INDIAN – AND COULD BE REGARDED AS MELAKA IN A POT.

SERVES FOUR

INGREDIENTS

For the rempah
 6–8 dried red chillies, soaked in
   warm water until soft, squeezed dry
   and seeded
 6–8 shallots, chopped
 4–6 garlic cloves, chopped
 25g/1oz fresh root ginger, chopped
 5ml/1 tsp shrimp paste
 10ml/2 tsp ground turmeric
 10ml/2 tsp Chinese
   five-spice powder
For the curry
 15–30ml/1–2 tbsp tamarind pulp
 1 fresh coconut, grated (shredded)
 30–45ml/2–3 tbsp vegetable or
   groundnut (peanut) oil
 1–2 cinnamon sticks
 12 chicken thighs, boned and cut
   into bitesize strips lengthways
 600ml/1 pint/2½ cups coconut milk
 15ml/1 tbsp palm sugar (jaggery)
 salt and ground black pepper

For the relish
 1 green chilli, seeded and finely sliced
 1 red chilli, seeded and finely sliced
 fresh coriander (cilantro) leaves,
   finely chopped (reserve a few leaves
   for garnishing)
 2 limes
 steamed rice, to serve

1 First make the rempah. Using a mortar and pestle or food processor, grind the chillies, shallots, garlic and ginger to a paste. Beat in the shrimp paste and stir in the dried spices.

2 Soak the tamarind pulp in 150ml/ ¼ pint/⅔ cup warm water until soft. Squeeze the pulp to soften it, then strain to extract the juice and discard the pulp.

3 In a heavy pan, dry roast half the grated coconut over a medium heat until it is just turning golden brown and emits a nutty aroma. Be careful not to burn it.

4 Using a mortar and pestle or food processor, grind the roasted coconut until it resembles sugar grains.

COOK'S TIP
Palm sugar lends a unique, caramelized flavour to the dish. As a substitute, you could try muscovado sugar.

5 Heat the oil in a wok or earthenware pot, and stir in the rempah and cinnamon sticks until fragrant. Add the chicken strips.

6 Pour in the coconut milk and tamarind water, and stir in the sugar. Reduce the heat and cook gently for about 10 minutes. Stir in half the ground roasted coconut and season.

7 In a bowl, mix the remaining grated coconut with the chillies, coriander and juice of 1 lime to serve as a relish.

8 Cut the other lime into wedges. Spoon the chicken curry into a serving dish and garnish with a few coriander leaves. Serve with the coconut and chilli relish, the lime wedges to squeeze over it and a bowl of steamed rice.

Per Portion Energy 487Kcal/2024kJ; Protein 29.2g; Carbohydrate 11.3g, of which sugars 10.6g; Fat 36.4g, of which saturates 19.2g; Cholesterol 150mg; Calcium 114mg; Fibre 4.4g; Sodium 267mg.

CHICKEN IN RED SAMBAL

THIS IS A POPULAR DISH AMONG SINGAPORE MALAYS, WHO CALL IT AYAM MASAK MERAH. THE METHOD IS IN FACT GENERIC, AND MANY MEAT AND SEAFOOD DISHES ARE COOKED THIS WAY. IT IS AN EVOCATIVE DISH, ALL RED AND VERY FIERY IF YOU USE AS MANY CHILLIES AS MALAY COOKS LIKE TO. HOWEVER, IT CAN BE TEMPERED TO YOUR OWN TASTE, AS MORE OR LESS HEAT DOES NOT ALTER THE INTRINSIC TASTE. IT'S DELICIOUS SERVED WITH BREAD OR RICE.

SERVES FOUR

INGREDIENTS

    4 chicken legs
    150ml/¼ pint/⅔ cup vegetable or
        groundnut (peanut) oil
    15ml/1 tbsp chilli oil
    5ml/1 tsp salt
    10ml/2 tsp sugar
    4 lime leaves, finely shredded
    15ml/1 tbsp tamarind concentrate
    200ml/7fl oz/scant 1 cup water
For the spice paste
    4–6 dried red chillies, soaked in
        warm water until soft, squeezed dry
        and seeded
    ½ large onion, chopped
    4 garlic cloves, chopped
    15ml/1 tbsp shrimp paste
    4 candlenuts

1 Cut each chicken leg into thigh and drumstick joints and trim off any excess fat. Wash and pat dry.

2 Heat the oil in a wok or large pan and fry the chicken pieces, turning several times, until the skin is well browned. Lift out with a slotted spoon and set aside. Remove all but 45ml/3 tbsp of the fat.

3 Grind the ingredients for the spice paste until fine. Fry until fragrant. Add the chilli oil, salt, sugar, lime leaves and tamarind concentrate. Continue to fry for 3 minutes.

4 Add the chicken and water and simmer for 25–30 minutes, until the chicken is done and the sauce is thick.

Per portion Energy 290Kcal/1214kJ; Protein 33.5g; Carbohydrate 3.8g, of which sugars 3.5g; Fat 15.8g, of which saturates 3.1g; Cholesterol 123mg; Calcium 58mg; Fibre 0.2g; Sodium 736mg.

PANDAN WRAPPED CHICKEN

UNIQUE TO SOUTH-EAST ASIA, THIS DISH HAS MANY REGIONAL VARIATIONS, PRIMARILY IN THAILAND WHERE IT IS OFTEN FEATURED AS AN APPETIZER ON RESTAURANT MENUS. TRY TO FIND PANDAN LEAVES THAT ARE AS WIDE AS POSSIBLE SO THAT YOU CAN MAKE DECENT WRAPS. THE LEAVES PROTECT AND PERFUME THE DELICATE CHICKEN, AS WELL AS KEEPING IN ALL THE FLAVOUR. THERE IS LITTLE NEED TO SERVE A DIPPING SAUCE WITH THIS, AS THE CHICKEN IS STEEPED IN SPICES.

SERVES FOUR TO SIX

INGREDIENTS
   500g/1¼lb skinless, boneless
     chicken breast
   6–8 pandan (screwpine) leaves
   vegetable or groundnut (peanut) oil
     for deep-frying
For the marinade
   15ml/1 tbsp ground coriander
   10ml/2 tsp chilli powder
   5ml/1 tsp ground turmeric
   30ml/2 tbsp lime juice
   5ml/1 tsp sugar

1 Cut the chicken into 3cm/1½in cubes, wash and dry thoroughly. Mix together the ingredients for the marinade. While the chicken is still damp, blend it with the marinade and set aside for 20 minutes.

2 Cut the pandan leaves into 15cm/6in lengths. Put them into a bowl and pour over boiling water. Leave them for about a minute so that they blanch and soften, and release their perfume.

3 Wrap each piece of chicken in a pandan leaf and secure with cocktail sticks (toothpicks), snipping off any protruding ends.

4 Heat the oil in a wok or large pan, deep-fry the parcels until they are golden brown, and serve for diners to unwrap each piece at the table.

Per portion Energy 199Kcal/832kJ; Protein 21.3g; Carbohydrate 4.4g, of which sugars 2.3g; Fat 10.9g, of which saturates 1.4g; Cholesterol 58mg; Calcium 31mg; Fibre 0.7g; Sodium 54mg.

SOY BRAISED CHICKEN

THIS WAS ORIGINALLY A CLASSIC CANTONESE RESTAURANT DISH, FLAVOURED WITH FIVE-SPICE POWDER, BUT THE NONYA TAKE ON IT, AS IS TYPICAL, INCLUDES A LARGE, BRUISED KNOB OF GALANGAL INSTEAD. IT IS A VERY GOOD DISH TO SERVE WHEN ENTERTAINING, AS IT CAN BE COOKED UP TO A DAY IN ADVANCE AND SIMPLY REHEATED. ALWAYS SERVE IT WITH A SHARP CHILLI, GARLIC AND VINEGAR DIP AND PLENTY OF SLICED CUCUMBER AND RICE.

SERVES SIX TO EIGHT

INGREDIENTS

   1 whole chicken (about 1.3kg/3lb)
   25g/1oz sugar
   90ml/6 tbsp dark soy sauce
   25g/1oz galangal, bruised
   1.5 litres/2½ pints/6¼ cups water
   10ml/2 tsp salt
   15ml/1 tbsp cornflour (cornstarch)
   steamed rice and sliced cucumber,
     to serve

1 Remove any excess fat from the chicken, wash it and pat dry. In a dry, heavy pan, heat the sugar until frothy and caramelized to a rich, dark brown colour. Add the chicken and turn it several times in the pan until well sealed.

2 Add the soy sauce, galangal and water. Bring to the boil and simmer, covered, for 30 minutes, turning several times so the chicken is evenly cooked.

3 Add salt and continue to cook for another 15–20 minutes until tender. Remove and set aside.

4 Increase the heat and boil until the sauce is well reduced and glossy. Blend the cornflour with a little water and add to the sauce to thicken it.

5 Chop the chicken into bitesize pieces and serve with rice and sliced cucumber, with the sauce on the side.

Per portion Energy 255Kcal/1058kJ; Protein 20.2g; Carbohydrate 5.9g, of which sugars 4.1g; Fat 16.8g, of which saturates 4.9g; Cholesterol 104mg; Calcium 12mg; Fibre 0g; Sodium 883mg.

MALAY BRAISED DUCK IN AROMATIC SAUCE

THE CHINESE COMMUNITIES IN MALAYSIA AND SINGAPORE OFTEN BRAISE DUCK, GOOSE, CHICKEN OR PORK IN SOY SAUCE AND WARM FLAVOURINGS, SUCH AS STAR ANISE AND CINNAMON. SUCH DISHES ARE FOUND AT CHINESE HAWKER STALLS AND COFFEE SHOPS, AND THERE ARE MANY VARIATIONS ON THE THEME. THE MALAYS LIKE TO ADD TURMERIC AND LEMON GRASS TO THE FLAVOURINGS AND, TO ACHIEVE THEIR DESIRED FIERY KICK, CHILLIES ARE ALWAYS TUCKED INTO THE RECIPE SOMEWHERE.

SERVES FOUR TO SIX

INGREDIENTS

1 duck (about 2kg/4½ lb), washed
  and trimmed
15–30ml/1–2 tbsp Chinese
  five-spice powder
25g/1oz fresh turmeric, chopped
25g/1oz galangal, chopped
4 garlic cloves, chopped
30ml/2 tbsp sesame oil
12 shallots, peeled and left whole
2–3 lemon grass stalks, halved and
  lightly crushed
4 cinnamon sticks
8 star anise
12 cloves
600ml/1 pint/2½ cups light soy sauce
120ml/4fl oz/½ cup dark soy sauce
30–45ml/2–3 tbsp palm sugar (jaggery)
coriander (cilantro) leaves, to garnish
  2 green and 2 red chillies,
  seeded and quartered lengthways,
  to garnish
steamed jasmine rice and salad,
  to serve

1 Rub the duck, inside and out, with the five-spice powder and place in the refrigerator, uncovered, for 6–8 hours to absorb the flavours.

2 Using a mortar and pestle or food processor, grind the turmeric, galangal and garlic to a smooth paste. Heat the oil in a heavy pan and stir in the spice paste until it becomes fragrant. Stir in the shallots, lemon grass, cinnamon sticks, star anise and cloves. Pour in the soy sauces and stir in the sugar until dissolved.

3 Place the duck in the pan, baste with the sauce, and add 550ml/18fl oz/ 2½ cups water. Bring to the boil, reduce the heat and cover the pan. Simmer gently for 4–6 hours, basting from time to time, until the duck is very tender. Garnish with coriander and chillies, and serve with rice and salad.

Per Portion Energy 119Kcal/498kJ; Protein 10.2g; Carbohydrate 4.6g, of which sugars 3.4g; Fat 6.9g, of which saturates 1.5g; Cholesterol 50mg; Calcium 35mg; Fibre 1.1g; Sodium 412mg.

CORIANDER BRAISED DUCK

This glorious dish has been a Nonya mainstay for generations. It is believed to have evolved from an even older Javanese method of preparing poultry, called golek, in which the spice paste is a rich combination of cumin, pepper, coriander and coconut milk. It requires long cooking. A pressure cooker is useful for this, but if you use one you should cook the dish without using pressure for the last half hour to reduce and concentrate the spicy juices that characterize the dish. If you can find lengths of sugar cane, they can take the place of ordinary sugar for a really authentic result.

SERVES SIX TO EIGHT

INGREDIENTS

    1 prepared duck (about 1.5kg/3½lb),
        trimmed of excess fat
    45ml/3 tbsp vegetable oil
    45g/3 tbsp minced (ground) onions
    30g/2 tbsp garlic purée
    30g/2 tbsp ground coriander
    5ml/1 tsp black pepper
    30ml/2 tbsp dark soy sauce
    20cm/8in sugar cane, cut into 6
        pieces or 30ml/2 tbsp sugar
    60ml/4 tbsp finely chopped fresh
        coriander (cilantro)
    2 cinnamon sticks, 10cm/4in long
    6 cloves
    1.5 litres/2½ pints/6 cups water,
        or more

1 Wash the duck and and dry it well. Heat the oil in a deep wok or pan and add the onions, garlic purée and coriander. Fry gently for 5 minutes.

2 Put the duck into the pan and fry for about 10 minutes, turning several times, to brown the skin all over.

3 Stir in all the other ingredients, cover the pan and cook over a very low heat for about 2 hours, until the duck is very tender. Alternatively, transfer the duck and other ingredients to a pressure cooker and cook under high pressure for 30 minutes, then de-pressurize and braise for a further 30 minutes.

4 Remove the duck from the pan and keep it warm. Raise the heat and bring the sauce to a furious boil to reduce it to a syrupy consistency.

5 Cut the duck into large serving pieces, removing any large bones. Arrange on a serving dish and pour the sauce over it. Serve with plain rice.

COOK'S TIP
Sizzling the duck skin in the hot oil is an important step, so don't rush it. It should be well browned and crisp on all sides before the cooking liquid is added.

Per portion Energy 510Kcal/2120kJ; Protein 17.8g; Carbohydrate 26.9g, of which sugars 26.8g; Fat 47.5g, of which saturates 10.5g; Cholesterol 87mg; Calcium 35mg; Fibre 0.1g; Sodium 380mg.

CANTONESE ROAST DUCK

*POSSIBLY ONE OF THE BEST KNOWN DUCK DISHES AROUND THE WORLD, THIS SITS NEXT TO THE OTHER
TWO UNIVERSALLY ACCLAIMED DISHES, PEKING DUCK AND CRISPY AROMATIC DUCK, AS A GRAND
BANQUET DISH. THE FACT THAT IT CAN BE SEEN HANGING FROM JUST ABOUT EVERY CHINESE
RESTAURANT WINDOW DOES NOT REDUCE ITS CULINARY CACHET. THE BEST ROAST DUCK SHOULD HAVE
REALLY CRACKLY, CRISP SKIN AND FOR THIS, THE TRADITIONAL METHOD USED IN CHINESE COOKING
FOR PEKING DUCK IS TO DRY THE DUCK IN THE SUN FOR AT LEAST SIX HOURS.*

SERVES SIX TO EIGHT

INGREDIENTS
    1 prepared duck (about 1.5kg/3½lb),
      trimmed of excess fat
    30ml/2 tbsp hoisin sauce
    30ml/2 tbsp Chinese rice wine
      or sherry
    1 small cube preserved red soy bean,
      mashed fine
    few drops cochineal, or red food
      colouring

1 Tie a length of string under the wings
and around the neck of the duck to
make a loop.

2 Bring a large pot of water to the boil
and use the string to immerse the duck
several times to shrink the skin and
remove some of the fat.

3 Hang up the duck in an airy spot for
several hours, if possible for the whole
day if you are cooking it in the evening.
During this time, the skin will take on a
parchment-like texture as it dries out.

COOK'S TIPS
• Unlike chicken, duck may be eaten
slightly pink in the middle.
• You can buy various chilli sauces in
any supermarket. This dish goes well
with a sweet chilli dip, or you could serve
it with plum sauce.

4 Preheat the oven to 220°C/425°F/
Gas 7. Blend the hoisin sauce with the
wine, preserved red soy bean and red
colouring and rub it all over the duck.

5 Place the duck on a rack in a large
roasting pan and roast for 30 minutes.
Reduce the heat to 180°C/350°F/Gas 4
and cook for another 30 minutes. Push
a metal skewer into the deepest part
between the thigh and breast – if the
juice runs clear the duck is done.

6 Turn off the heat and leave the duck
in the oven for 20 minutes to continue
cooking in the residual heat.

7 Chop the duck into serving pieces
and serve with sliced cucumber and a
chilli sauce dip.

Per portion Energy 384kcal/1581kJ; Protein 10g; Carbohydrate 0.7g, of which sugars 0.7g; Fat 37.4g, of which saturates 10.2g; Cholesterol 0mg; Calcium 11mg; Fibre 0g; Sodium 232mg.

MEAT

The meat dishes of Malaysia and Singapore divide along ethnic lines, as the types of meat eaten are subject to the dietary codes of Islam, Hinduism and Buddhism. Malay dishes concentrate on beef, mutton or goat, as Muslims do not eat pork, while pork is a staple of Chinese cookery and appears in many Singapore specialities. Prime cuts are used for speedy stir-fries, for which the meat is usually sliced thinly for quick cooking, while rich, tasty curries call for long, gentle cooking.

RENDANG

IN THE 15TH CENTURY, WHEN THE MINANGKABAU PEOPLE FIRST CAME FROM SUMATRA TO SETTLE IN THE SMALL STATE OF NEGERI SEMBILAN, THEY BROUGHT WITH THEM THEIR TRADITIONAL SOCIAL CUSTOMS AND FIERY COOKING STYLES. ALTHOUGH THE CUSTOMS HAVE BEEN DILUTED OVER TIME, MANY OF THE UNIQUE DISHES HAVE SURVIVED, AND RENDANG IS ONE OF THEM. MADE WITH BEEF OR, TRADITIONALLY, WITH THE MEAT OF WATER BUFFALO, THIS DISH MUST BE SLOW-COOKED TO ACHIEVE THE REQUIRED TENDERNESS AND TO REDUCE THE SAUCE TO A SYRUPY THICKNESS.

SERVES SIX

INGREDIENTS

1kg/2¼lb beef topside (pot roast) or rump (round) steak, cut into bitesize cubes

115g/4oz fresh coconut, grated, or 50g/2oz desiccated (dry unsweetened shredded) coconut

15ml/1 tbsp tamarind pulp, soaked in 90ml/6 tbsp water until soft

45ml/3 tbsp vegetable or groundnut (peanut) oil

2 onions, halved lengthways, and sliced along the grain

3 lemon grass stalks, trimmed, halved and bruised

2 cinnamon sticks

1.2 litres/2 pints/5 cups coconut milk

15ml/1 tbsp sugar

salt and ground black pepper

steamed rice or bread and salad, to serve

For the spice paste

8–10 dried red chillies, soaked in warm water until soft, squeezed dry and seeded

8 shallots, chopped

4–6 garlic cloves, chopped

50g/2oz fresh galangal, chopped

25g/1oz fresh turmeric, chopped

15ml/1 tbsp coriander seeds

10ml/2 tsp cumin seeds

5ml/1 tsp black peppercorns

COOK'S TIP

In Malaysia, rendang is often served with *roti jala* to mop up the deliciously rich sauce. These are thin Indian pancakes made with coconut milk. They have a lacy, net-like appearance, which is achieved by swirling a small amount of the batter around in a hot pan.

1 First make the spice paste. Using a mortar and pestle or food processor, grind the soaked chillies, shallots, garlic, galangal and turmeric to a smooth paste.

2 In a small heavy pan, dry-roast the coriander and cumin seeds with the peppercorns, until they start to give off a nutty aroma. Grind the roasted spices to a powder and stir this into the spice paste.

3 Coat the beef in the spice paste and set aside to marinate for about 1 hour.

4 Meanwhile, dry-roast the grated coconut in a heavy pan, until it is brown and emits a nutty aroma. Using a mortar and pestle or food processor, grind the roasted coconut until it resembles brown sugar and set it aside.

5 Squeeze the tamarind to help soften it, then strain it to extract the juice. Discard the pulp.

6 Heat the oil in a wok or heavy pan. Add the onions, lemon grass and cinnamon sticks, and fry until the onions begin to colour. Add the beef with all the spice paste and toss it around the wok, until lightly browned.

7 Pour the coconut milk and tamarind juice into the pan and bring to the boil, stirring all the time. Reduce the heat and simmer gently, until the sauce begins to thicken.

8 Stir in the sugar and the ground roasted coconut, and continue to simmer very gently, stirring from time to time, until the meat is tender and the reduced sauce is very thick. This may take 2–4 hours, depending on the cut and type of meat.

9 Season with salt and black pepper to taste, and serve hot with rice or bread and a salad.

Per Portion Energy 439Kcal/1842kJ; Protein 41g; Carbohydrate 19.4g, of which sugars 17.4g; Fat 22.7g, of which saturates 13.1g; Cholesterol 83mg; Calcium 94mg; Fibre 3.8g; Sodium 356mg.

OXTAIL IN HOT TANGY SAUCE

CONSIDERED A DELICACY IN SOME PARTS OF SOUTH-EAST ASIA, OXTAIL AND THE TAILS OF WATER BUFFALO ARE GENERALLY COOKED FOR SPECIAL FEASTS AND CELEBRATIONS. IN MALAYSIA AND SINGAPORE, OXTAIL IS COOKED IN EUROPEAN-STYLE STEWS BY THE EURASIANS AND HAINANESE, BUT THE MALAYS AND INDONESIANS PREFER TO COOK IT SLOWLY IN A HOT, TANGY SAUCE. SERVED WITH STEAMED RICE, OR CHUNKS OF FRESH, CRUSTY BREAD, IT MAKES A VERY TASTY SUPPER DISH.

SERVES FOUR TO SIX

INGREDIENTS

8 shallots, chopped
8 garlic cloves, chopped
4–6 red chillies, seeded and chopped
25g/1oz fresh galangal, chopped
30ml/2 tbsp rice flour or plain (all-purpose) flour
15ml/1 tbsp ground turmeric
8–12 oxtail joints, cut roughly the same size and trimmed of fat
45ml/3 tbsp vegetable oil
400g/14oz can plum tomatoes, drained
2 lemon grass stalks, halved and bruised
a handful of fresh kaffir lime leaves
225g/8oz tamarind pulp, soaked in 600ml/1 pint/2½ cups water, squeezed and strained
30–45ml/2–3 tbsp sugar
salt and ground black pepper
fresh coriander (cilantro) leaves, roughly chopped

1 Using a mortar and pestle or food processor, grind the shallots, garlic, chillies and galangal to a coarse paste. Mix the flour with the ground turmeric and spread it on a flat surface or a large plate. Roll the oxtail in the flour to coat thoroughly and set aside.

2 Heat the oil in a heavy pan or earthenware pot. Stir in the spice paste and cook until fragrant and golden. Add the oxtail joints and brown on all sides. Add the tomatoes, lemon grass stalks, lime leaves and tamarind juice. Add enough water to cover the oxtail, and bring it to the boil. Skim off any fat from the surface. Reduce the heat, put the lid on the pan and simmer the oxtail for about 2 hours.

3 Stir in the sugar, season to taste with salt and pepper and continue to cook, uncovered, for a further 30–40 minutes, until the meat is very tender. Sprinkle with the coriander and serve straight from the pan.

Per Portion Energy 386Kcal/1611kJ; Protein 34.5g; Carbohydrate 11.3g, of which sugars 6.6g; Fat 22.6g, of which saturates 7.7g; Cholesterol 125mg; Calcium 31mg; Fibre 1.2g; Sodium 191mg.

BEEF SEMUR

THE INDONESIAN-COINED TERM SEMUR OR SMOOR, ALSO USED IN MALAYSIA AND SINGAPORE, REFERS TO ANY DISH COOKED IN SOY SAUCE IN TANDEM WITH A TART SEASONING SUCH AS TAMARIND OR LIME JUICE. THIS IS A DRY DISH THAT TASTES EVEN BETTER A DAY OR TWO AFTER IT IS MADE. USE A FAIRLY TENDER CUT OF BEEF SUCH AS SIRLOIN, RUMP OR EVEN JAPANESE-CUT SUKIYAKI BEEF TO REDUCE THE COOKING TIME, ALTHOUGH TRADITIONALLY INDONESIANS USE TOUGHER CUTS, COOKED SLOWLY.

SERVES FOUR

INGREDIENTS
  600g/1lb 6oz beef sirloin or rump
    (round) steak
  30ml/2 tbsp dark soy sauce
  15ml/1 tbsp lime juice
  45ml/3 tbsp vegetable or groundnut
    (peanut) oil
  1 large onion, chopped
  30ml/2 tbsp tamarind
    concentrate
  600ml/1 pint/2½ cups water
  5 cloves
  5ml/1 tsp salt
  5ml/1 tsp sugar
For the spice paste
  15ml/1 tbsp ground coriander
  5ml/1 tsp ground cumin
  5ml/1 tsp ground fennel
  3 candlenuts
  10ml/2 tsp black peppercorns

1 Slice the beef 1cm/½in thick. Whisk the soy sauce and lime juice together, pour over the beef in a non-metallic container and marinate for half an hour.

2 Heat the oil in a wok or heavy pan and fry the onion for 2 minutes, until softened. Blend the ground spices for the spice paste with a little water then add the remaining ingredients and grind to a paste.

3 Add the spice paste to the pan and fry for 2 minutes. Add the beef with its marinade, the tamarind, water, cloves, salt and sugar. Reduce the heat and simmer, covered, for 40 minutes.

4 At the end of the cooking time the liquid should have reduced by half. Remove the beef to a serving plate. Correct the seasoning if necessary and serve the gravy on the side.

Per portion Energy 400Kcal/1664kJ; Protein 36.7g; Carbohydrate 11.1g, of which sugars 5.8g; Fat 23.7g, of which saturates 6.9g; Cholesterol 87mg; Calcium 46mg; Fibre 1.1g; Sodium 1127mg.

STIR-FRIED BEEF IN OYSTER SAUCE

THIS SIMPLE BUT DELICIOUS RECIPE IS OFTEN MADE WITH JUST STRAW MUSHROOMS, WHICH ARE READILY AVAILABLE FRESH IN SOUTH-EAST ASIA, BUT OYSTER MUSHROOMS MAKE A GOOD SUBSTITUTE AND USING A MIXTURE MAKES THE DISH EXTRA INTERESTING.

SERVES FOUR TO SIX

INGREDIENTS

    450g/1lb rump (round) steak
    30ml/2 tbsp soy sauce
    15ml/1 tbsp cornflour (cornstarch)
    45ml/3 tbsp vegetable oil
    15ml/1 tbsp chopped garlic
    15ml/1 tbsp chopped fresh
      root ginger
    225g/8oz/3¼ cups mixed
      mushrooms such as shiitake,
      oyster and straw
    30ml/2 tbsp oyster sauce
    5ml/1 tsp granulated (white) sugar
    4 spring onions (scallions), cut into
      short lengths
    ground black pepper
    2 fresh red chillies, seeded and cut
      into strips, to garnish

1 Place the steak in the freezer for 30–40 minutes, until firm, then, using a sharp knife, slice it on the diagonal into long thin strips.

2 Mix together the soy sauce and cornflour in a large bowl. Add the steak, turning to coat well, cover with clear film (plastic wrap) and leave to marinate at room temperature for 1–2 hours.

3 Heat half the oil in a wok or large, heavy frying pan. Add the garlic and ginger and cook for 1–2 minutes, until fragrant. Drain the steak, add it to the wok or pan and stir well to separate the strips. Cook, stirring frequently, for a further 1–2 minutes, until the steak is browned all over and tender. Remove from the wok or pan and set aside.

4 Heat the remaining oil in the wok or pan. Add the shiitake, oyster and straw mushrooms. Stir-fry over a medium heat until golden brown.

5 Return the steak to the wok and mix it with the mushrooms. Spoon in the oyster sauce and sugar, mix well, then add ground black pepper to taste. Toss over the heat until all the ingredients are thoroughly combined.

6 Stir in the spring onions. Tip the mixture on to a serving platter, garnish with the strips of red chilli and serve.

Per portion Energy 171Kcal/717kJ; Protein 20g; Carbohydrate 8.3g, of which sugars 5.6g; Fat 6.6g, of which saturates 1.9g; Cholesterol 52mg; Calcium 28mg; Fibre 1.1g; Sodium 343mg.

MALAY LAMB KORMA

ADAPTED FROM THE TRADITIONAL INDIAN KORMA, THE CREAMY MALAY VERSION IS FLAVOURED WITH COCONUT MILK. SERVED AT THE MALAY AND MUSLIM HAWKER STALLS, THIS TASTY LAMB KORMA IS OFTEN ACCOMPANIED BY FRAGRANT RICE OR FLATBREAD AND A MALAY SALAD OR SAMBAL.

SERVES FOUR TO SIX

INGREDIENTS

  25g/1oz fresh root ginger, peeled and chopped
  4 garlic cloves, chopped
  2 red chillies, seeded and chopped
  10ml/2 tsp garam masala
  10ml/2 tsp ground coriander
  5ml/1 tsp ground cumin
  5ml/1 tsp ground turmeric
  675g/1½lb lamb shoulder, cut into bitesize cubes
  45ml/3 tbsp ghee, or 30ml/2 tbsp vegetable oil and 15g/½oz/1 tbsp butter
  2 onions, halved lengthways and sliced along the grain
  2.5ml/½ tsp sugar
  4–6 cardamom pods, bruised
  1 cinnamon stick
  400ml/14fl oz/1⅔ cups coconut milk
salt and ground black pepper
  30ml/2 tbsp roasted peanuts, crushed, and fresh coriander (cilantro) and mint leaves, coarsely chopped, to garnish

1 Using a mortar and pestle or food processor, grind the ginger, garlic and chillies to a paste. Stir in the garam masala, ground coriander, cumin and turmeric. Put the lamb into a shallow dish and rub the paste into it. Cover and leave to marinate for 1 hour.

2 Heat the ghee or oil and butter in a heavy pan or flameproof earthenware pot. Add the onions and sugar, and cook until brown and almost caramelized. Stir in the cardamom pods and cinnamon stick and add the lamb with all the marinade. Mix well and cook until the meat is browned all over.

3 Pour in the coconut milk, stir well and bring to the boil. Reduce the heat, cover the pan and cook gently for 30–40 minutes until the meat is tender. Make sure the meat doesn't become dry – stir in a little extra coconut milk, or water, if necessary.

4 Season to taste with salt and pepper. Scatter the peanuts over the top and garnish with the coriander and mint. Serve immediately.

COOK'S TIP
Homemade clarified butter can be used in place of ghee.

Per Portion Energy 267Kcal/1117kJ; Protein 24.3g; Carbohydrate 8.5g, of which sugars 6.8g; Fat 15.4g, of which saturates 6.4g; Cholesterol 86mg; Calcium 46mg; Fibre 1.2g; Sodium 211mg.

SIZZLING LAMB <u>WITH</u> WINE SAUCE

THIS IS A WELL-KNOWN RESTAURANT DISH IN MALAYSIA AND SINGAPORE, WHERE IT IS SERVED WITH PANACHE IN A CAST IRON HOT PLATE MOUNTED ON A WOODEN BASE. OF NORTH CHINESE ORIGIN, IT IS STEEPED IN CHINESE WINE, GINGER JUICE AND SESAME OIL AND IS USUALLY SERVED AS A WINTER WARMER IN COLD CLIMATES. USING GINGER WINE OBVIATES THE NEED TO SQUEEZE OUT THE JUICE FROM FRESH GINGER. IF YOU CANNOT FIND THIS PRODUCT, CRUSH OR GRIND A THUMB-SIZED PIECE OF FRESH ROOT GINGER TO EXTRACT ITS JUICE AND BLEND THIS WITH 30ML/2 TBSP CHINESE RICE WINE. YOU CAN ADD SOME FRESH GRATED GINGER FOR GOOD MEASURE.

SERVES FOUR

INGREDIENTS
500g/1¼lb lean lamb
45ml/3 tbsp ginger wine
45ml/2 tbsp sesame oil
2.5ml/½ tsp black pepper
30ml/2 tbsp oyster sauce
30ml/2 tbsp vegetable or groundnut (peanut) oil
25g/1oz grated fresh root ginger
4 garlic cloves, crushed
3 spring onions (scallions), chopped
10ml/2 tsp cornflour (cornstarch)

1 Cut the lamb into thin strips and tenderize by beating them with the blunt edge of a cleaver or meat mallet.

2 Blend the ginger wine with the sesame oil, pepper and oyster sauce and stir well to incorporate. Set aside.

3 Heat the oil and fry the ginger and garlic for 2 minutes until they are just starting to brown.

4 Add the lamb strips and stir-fry for 3 minutes. Add the ginger wine mixture and bring to a fast boil. When the lamb is nearly done, add the chopped spring onions and stir for 1 minute. Blend the cornflour with a little water to make a smooth paste and add to the pan. Stir until the sauce is thick.

5 If you have a cast iron plate, heat it over a flame for 5 minutes and replace it on the wooden base, being careful to handle it with special tongs. Heap the lamb on the hot plate and serve immediately as the sizzling will die down very quickly.

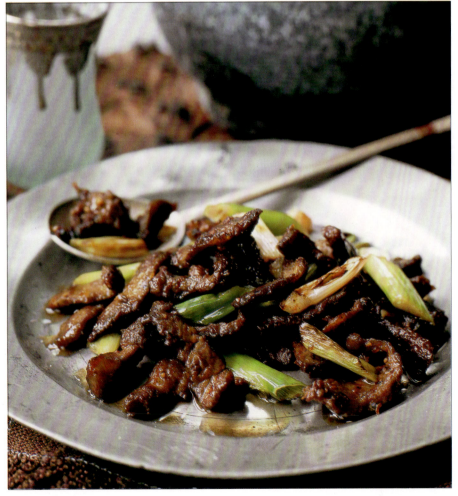

Per portion Energy 386Kcal/1607kJ; Protein 24.9g; Carbohydrate 6.5g, of which sugars 4.1g; Fat 27.8g, of which saturates 8.4g; Cholesterol 95mg; Calcium 17mg; Fibre 0.2g; Sodium 294mg.

NONYA SAMBAL PORK

THIS IS A LOVELY TRADITIONAL NONYA DISH. IT IS COOKED WITHOUT WATER, WITH THE RESULT THAT THE PORK IS ALMOST PICKLED. IT WILL KEEP FOR WEEKS, TASTING BETTER WITH EACH DAY AS THE FLAVOURS BLEND TOGETHER AND MATURE. BE CAREFUL TO USE A DRY SPOON WHEN YOU SERVE IT, OTHERWISE YOU WILL INTRODUCE MOISTURE. AS THE PORK BECOMES MORE FLAVOURSOME AND TENDER WITH KEEPING, IT MAKES A DELICIOUS SANDWICH SPREAD, RATHER LIKE A COARSE PÂTÉ. THE ONLY CUT OF PORK TO USE FOR THIS IS BELLY, AS IT HAS THE CORRECT PROPORTION OF LEAN MEAT AND FAT. IT IS WORTH COOKING A LARGE BATCH AS IT KEEPS SO WELL.

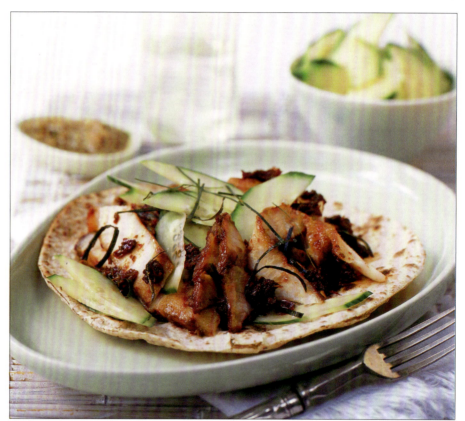

SERVES FOUR

INGREDIENTS
  1kg/2¼lb belly pork
  500ml/17fl oz/generous
    2 cups water
  45ml/3 tbsp vegetable oil
  2.5ml/1 tsp salt
  10ml/2 tsp sugar
  6 kaffir lime leaves
  30ml/2 tbsp dark soy sauce
For the spice paste
  1 large onion or 20 shallots,
    roughly chopped
  3 stalks lemon grass, trimmed to
    leave 7.5cm/3in of the root end
  10g/¼oz galangal, chopped
  10 dried chillies, soaked until soft
    and seeds removed (optional for
    milder flavour)
  4 garlic cloves, chopped
  40g/1½oz shrimp paste
  8 candlenuts

1 First make the spice blend. Grind all the paste ingredients in a mortar and pestle or food processor until fine.

COOK'S TIP
When making the spice paste, it will reduce splattering if you process the onions separately first, then add the other spices, as the onion purée will facilitate the grinding process.

2 Put the pork in a pan and add the water. Bring to the boil and cook for 15 minutes. Remove the pork and drain well. Holding the meat firmly, insert a sharp knife between the skin and the meat, and remove the skin in one piece. Cut the pork into 3cm/1in wide strips trimming off any excess fat.

3 Heat the oil in a wok or heavy pan and fry the spice paste over low heat for 10 minutes. Do not rush this step.

4 Add the pork and fry over low heat for 10 minutes until evenly browned. Add salt, sugar and soy sauce and continue to fry for 5 minutes, making sure every piece is well coated. The pork will take on a mahogany hue.

5 Remove the central spine of each lime leaf and shred very finely with a sharp knife or scissors. Add the shredded leaves to the pork in the last minutes of frying. Leave to cool before storing in an airtight container, if not serving immediately. It goes very well with sliced cucumber.

Per portion Energy 703Kcal/2917kJ; Protein 49.2g; Carbohydrate 13.3g, of which sugars 8.8g; Fat 50.8g, of which saturates 16.6g; Cholesterol 183mg; Calcium 172mg; Fibre 1.4g; Sodium 5314mg.

FENG

Portuguese Eurasians eat feng at Christmas. Traditionally made with offal, this curry represents a mix of Malay and Portuguese culinary traditions. If you are not a fan of offal, use lean pork from the hind leg — this version of the curry is popular in Singapore.

SERVES FOUR

INGREDIENTS
1kg/2¼lb mixed pork offal (such as
    liver, lungs, intestines and heart),
    thoroughly cleaned and trimmed
30ml/2 tbsp vegetable oil
50g/2oz fresh root ginger, peeled
    and shredded
15–30ml/1–2 tbsp white wine
    vinegar or rice vinegar
salt
bread or steamed rice, to serve
For the spice paste
8 shallots, chopped
4 garlic cloves, chopped
25g/1oz fresh root ginger, peeled
    and chopped
30ml/2 tbsp coriander seeds
10ml/2 tsp cumin seeds
10ml/2 tsp fennel seeds
10ml/2 tsp black peppercorns
5ml/1 tsp ground turmeric

1 First make the spice paste. Using a mortar and pestle or food processor, grind the shallots, garlic and ginger to a paste.

2 In a heavy pan, dry-roast the coriander, cumin and fennel seeds with the peppercorns until they emit a nutty aroma. Grind the roasted spices to a powder and stir them into the spice paste with the ground turmeric.

3 Put the offal, except the liver, in a pan with water to cover. Bring to the boil, lower the heat and cook for 40 minutes.

4 Add the liver and cook for a further 5 minutes, until all the offal is tender. Drain the offal but reserve the cooking broth. Cut the offal into bitesize pieces.

5 Heat the oil in a wok or earthenware pot. Stir in the ginger and fry until crisp. Lift the ginger out and set aside.

6 Stir the spice paste into the oil and fry until fragrant. Add the offal and toss it to brown lightly. Stir in the vinegar over a high heat and season. Stir in half the crispy fried ginger and scatter the rest over the top.

7 Serve the dish hot with fresh, crusty bread or steamed rice and some simple steamed green vegetables.

Per Portion Energy 444Kcal/1858kJ; Protein 53.6g; Carbohydrate 7.2g, of which sugars 1.4g; Fat 13.3g, of which saturates 5.9g; Cholesterol 650mg; Calcium 21mg; Fibre 0.4g; Sodium 218mg.

PORK RIBS IN BLACK BEAN SAUCE

BLACK BEANS AND BLACK BEAN SAUCE ARE ALMOST EXCLUSIVE TO MALAYSIAN AND SINGAPORE CHINESE COOKING, AND GO PARTICULARLY WELL WITH PORK. BOILING THE RIBS FIRST ENSURES A MORE SUCCULENT TEXTURE AND THE MEAT ABSORBS THE SEASONINGS BETTER.

SERVES FOUR

INGREDIENTS

- 8 large meaty pork spare ribs
- 500ml/17 fl oz/generous 2 cups water
- 30ml/2 tbsp light soy sauce
- 15g/½oz fresh root ginger
- 3 garlic cloves
- 2 red chillies
- 45ml/3 tbsp sesame oil
- 30ml/2 tbsp black bean sauce

1 Cut each rib into 6cm/2½in pieces. Bring the water to the boil in a wok or heavy pan and add the soy sauce. Add the ribs and cook for 20 minutes. Drain, reserving the stock for another dish.

2 Finely chop the ginger, garlic and chillies. Blend the sesame oil with the black bean sauce and add the ginger, garlic and chillies. Pour the mixture over the cooked ribs in a shallow dish and leave to marinate for several hours.

3 When ready to cook, lift the ribs out of the marinade and arrange them in a shallow dish. Put the dish in a bamboo steamer, cover and steam the ribs for about 15 minutes until they are heated through and tender.

Per portion Energy 722Kcal/3012kJ; Protein 61.8g; Carbohydrate 2.6g, of which sugars 1g; Fat 51.9g, of which saturates 18.1g; Cholesterol 215mg; Calcium 59mg; Fibre 0.7g; Sodium 897mg.

PORK RIBS IN PANDAN LEAVES

THE MALAYS HAVE A PENCHANT FOR SWEET TASTES AND PORK IS OFTEN MARRIED WITH SWEET FLAVOURINGS IN MALAYSIA. THE DAYAKS LOVE PORK COATED IN HONEY AND GRILLED, STIR-FRIED OR ROASTED. IN THIS CHINESE-STYLE SINGAPORE DISH, THE PORK IS MARINATED IN HONEY AND WESTERN FLAVOURINGS, BEFORE BEING WRAPPED IN LONG, THIN PANDAN LEAVES AND DEEP-FRIED. SERVE THESE PORK RIBS AS AN APPETIZER OR AS A MAIN COURSE WITH STIR-FRIED RICE OR NOODLES.

SERVES FOUR TO FIVE

INGREDIENTS
    675g/1½lb meaty pork ribs, cut into
       bitesize pieces
    25 pandan (screwpine) leaves
    vegetable oil, for deep-frying
    2 limes, cut into wedges, to serve
For the marinade
    6 shallots, chopped
    4 garlic cloves, chopped
    25g/1oz fresh root ginger, peeled
       and chopped
    30ml/2 tbsp clear honey
    45ml/3 tbsp Worcestershire sauce
    30ml/2 tbsp tomato ketchup
    30ml/2 tbsp sour plum sauce
    15ml/1 tbsp sesame oil

1 First make the marinade. Using a mortar and pestle or food processor, grind the shallots, garlic and ginger to a smooth paste. Beat in the honey, Worcestershire sauce, tomato ketchup, sour plum sauce and sesame oil, mixing thoroughly until fully blended.

2 Put the pork ribs in a shallow dish and smear the marinade all over them. Set aside for 2–3 hours.

3 Lay the pandan leaves on a flat surface and place a marinated pork rib in the centre of each one. Tie a tight knot over each rib so that the ends poke out.

4 Heat enough oil in a wok or heavy pan for deep-frying and fry the wrapped ribs in batches for 4–5 minutes until cooked. Serve immediately, still wrapped in the leaves, with lime wedges for squeezing, so that each diner can open their own parcels.

COOK'S TIP
Pandan leaves lend a unique fragrance to this dish, but if they are not available you can substitute banana or bamboo leaves cut into strips. Pandan leaves are always used when slightly withered, as the fresh leaves have very little scent.

Per Portion Energy 299Kcal/1250kJ; Protein 25.5g; Carbohydrate 4.1g, of which sugars 3.8g; Fat 20.3g, of which saturates 7.3g; Cholesterol 89mg; Calcium 24mg; Fibre 0.2g; Sodium 182mg.

TIFFIN PORK CHOPS

THIS DISH IS STEEPED IN SINGAPORE'S COLONIAL HISTORY. TIFFIN IS BELIEVED TO DERIVE FROM MEALS ORDERED FROM INDIAN COOKS BY BRITISH ARMY OFFICERS, WHICH WERE DELIVERED IN METAL TIFFIN CARRIERS. WHEN THESE MEN MARRIED AND SET UP HOME, THEY WOULD HIRE HAINANESE COOKS AND PROBABLY INSTRUCTED THEM TO COOK SIMILAR ALL-IN-ONE DISHES, WITH PORK AND POTATOES IN GRAVY MADE WITH TOMATO KETCHUP AND THE VERY BRITISH WORCESTERSHIRE SAUCE.

SERVES FOUR

INGREDIENTS

4 thick boneless pork chops
10ml/2 tsp cornflour (cornstarch)
60ml/4 tbsp vegetable or groundnut (peanut) oil
2 large potatoes, peeled and cut into 5mm/¼in slices
1 large onion, sliced
30ml/2 tbsp Worcestershire sauce
30ml/2 tbsp tomato ketchup
200ml/7fl oz/scant 1 cup water
2.5ml/½ tsp ground black pepper
mushy peas and extra Worcestershire sauce, to serve (optional)

1 Slice the pork chops horizontally to make thin escalopes, to facilitate cooking. Beat them with a meat mallet to tenderize them and dust them lightly with cornflour.

2 Heat 15ml/1 tbsp of the oil in a wok or heavy pan and fry the pieces of pork quickly on both sides until they are lightly browned. Remove to a plate and set aside.

3 Heat the remaining oil in the pan and fry the sliced onion until soft and golden but not brown. Remove and set aside.

4 Meanwhile, blend the Worcestershire sauce with the tomato ketchup, water and pepper and stir until smooth.

5 Fry the sliced potatoes in the onion cooking oil in a single layer, cooking them in batches if necessary, until they are browned on both sides and partially cooked. Remove them with a slotted spoon and drain on kitchen paper.

6 Return the pork, onion and potatoes to the pan and add the sauce. Bring to a quick boil and cook, stirring, until the sauce is rich and glossy. If you want to serve the dish in British colonial style, serve with mushy peas and more Worcestershire sauce on the side.

Per portion Energy 517Kcal/2164kJ; Protein 51.6g; Carbohydrate 29.6g, of which sugars 10.1g; Fat 22.1g, of which saturates 6.5g; Cholesterol 165mg; Calcium 60mg; Fibre 2.5g; Sodium 354mg.

PORK CURRY

Although most curries originate from the Indian or Indonesian kitchen, Chinese cooks have created their own version, which sits somewhere between the two. Generally mild, this curry resembles Japanese-style curry in that it is sweet rather than hot. Coconut milk is rarely present in Chinese cooking – unless it is used by Nonyas who are of Chinese stock – and this is one of the few recipes that includes it. The addition of potatoes is believed to have been inspired by colonial plantation owners, who would have instructed their Chinese cooks to include their favourite staple.

SERVES FOUR

INGREDIENTS
    500g/1¼lb boneless pork chops
    4 tomatoes
    2 large potatoes
    45ml/3 tbsp vegetable oil
    30ml/2 tbsp mild curry powder
    15g/½oz ground ginger
    400ml/14 fl oz/1⅔ cups
      coconut milk
    10ml/2 tsp sugar
    15ml/1 tbsp light soy sauce
    15ml/1 tbsp lime juice
    steamed rice, to serve

1 Slice the pork horizontally into thin escalopes, then cut into 5cm/2in squares. Tenderize with a meat mallet. Skin, quarter and deseed the tomatoes.

2 Peel the potatoes and cut them into chunks. Heat the oil in a wok or heavy pan and fry the potatoes over high heat, turning them constantly so that they brown lightly on all sides. This will help to prevent them breaking up while being simmered with the pork. Remove them with a slotted spoon and drain on kitchen paper.

3 Blend the curry powder to a paste with a little water. Stir the ginger into the remaining oil and add the curry paste. Fry for 4 minutes until fragrant.

4 Add the coconut milk, sugar and soy sauce. Bring to the boil, add the pork and potatoes and simmer for 15 minutes. Add the lime juice and serve.

Per portion Energy 373Kcal/1569kJ; Protein 30.9g; Carbohydrate 30.4g, of which sugars 13g; Fat 15.2g, of which saturates 3.3g; Cholesterol 79mg; Calcium 68mg; Fibre 2.3g; Sodium 490mg.

PENANG SPRING ROLLS

THESE SPRING ROLLS, WHICH ARE CALLED CHUEN PIAH, *ARE A SPECIALITY OF* PENANG *COOKING. THEIR GENERIC NAME DOES THEM LITTLE JUSTICE, AS THEY ARE QUITE DIFFERENT FROM THE ORDINARY* CHINESE *VARIETY OF SPRING ROLL. COMMONLY CALLED* LOBAK, *THEY ARE ACTUALLY A MEAT-FILLED VERSION OF POPIAH, USING TOFU (BEAN CURD) INSTEAD OF FLOUR WRAPPERS. SOME RESTAURANTS IN* PENANG *SERVE A CROSS BETWEEN* CHUEN PIAH *AND* POPIAH, *USING FRESHLY MADE POPIAH SKINS. AS THE ROLLS REQUIRE A COARSELY GROUND PORK, IT'S ESSENTIAL TO CHOP THE MEAT YOURSELF, RATHER THAN USING SUPERMARKET MINCE, TO GET THE CORRECT TEXTURE.*

SERVES FOUR

INGREDIENTS
    500g/1¼lb leg of pork
    1 large leek
    2 large sheets tofu (bean curd) skin
    1 egg, lightly beaten
    5ml/1 tsp five-spice powder
    15ml/1 tbsp light soy sauce
    15ml/1 tbsp dark soy sauce
    15ml/1 tbsp sesame oil
    2.5ml/½ tsp black pepper
    oil for deep-frying
    lettuce leaves and chilli and garlic
      dip, to serve

COOK'S TIP
Tofu sheets are sold in Asian markets. They should be moistened before use so they can be rolled up without cracking.

1 With a heavy cleaver, chop the pork until it is fine and crumbly but not minced. Slice the leek very finely, discarding most of the green part.

2 Mix the pork with the leek, beaten egg, five-spice powder, sesame oil, soy sauces and pepper.

3 Spread out a tofu sheet on a flat surface and, with a damp cloth, lightly wipe it down to soften any crackly areas. Cut it into rectangles measuring 20 x 13cm/8 x 5in.

4 Place 30ml/2 tbsp of the pork mixture at one end of a rectangle, about 6cm/2½in from the edge. Roll the edge over the filling and pat in firmly. Roll once more and tuck in both sides before completing the rolling.

5 Repeat with the remaining wrappers and allow to rest for 10 minutes. Heat the oil and deep-fry the rolls for 4–5 minutes, until golden brown. Serve on a bed of lettuce with a sharp chilli and garlic dip.

Per portion Energy 207Kcal/872kJ; Protein 23.7g; Carbohydrate 19.7g, of which sugars 3.4g; Fat 4.2g, of which saturates 1g; Cholesterol 121mg; Calcium 241mg; Fibre 1.2g; Sodium 161mg.

SINGAPORE FIVE-SPICE MEAT ROLLS

A GREAT FAVOURITE AT THE CZE CHA HAWKER STALLS IN SINGAPORE, THESE DEEP-FRIED STEAMED ROLLS ARE DELICIOUS WITH A DIPPING SAUCE. WRAPPED IN TRADITIONAL TOFU SHEETS, THEY CAN BE SERVED AS A SNACK, OR EATEN AS PART OF A LIGHT MEAL WITH RICE, PIQUANT SAUCE AND A SALAD.

SERVES FOUR

INGREDIENTS
225g/8oz minced (ground) pork
150g/5oz fresh prawns (shrimp), peeled and finely chopped
115g/4oz water chestnuts, finely chopped
15ml/1 tbsp light soy sauce
15ml/1 tbsp dark soy sauce
15ml/1 tbsp sour plum sauce
7.5ml/1½ tsp sesame oil
10ml/2 tsp five-spice powder
5ml/1 tsp glutinous rice flour or cornflour (cornstarch)
1 egg, lightly beaten
4 fresh tofu sheets, 18–20cm/7–8in square, soaked in warm water
vegetable oil, for deep-frying
chilli oil, for drizzling
soy sauce mixed with chopped chillies, to serve

1 Put the minced pork, chopped prawns and water chestnuts in a bowl. Add the soy sauces, sour plum sauce and sesame oil and mix well.

2 Stir in the five-spice powder, glutinous rice flour or cornflour, and egg. Mix well to blend thoroughly.

3 Lay the tofu sheets on a flat surface and divide the pork mixture between them, placing spoonfuls towards the edge nearest you.

4 Pull the nearest edge up over the filling, tuck in the sides and roll into a log, just like a spring roll. Moisten the last edge with a little water to seal the roll. Repeat to make four rolls.

5 Fill a wok one-third of the way up with water and place a bamboo steamer in it. Bring the water to the boil and place the tofu rolls in the steamer. Cover and steam for 15 minutes.

6 Remove the steamed rolls with tongs and place them on a clean dish towel.

7 Heat enough oil for deep-frying in a wok. Fry the steamed rolls in batches until crisp and golden. Drain them on kitchen paper.

8 Serve the rolls hot, whole or sliced. Drizzle them with chilli oil and serve with a little dipping bowl of soy sauce mixed with finely chopped red chillies or a ready-made chilli dip.

COOK'S TIP
Tofu sheets are available in Chinese and Asian markets and large supermarkets, but if you cannot find them, try making these rolls with Asian rice sheets or even with filo pastry.

Per Portion Energy 339Kcal/1413kJ; Protein 24.4g; Carbohydrate 12.5g, of which sugars 2.7g; Fat 21.6g, of which saturates 4.2g; Cholesterol 158mg; Calcium 343mg; Fibre 1.2g; Sodium 65mg.

SARAWAK GOAT CURRY

GIVEN THEIR PROXIMITY, IT IS NO SURPRISE THAT SARAWAK, SABAH AND INDONESIA SHARE MANY DISHES, ALTHOUGH THERE ARE REGIONAL OR TRIBAL VARIATIONS ON A THEME. ONE THING THEY ALL HAVE IN COMMON IS THEIR ENJOYMENT OF MUTTON AND GOAT, WHICH THEY USUALLY COOK IN A CURRY OR CHARGRILL AS A SPICY SATAY. IN SARAWAK, THIS CURRY WOULD NORMALLY BE SERVED WITH THE LOCAL SAGO PORRIDGE, BUT IT IS EQUALLY DELICIOUS SERVED WITH STEAMED JASMINE RICE, AN INDIAN PILAFF OR CHUNKS OF FRESH CRUSTY BREAD AND A GREEN MANGO OR PAPAYA SALAD.

SERVES FOUR

INGREDIENTS

30ml/2 tbsp vegetable or groundnut (peanut) oil

2 cinnamon sticks

1kg/2¼lb lean goat meat, from the leg or shoulder, cut into bitesize strips

4 tomatoes, skinned, seeded and chopped

15–30ml/1–2 tbsp palm sugar (jaggery)

900ml/1½ pints/ 3¾ cups coconut milk

a handful of kaffir lime leaves

salt

fresh coriander (cilantro) leaves, roughly chopped, to garnish

3–4 green chillies, seeded and quartered lengthways, and bread, to serve

For the spice paste

8 shallots, chopped

6 garlic cloves, chopped

4 red chillies, seeded and chopped

50g/2oz galangal, chopped

25g/1oz fresh turmeric, chopped

2 lemon grass stalks, trimmed and chopped

4 candlenuts or macadamia nuts

15ml/1 tbsp coriander seeds

5ml/1 tsp cumin seeds

1 First make the spice paste. Using a mortar and pestle or food processor, grind the shallots, garlic, chillies, galangal, turmeric, lemon grass and nuts to a coarse paste. Grind the coriander and cumin seeds separately and stir them into the spice paste.

2 Heat the oil in a wok and stir in the spice paste. Add the cinnamon sticks. Once they start to emit a fragrant aroma, add the strips of goat, tossing them around the wok to brown them lightly. Stir in the tomatoes with the sugar and cook for 2 minutes before pouring in the coconut milk. Bring to the boil, stir in the lime leaves and reduce the heat.

3 Cover and simmer gently for about 1½ hours, until the meat is tender. Add more coconut milk if necessary to prevent the curry becoming too dry. Season to taste with salt, sprinkle with coriander and serve with chillies and crusty bread.

Per Portion Energy 625Kcal/2614kJ; Protein 51.3g; Carbohydrate 19.8g, of which sugars 19.2g; Fat 38.5g, of which saturates 14.7g; Cholesterol 190mg; Calcium 126mg; Fibre 2g; Sodium 88mg.

INDIAN DRY MUTTON CURRY

IN MALAYSIA AND SINGAPORE, A REFERENCE TO MUTTON USUALLY MEANS GOAT MEAT, AND NOT SHEEP MEAT AS IN THE WEST. SHEEP ARE NOT REARED IN ASIA, SO WHEN LAMB IS REQUIRED IT IS USUALLY IMPORTED FROZEN. MOST INDIANS IN THE REGION ARE EITHER HINDUS WHO ESCHEW BEEF OR MUSLIMS WHO DO NOT EAT PORK. GOAT MEAT CAN BE TOUGH AND NEEDS LONG SIMMERING, BUT HAS A MUCH STRONGER FLAVOUR THAN LAMB. THE BEST CUTS ARE BONELESS CHOPS, BUT MALAYSIANS OFTEN PREFER THE MEAT LEFT ON THE BONE. THIS DISH CAN BE SERVED WITH PILAFF OR BIRYANI.

SERVES FOUR

INGREDIENTS

500g/1¼lb mutton chops
5ml/1 tsp cumin seeds
15ml/1 tbsp chilli powder
15ml/1 tbsp ground coriander
5ml/1 tsp ground turmeric
75ml/5 tbsp water
45ml/3 tbsp oil
250ml/8fl oz/1 cup thin
  coconut milk
salt and ground black pepper
small bunch of fresh coriander
  (cilantro), to garnish

COOK'S TIP
Thin coconut milk is recommended for this slow-cooked dish, as thick coconut milk can render down to oil over long cooking. Canned coconut milk is quite thick, so thin down the contents of the can with ½ can water.

1 Cut the mutton into 3cm/1¼in cubes. Soak the cumin seeds in water, then drain them and crush coarsely using a mortar and pestle or in a food processor. Blend the cumin with the chilli powder, ground coriander, turmeric and a generous grinding of pepper, and add a little water to make a paste.

2 Stir the paste into the mutton and leave to marinate for 30 minutes.

3 Heat the oil and fry the mutton for about 4 minutes, until fragrant. Add the coconut milk and salt and simmer over low heat, covered, for about 1 hour.

4 The curry should be almost dry when cooked. You may have to top up with coconut milk if the evaporation rate is high, so have extra standing by.

Per portion Energy 581Kcal/2403kJ; Protein 19.6g; Carbohydrate 5.7g, of which sugars 3.1g; Fat 53.7g, of which saturates 23.2g; Cholesterol 96mg; Calcium 41mg; Fibre 0g; Sodium 148mg.

VEGETABLES AND SALADS

The tropical climate of Malaysia and Singapore means that most vegetables are available all year round. Cool, colourful salads act as a foil for spicy snacks and curries, and often incorporate fresh fruits such as pineapple and mango as well as crunchy vegetables. Exotic local vegetables such as water spinach and bamboo shoots are tossed into stir-fries and briefly cooked to retain all their colour and flavour, while Indian influences are revealed in slow-cooked vegetable curries.

GADO-GADO

THIS CLASSIC MIXED SALAD IS OF INDONESIAN ORIGIN, BUT IT IS ALSO VERY POPULAR IN MALAYSIA AND SINGAPORE. IT IS DISTINGUISHED BY THE CRUNCHY PEANUT AND COCONUT SAUCE SERVED WITH IT, AND MAKES A PERFECT ACCOMPANIMENT TO A VARIETY OF SPICY DISHES AND CURRIES WITH ITS CLEAN TASTE AND BRIGHT, JEWEL-LIKE COLOURS.

SERVES SIX

INGREDIENTS
  ½ cucumber
  2 pears (not too ripe) or 175g/
    6oz wedge of yam bean
  1–2 eating apples
  juice of ½ lemon
  mixed salad leaves
  6 small tomatoes, cut in wedges
  3 slices fresh pineapple, cored and
    cut in wedges
  3 eggs, hard-boiled and shelled
  175g/6oz egg noodles, cooked,
    cooled and chopped
  deep-fried onions, to garnish
For the peanut sauce
  2–4 fresh red chillies, seeded
    and ground, or 15ml/
    1 tbsp chilli sambal
  300ml/½ pint/1¼ cups coconut milk
  350g/12oz/1¼ cups crunchy
    peanut butter

15ml/1 tbsp dark soy sauce or dark
  brown sugar
5ml/1 tsp tamarind pulp, soaked in
  45ml/3 tbsp warm water
coarsely crushed peanuts
salt

2 Simmer gently until the sauce thickens, then stir in the soy sauce or sugar. Strain in the tamarind liquid, add salt to taste and stir well. Spoon into a bowl and sprinkle with a few coarsely crushed peanuts.

1 To make the peanut sauce, put the ground chillies or chilli sambal in a pan. Pour in the coconut milk, then stir in the peanut butter. Heat gently, stirring, until well blended.

3 To make the salad, core the cucumber and peel the pears or yam bean. Cut them into matchsticks. Finely shred the apples and sprinkle them with the lemon juice.

4 Spread a bed of lettuce leaves on a flat platter or a section of banana leaf, then pile the prepared fruit and vegetables on top.

5 Add the sliced or quartered hard-boiled eggs, the chopped noodles and the deep-fried onions. Serve at once, with the sauce.

COOK'S TIP
Quail's eggs can be used instead of normal eggs and look very attractive in this dish. Hard boil for 3 minutes and halve or leave whole.

Per portion Energy 490Kcal/2043kJ; Protein18.9g; Carbohydrate 28.5g, of which sugars 21g; Fat 34.3g, of which saturates 8.6g; Cholesterol 116mg; Calcium 80mg; Fibre 6.2g; Sodium 493mg.

SPICY KANGKUNG WITH DRIED SHRIMP

KANGKUNG IS THE MALAY NAME FOR WATER SPINACH, OR MORNING GLORY, WHICH IS A WONDERFUL GREEN VEGETABLE WITH SPEAR-SHAPED LEAVES. THE VERSATILITY OF WATER SPINACH IS MUCH APPRECIATED THROUGHOUT SOUTH-EAST ASIA, WHERE IT IS USED IN SOUPS, FILLINGS AND BRAISED DISHES, OR SIMPLY STIR-FRIED ON ITS OWN. THIS DISH SERVES TWO AS A MAIN DISH OR FOUR AS A SIDE DISH.

SERVES TWO TO FOUR

INGREDIENTS

 4 garlic cloves, chopped
 25g/1oz fresh root ginger, peeled
  and chopped
 2 red chillies, seeded and chopped
 30ml/2 tbsp dried shrimp, soaked in
  warm water to soften and drained
 5ml/1 tsp shrimp paste
 30ml/2 tbsp vegetable or groundnut
  (peanut) oil
 7.5ml/1½1/2 tsp palm sugar (jaggery)
 15–30ml/1–2 tbsp light soy sauce
 500g/1¼lb fresh kangkung or
  water spinach leaves, washed
  and trimmed
 salt and ground black pepper
 1 red chilli, seeded and sliced,
  to garnish

1 Using a mortar and pestle or food processor, grind the garlic, ginger and chillies to a smooth paste. Add the dried shrimp and grind them to a paste. Beat in the shrimp paste and bind with a little of the oil.

2 Heat the rest of the oil in a wok or heavy pan. Stir in the spicy shrimp paste and cook over a low heat for 2–3 minutes until it is fragrant and beginning to colour. Stir in the sugar and soy sauce until well mixed.

3 Add the kangkung, tossing it around the pan so that all the leaves are coated in the spicy juices.

4 Cover with the lid for a few minutes to let the leaves wilt in the steam, then remove it and toss them around once more. Season to taste with salt and pepper, scatter the slices of red chilli over the top and serve immediately.

COOK'S TIP
Bundles of water spinach are sold in Chinese markets, but if it is not available you could replace it with ordinary garden spinach to make this dish. Serve it as a snack with bread and sliced chillies or as a side dish to accompany grilled or fried meats.

Per Portion Energy 107Kcal/441kJ; Protein 7.7g; Carbohydrate 4g, of which sugars 3.8g; Fat 6.7g, of which saturates 0.8g; Cholesterol 38mg; Calcium 304mg; Fibre 2.6g; Sodium 500mg.

KANGKUNG AND SWEET POTATO LEMAK

RARELY FOUND OUTSIDE THE NONYA HOME, THIS IS AN UNUSUAL DISH IN THAT IT IS ONE OF THE VERY FEW SPICY DISHES TO FEATURE SWEET POTATO. A ROOT VEGETABLE ASSOCIATED WITH THE REGION'S HUNGRY POSTWAR YEARS, IT HAS NOW GAINED RESPECT AS A GOOD CARBOHYDRATE THAT ALSO HAS A DISTINCTIVE SWEETNESS WITHOUT BEING CLOYING. WITH THE KANGKUNG AND RICH, COCONUT MILK-BASED SAUCE, IT MAKES A VERY SATISFYING MAIN COURSE.

SERVES FOUR

INGREDIENTS
  225g/8oz kangkung
  150g/5oz sweet potato
  45ml/3 tbsp vegetable or groundnut
    (peanut) oil
  400ml/14fl oz/1⅔ cups coconut milk
  5ml/1 tsp salt
  5ml/1 tsp sugar
For the spice paste
  5 candlenuts
  8 shallots
  15g/½oz shrimp paste
  15ml/1 tbsp dried shrimps,
    soaked until soft
  15g/½oz fresh turmeric, chopped
  3 garlic cloves, chopped
  5 red chillies, chopped
  steamed rice, to serve

1 Wash the kangkung well. Slice the stalks thinly and tear off the leaves in small bunches. Peel the sweet potato and cut into chunks, wash and dry.

2 Grind together all the ingredients for the spice paste. Heat the oil in a wok or heavy pan and fry the ground spices for 3 minutes, until fragrant.

3 Add the coconut milk, kangkung and sweet potatoes. Bring to the boil and add salt and sugar.

4 Cook for 10-15 minutes until the sweet potato is soft. Kangkung cooks very quickly but is unique in that it never becomes mushy with long simmering. Serve with rice.

Per portion Energy 194Kcal/812kJ; Protein 7.7g; Carbohydrate 20.1g, of which sugars 11.7g; Fat 9.9g, of which saturates 1.4g; Cholesterol 38mg; Calcium 244mg; Fibre 2.8g; Sodium 1023mg.

SARAWAK AUBERGINES WITH LEMON GRASS

THIS IS A GREAT WAY TO SERVE ANY AUBERGINE AVAILABLE. IF YOU CAN, TRY THE ROUND, ORANGE AUBERGINES GROWN BY DAYAK FARMERS, WHICH ARE PRETTY AND DELICATE IN FLAVOUR, AND PARTICULARLY TASTY COOKED IN COCONUT MILK WITH LOTS OF CHILLIES, GINGER AND LEMON GRASS. THE DAYAKS SERVE THIS DISH WITH THEIR LOCAL STAPLE, SAGO PORRIDGE, AND A HANDFUL OF FRESH CHILLIES FOR EXTRA FIRE, BUT IT IS DELICIOUS WITH PLAIN RICE OR CHUNKS OF CRUSTY BREAD.

SERVES FOUR

INGREDIENTS

15ml/1 tbsp ground turmeric
5ml/1 tsp chilli powder
3 slender orange aubergines
   (eggplants) or 8 baby aubergines,
   cut in wedges
45ml/3 tbsp vegetable or groundnut
   (peanut) oil
2 lemon grass stalks, trimmed,
   halved and bruised
600ml/1 pint/2½ cups
   coconut milk
salt and ground black pepper
a small bunch fresh coriander
   (cilantro), roughly chopped,
   to garnish
jasmine or coconut rice and
   2 green chillies, seeded and
   quartered lengthways (optional),
   to serve

For the spice paste
4–6 dried red chillies, soaked in
   warm water until soft, squeezed dry
   and seeded
4 garlic cloves, chopped
4 shallots, chopped
25g/1oz fresh root ginger, peeled
   and chopped
2 lemon grass stalks, trimmed
   and chopped
30ml/2 tbsp dried shrimp,
   re-hydrated in warm water
   and drained
5ml/1 tsp shrimp paste

1 First make the spice paste. Using a mortar and pestle or food processor, grind the chillies, garlic, shallots, ginger and lemon grass to a coarse paste. Grind in the dried shrimp and beat in the shrimp paste.

2 Mix the turmeric and chilli powder together. Rub the mixture all over the aubergine wedges.

COOK'S TIP
If you cannot find the orange aubergines used in this recipe, small purple ones can be substituted.

3 Heat the oil in a wok or heavy pan. Stir in the spice paste and lemon grass. Add the aubergine wedges, and cook until lightly browned. Pour in the coconut milk, stir well, and bubble it up to thicken.

4 Reduce the heat and cook gently for 15–20 minutes until the aubergine is tender but not mushy. Season with salt and pepper to taste. Sprinkle the coriander over the top and serve straight from the wok with the extra chillies to munch on, if you like. Serve with jasmine or coconut rice.

Per Portion Energy 154Kcal/644kJ; Protein 6.2g; Carbohydrate 11.9g, of which sugars 11g; Fat 9.5g, of which saturates 1.4g; Cholesterol 38mg; Calcium 175mg; Fibre 3g; Sodium 497mg.

STIR-FRIED SPICY AUBERGINE

THIS DISH IS BELIEVED TO HAVE COME FROM THE CHINESE PROVINCE OF HUPEI OR HUNAN, WHERE THE SAUCE USED HERE, CALLED DOU BANJIANG, IS VERY POPULAR. IT IS A BEAN PASTE INFUSED WITH SICHUAN PEPPERCORNS AND CHILLIES. AS IT IS A PUNGENT SAUCE, IT NEEDS TO BE TEMPERED WITH A LITTLE SUGAR TO STRIKE A YIN-YANG BALANCE. DOU BANJIANG, WHICH IS COMMONLY CALLED CHILLI BEAN SAUCE, IS SOLD IN EVERY CHINESE STORE, BUT YOU CAN MAKE YOU OWN BY SIMPLY BLENDING YELLOW BEAN SAUCE WITH GROUND CHILLIES, SICHUAN PEPPERCORNS AND SESAME OIL.

SERVES FOUR

INGREDIENTS
2 large aubergines (eggplants)
30ml/2 tbsp vegetable oil
2 garlic cloves, crushed
30ml/2 tbsp dou banjiang
200ml/7fl oz/scant 1 cup water
30ml/2 tbsp sesame oil
5ml/1 tsp sugar

COOK'S TIP
To quickly make your own dou banjiang, or chilli bean sauce, blend 60ml/ 4 tbsp yellow bean sauce with 15ml/ 1 tbsp chilli sauce, 5ml/1 tsp ground Sichuan peppercorns and 30ml/2 tbsp sesame oil. This makes four times the quantity needed for this spicy aubergine dish. Store the sauce in a screw-top jar in the refrigerator.

1 Slice the aubergines in quarters lengthways then cut them across the grain into small chunks.

2 Bring a large pan of water to the boil and blanch the aubergines for 3 minutes, then drain thoroughly. This will loosen the cottony texture of the flesh to help it absorb the seasonings better.

3 Heat the oil and fry the garlic for 2 minutes. Add the dou banjiang and cook rapidly for 1 minute, stirring.

4 Add the aubergines and stir-fry for 2 minutes. Add the water and bring to a fast boil. Because they have been blanched, the aubergines will absorb the liquid more easily, hastening the cooking time. Simmer for 4 minutes until the sauce has thickened a little.

5 Add the sesame oil and stir for 30 seconds. Season with sugar to taste, and serve the dish piping hot with rice or noodles.

Per portion Energy 121kcal/501kJ; Protein 1g; Carbohydrate 3.9g, of which sugars 3.4g; Fat 11.6g, of which saturates 1.6g; Cholesterol 0mg; Calcium 12mg; Fibre 2g; Sodium 73mg.

Deep-fried Aubergine with Garlic Sauce

This dish, terung sambal, is often served at the rice stalls in Singapore as an accompaniment to a main rice dish such as nasi lemak, Malay coconut rice. Many cooks at the stalls, and in the home, make up batches of different sambals to be stored and used for quickly made dishes like this one. At the hawker stalls the aubergines are generally deep-fried, but they could be baked in the oven instead. Serve terung sambal as a snack with bread or as a side dish with rice or grilled meats.

SERVES TWO TO FOUR

INGREDIENTS

- 6 shallots, chopped
- 4 garlic cloves, chopped
- 2 red chillies, seeded and chopped
- 1 lemon grass stalk, trimmed and chopped
- 5ml/1 tsp shrimp paste
- 15ml/1 tbsp sesame oil
- 15–30ml/1–2 tbsp soy sauce
- 7.5ml/1½ tsp sugar
- 2 slender, purple aubergines (eggplants), partially peeled in strips and halved lengthways
- vegetable oil, for deep-frying

To garnish

- 1 green chilli, seeded and finely chopped
- a small bunch each of fresh mint and coriander (cilantro), stalks removed, finely chopped

1 Using a mortar and pestle or food processor, grind the shallots, garlic, chillies and lemon grass to a paste. Beat in the shrimp paste and mix well.

2 Heat the sesame oil in a small wok or heavy pan. Stir in the spice paste and cook until fragrant and brown. Stir in the soy sauce and sugar and cook until smooth. Remove from the heat.

3 Heat enough oil for deep-frying in a wok or heavy pan. Drop in the aubergine halves and fry until tender. Drain on kitchen paper, then press down the centre of each half to make a dip or shallow pouch. Arrange the aubergine halves on a plate and smear or brush them with the spicy sauce. Garnish with the chopped green chilli, mint and coriander leaves, and serve at room temperature.

Per Portion Energy 158Kcal/654kJ; Protein 1.6g; Carbohydrate 6.5g, of which sugars 5.1g; Fat 14.2g, of which saturates 1.8g; Cholesterol 0mg; Calcium 24mg; Fibre 2.7g; Sodium 271mg.

STIR-FRIED BITTER GOURD WITH SAMBAL

ACCORDING TO THE PRINCIPLES OF TRADITIONAL CHINESE MEDICINE, ANY FOOD THAT HAS A BITTER EDGE IS GOOD FOR CLEANSING THE LIVER AND CAN HELP TO BRING DOWN RAISED BLOOD PRESSURE. BITTER GOURD, ALSO KNOWN AS BITTER MELON, FULFILS THIS ROLE BRILLIANTLY. ITS TANGINESS, WHICH COMES FROM THE HIGH LEVELS OF QUININE IT CONTAINS, IS APPETIZING AS WELL AS BENEFICIAL, AND THE PIQUANT SAMBAL ENHANCES THE TASTE GREATLY.

SERVES FOUR

INGREDIENTS
1 whole bitter gourd
30ml/2 tbsp oil
30ml/2 tbsp sambal goreng (fried chilli paste)
100ml/3½fl oz/scant ½ cup water
5ml/1 tsp sugar
15ml/1 tbsp lime juice

1 Cut the bitter gourd in half down its length. Use a spoon to scoop out the pith and red seeds. Slice into half moon pieces each 1cm/¹/₂in wide.

2 Bring a pan of water to the boil and blanch the bitter gourd for 2 minutes. Drain. This removes some bitterness and shortens the cooking time.

3 Heat the oil and fry the sambal goreng for just 1 minute, as it is already cooked. Add the pieces of gourd and stir-fry rapidly for 3 minutes.

4 Add the water, sugar and lime juice and continue to stir for another 2 minutes until the ingredients are well blended. Serve hot.

Per portion Energy 72Kcal/299kJ; Protein 1.3g; Carbohydrate 3.9g, of which sugars 3.3g; Fat 5.8g, of which saturates 0.8g; Cholesterol 0mg; Calcium 41mg; Fibre 1.3g; Sodium 1mg.

NONYA CABBAGE IN COCONUT MILK

IN MELAKA AND JOHOR, WHERE THE CULINARY CULTURE IS DOMINATED BY THE CHINESE, MALAYS AND PERANAKANS, NONYA CUISINE FLOURISHES. WITH GOOD AGRICULTURAL GROUND, THERE IS AN ABUNDANCE OF VEGETABLES WHICH, IN THIS PART OF MALAYSIA, ARE OFTEN COOKED IN COCONUT MILK. FOR THIS DISH, YOU COULD USE GREEN BEANS, CURLY KALE, OR ANY TYPE OF CABBAGE, ALL OF WHICH ARE DELICIOUS SERVED WITH STEAMED, BRAISED OR GRILLED FISH DISHES.

SERVES FOUR

INGREDIENTS

4 shallots, chopped
2 garlic cloves, chopped
1 lemon grass stalk, trimmed
and chopped
25g/1oz fresh root ginger, peeled
and chopped
2 red chillies, seeded and chopped
5ml/1 tsp shrimp paste
5ml/1 tsp turmeric powder
5ml/1 tsp palm sugar (jaggery)
15ml/1 tbsp sesame or groundnut
(peanut) oil
400ml/14fl oz/1⅔ cups coconut milk
450g/1lb Chinese leaves (Chinese
cabbage) or kale, cut into thick
ribbons, or pak choi (bok choy),
separated into leaves, or a mixture
of the two
salt and ground black pepper

VARIATION
To make a one-pot vegetable dish,
include a mixture of vegetables such as
string beans, carrots and leeks. You
could also add toasted peanuts or
cashews for protein and crunch.

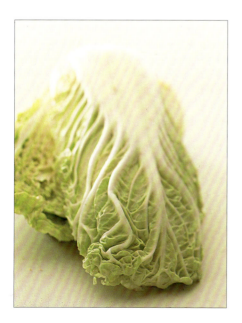

1 First prepare the paste. Using a mortar and pestle or food processor, grind the shallots, garlic, lemon grass, ginger and chillies. Beat in the shrimp paste, turmeric and sugar.

2 Heat the oil in a wok or heavy pan, and stir in the spice paste. Cook, stirring continuously until the fragrances are released and the paste is beginning to colour.

3 Slowly pour in the coconut milk, mixing well, and bring the mixture to the boil. Simmer it to allow it to thicken into a creamy sauce.

4 Drop in the cabbage leaves, coating them in the coconut milk, and cook for a minute or two until the leaves have wilted. Season to taste and serve immediately in a warmed dish.

Per Portion Energy 112Kcal/469kJ; Protein 2.1g; Carbohydrate 13g, of which sugars 12.6g; Fat 6.1g, of which saturates 1g; Cholesterol 0mg; Calcium 89mg; Fibre 2.6g; Sodium 119mg.

STIR-FRIED LONG BEANS <u>WITH</u> CHILLI SAUCE

YOU CAN USE LONG (SNAKE) BEANS, FRENCH (GREEN) BEANS OR EVEN MANGETOUTS FOR THIS NUTRITIOUS VEGETARIAN DISH, AND ADJUST THE AMOUNT OF CHILLI SAUCE TO YOUR OWN TASTE. AS WITH MOST STIR-FRIED VEGETABLE DISHES, IT IS ALWAYS BETTER TO BLANCH THE VEGETABLES BEFORE FRYING SO THAT THEY TAKE UP THE SEASONINGS EFFECTIVELY AND COOK QUICKLY.

<u>SERVES FOUR</u>

INGREDIENTS
    400g/14oz long (snake) beans
    30ml/2 tbsp oil
    2 garlic cloves, crushed
    5ml/1 tsp sugar
    30ml/2 tbsp chilli sauce, or amount
      to taste
    100ml/3½fl oz/scant ½ cup water

1 Trim the beans and cut them into 7.5cm/3in lengths. Bring a pan of water to the boil and blanch the beans for 2 minutes, then drain.

2 Heat the oil in a wok or heavy pan, add the garlic and fry until golden brown. Add the sugar and chilli sauce. Stir for 30 seconds then add the blanched beans. Stir rapidly for 2–3 minutes.

3 Add the water and bring quickly to the boil. Cook, stirring, until the beans are nearly dry. Serve hot with rice.

Per portion Energy 86Kcal/356kJ; Protein 2g; Carbohydrate 6.4g, of which sugars 5.4g; Fat 6g, of which saturates 0.8g; Cholesterol 0mg; Calcium 38mg; Fibre 2.3g; Sodium 122mg.

CHINESE STEAMED WINTER MELON WITH BARLEY

TO THE CHINESE, ALL PARTS OF THE WINTER MELON, INCLUDING THE SEEDS, RIND, PULP AND JUICE, ARE REGARDED AS MEDICINAL AND GOOD FOR THE TREATMENT OF URINARY AND KIDNEY DISEASES. THE SKIN ALSO HAS ANTISEPTIC AND ANALGESIC PROPERTIES. IN THIS RECIPE THE SKIN OF THE MELON CAN BE USED AS THE CONTAINER FOR A SIMPLE, WARMING SOUP THICKENED WITH BARLEY.

SERVES FOUR

INGREDIENTS

1 whole winter melon (about
  1.2kg/2½lb)
45ml/3 tbsp hulled or pearl barley
600ml/1 pint/2½ cups very
  hot water
15ml/1 tbsp preserved winter melon
  (tung chai)
5ml/1 tsp salt
15ml/1 tbsp sesame oil
ground black pepper

1 Soak the barley in enough water to cover for several hours, or boil for 20 minutes, to reconstitute the grain. Drain and discard the water.

2 If using the skin as a bowl, cut a slice about 4cm/1½in from the top of the melon and reserve. Cut around the edge of the melon flesh, about 2.5cm/1in away from the outer skin. Cut out the pith, leaving a deep hollow in the melon (be careful not to puncture the skin).

3 Place the whole melon in a deep dish, or use a deep bowl, and place in a steamer that has a high-domed lid. Pour the hot water into the bowl or shell and stir in the reserved melon flesh, barley, salt and sesame oil. Replace the melon "lid" or cover the bowl, and steam for 30 minutes.

4 At the end of the cooking time the barley grains should be plump and very soft. Season to taste with black pepper.

5 Serve the winter melon while piping hot, straight from the steamer in its steaming dish. Diners can eat the filling, then scoop out flesh from the sides of the melon shell for eating afterwards.

Per portion Energy 125Kcal/529kJ; Protein 2.2g; Carbohydrate 23.4g, of which sugars 14g; Fat 3.2g, of which saturates 0.4g; Cholesterol 0mg; Calcium 35mg; Fibre 1g; Sodium 569mg.

BRINJALS IN PEPPER GRAVY

THIS WAS ORIGINALLY A CLASSIC NONYA DISH CALLED KUAH LADA, CALLING FOR BRINJALS (AUBERGINE), SALT FISH AND MEAT IN A HEARTY, PEPPERY TAMARIND STOCK. THIS IS A MODIFIED VEGETARIAN VERSION BUT IT TASTES JUST AS GOOD. IN MALAYSIA AND SINGAPORE, THE LOCAL VARIETY OF AUBERGINE IS LONG AND THIN AND RANGES IN COLOUR FROM WHITE TO GREEN, YELLOW AND PURPLE, WITH A LESS COTTONY TEXTURE THAN THE NORMAL FAT PURPLE KIND.

SERVES FOUR

INGREDIENTS

45ml/3 tbsp vegetable oil
1 large aubergine (eggplant)
500ml/17fl oz/generous 2 cups water
30ml/2 tbsp tamarind concentrate
2 stalks lemon grass, trimmed to
   7.5cm/3in of the root end, bruised
5ml/1 tsp salt
For the spice paste
3 red chillies, seeded and chopped
5 candlenuts
3 garlic cloves, chopped
8 shallots, chopped
15ml/1 tbsp black peppercorns
15g/½oz galangal, chopped
15g/½oz fresh turmeric, chopped

1 Grind all the ingredients for the spice paste together until fine, using a mortar and pestle or a food processor. Heat the oil in a pan and fry this spice paste for about 2 minutes, then stir in the water and tamarind concentrate. Bring to the boil before adding the lemon grass and salt. Turn the heat down slightly.

2 Leave the stock to simmer for 3 minutes while you slice the aubergine in half lengthways and cut it into half moon shapes about 2cm/¾in thick.

3 Add the aubergine to the stock and simmer for 15 minutes until soft. Adjust the seasoning and serve hot with rice.

Per portion Energy 122Kcal/506kJ; Protein 2.3g; Carbohydrate 8.5g, of which sugars 5.8g; Fat 9.1g, of which saturates 1.1g; Cholesterol 0mg; Calcium 35mg; Fibre 2.6g; Sodium 6mg.

COCONUT VEGETABLE STEW

THIS DISH, KNOWN AS LODEH, IS OF INDONESIAN ORIGIN BUT HAS BEEN ENTRENCHED IN THE CUISINES OF MALAYSIA AND SINGAPORE FOR A LONG TIME. THERE IS A POPULAR MALAY HAWKER DISH CALLED LONTONG, A COMPRESSED STEAMED RICE ROLL, THAT IS OFTEN CUT INTO BITESIZE PIECES AND SERVED WITH A VEGETABLE STEW OF THIS KIND, SOMETIMES WITH CHICKEN ADDED. THE VEGETABLES YOU USE FOR THE STEW ARE A MATTER OF PERSONAL CHOICE.

SERVES FOUR

INGREDIENTS

    1 large potato
    1 large carrot
    150g/5oz cabbage
    1 green or purple aubergine
     (eggplant)
    45ml/3 tbsp vegetable oil
    500ml/17fl oz/generous 2 cups
     coconut milk
    5ml/1 tsp salt
    5ml/1 tsp sugar
For the spice paste
    4 candlenuts
    8 shallots, chopped
    10ml/2 tsp shrimp paste
    15ml/1 tbsp dried shrimp,
     soaked until soft
    15g/½oz fresh turmeric, chopped
    3 garlic, cloves
    5 dried red chillies, softened in
     warm water

1 Peel the potatoes and cut them into thick slices. Peel the carrot and cut into batons about 1cm/½in thick and 7.5cm/3in long. Cut the cabbage into chunky pieces and slice the aubergine into 1cm/½in thick rounds.

COOK'S TIP
As well as the vegetables listed here, you could use courgettes (zucchini), French (green) or long (snake) beans for this dish.

2 Grind all the ingredients for the spice paste together until smooth. Heat the oil in a pan and fry the spice paste for 2 minutes or until fragrant. Add the coconut milk, salt and sugar.

3 Stir in all the vegetables. Return the liquid to the boil then lower the heat and cover the pan. Simmer the stew for 30 minutes, checking often to see that the vegetables do not get overcooked. Serve the stew hot with rice or bread.

Per portion Energy 120Kcal/502kJ; Protein 1.8g; Carbohydrate 8.3g, of which sugars 8g; Fat 9.2g, of which saturates 1.3g; Cholesterol 0mg; Calcium 44mg; Fibre 3.4g; Sodium 107mg.

THREE VEGETABLES STIR-FRY

STIR-FRYING HAS CAUGHT ON ALL OVER THE WORLD IN RECENT DECADES, AND MOST CHEFS WILL ACKNOWLEDGE THAT IT IS ARGUABLY THE HEALTHIEST WAY TO COOK VEGETABLES. WHEN STIR-FRIED THEY TASTE CRUNCHY AND RETAIN THEIR NUTRIENTS, WHICH ARE MOSTLY SOLUBLE. THEY ALSO TAKE ONLY MINUTES TO PREPARE, LIKE THIS THREESOME, WHICH YOU CAN TWEAK TO YOUR PERSONAL TASTE USING THE VEGETABLES THAT YOU LIKE BEST.

SERVES FOUR

INGREDIENTS

    100g/3¾oz mangetouts (snow peas)
    100g/3¾oz baby corn cobs
    100g/3¾oz water chestnuts
    30ml/2 tbsp vegetable oil
    15ml/1 tbsp sesame oil
    2 garlic cloves
    30ml/2 tbsp yellow bean sauce

1 Top and tail the mangetouts. Cut each corn cob into two and slice the water chestnuts into thin rings.

2 Heat the oils in a wok or large, heavy pan. Crush the garlic and fry in the oil for 1 minute. Add all the prepared vegetables and the yellow bean sauce and stir-fry rapidly over high heat so that all the pieces cook evenly.

3 Sprinkle a scant 30ml/1 tbsp of water over the vegetables, just to moisten them – this dish is not meant to be water-logged – stir for 30 seconds and serve immediately.

Per portion Energy 103Kcal/427kJ; Protein 2.9g; Carbohydrate 3.9g, of which sugars 2g; Fat 8.6g, of which saturates 1.1g; Cholesterol 0mg; Calcium 24mg; Fibre 1.8g; Sodium 316mg.

CHINESE CHIVES WITH TOFU STIR-FRY

THESE CHIVES, ALSO KNOWN AS GARLIC CHIVES, ARE DIFFERENT FROM THE VARIETY USED AS A HERB IN THE WEST, BEING THICKER AND WITH A MORE PRONOUNCED AROMA. IN TRADITIONAL CHINESE MEDICINE THEY ARE VALUED FOR THEIR BLOOD-PURIFYING PROPERTIES AND ARE PURPORTED TO ALLEVIATE IMPOTENCE — A GOOD ENOUGH REASON TO EAT A WHOLE PLATEFUL EVERY NOW AND THEN. THE TOFU REQUIRED FOR THIS DISH IS THE FIRM VARIETY.

SERVES FOUR

INGREDIENTS

275g/10oz Chinese chives
8 pieces of firm tofu (bean curd),
  7.5cm/3in square and 4cm/1½in
  thick
30ml/2 tbsp vegetable oil
2 garlic cloves, crushed
30ml/2 tbsp light soy sauce
90ml/3 fl oz/¼ cup water

COOK'S TIP
Chinese or garlic chives are now widely available in supermarkets as well as in Asian markets. Both the leaves and the flower stems can be used.

1 Cut the chives into 7.5cm/3in lengths, wash and drain. Remove any that are tired-looking.

2 Cut each tofu cake into four. Heat the oil and fry them lightly until just brown.

3 Push the tofu aside and fry the garlic until light brown, then add the chives.

4 Stir-fry rapidly over high heat for 2 minutes. Add the soy sauce and water and stir for 2 minutes. Serve hot.

Per portion Energy 125Kcal/516kJ; Protein 8.2g; Carbohydrate 2.3g, of which sugars 1.8g; Fat 9.2g, of which saturates 1.1g; Cholesterol 0mg; Calcium 501mg; Fibre 1.5g; Sodium 633mg.

MUSHROOMS AND BAMBOO SHOOTS IN YELLOW BEAN SAUCE

YELLOW BEAN SAUCE HAS A LOVELY, NUTTY TANG THAT BLENDS WELL WITH MOST INGREDIENTS. IT IS EASILY OBTAINED FROM ASIAN MARKETS OR MANY LARGE SUPERMARKETS. THE MUSHROOMS CAN BE CHINESE DRIED CEPS, FRESH SHIITAKE OR FIELD MUSHROOMS, OR SEVERAL DIFFERENT TYPES.

SERVES FOUR

INGREDIENTS
150g/5oz mushrooms, any type, soaked until soft if dried
150g/5oz canned bamboo shoots
30ml/2 tbsp vegetable oil
2 spring onions (scallions), chopped
30g/2 tbsp yellow bean sauce
5ml/1 tsp sugar
175ml/6 fl oz/¾ cup water
5ml/1 tsp cornflour (cornstarch), blended with a little water
30ml/2 tbsp sesame oil

1 Cut each mushroom in half. Drain the bamboo shoots and rinse under cold running water, then drain again.

2 Heat the oil in a wok or large, heavy pan and fry the spring onions for 1 minute. Add the yellow bean sauce. Fry for 1 minute, then add the mushrooms and sliced bamboo shoots. Stir-fry over a high heat for about 2 minutes.

3 Add the sugar, water and cornflour blended with a little water. This will thicken the sauce very quickly. Stir for another minute.

4 Add the sesame oil, stir rapidly for 1 minute more and serve at once.

Per portion Energy 83Kcal/346kJ; Protein 2.4g; Carbohydrate 5.3g, of which sugars 2.4g; Fat 6g, of which saturates 0.7g; Cholesterol 0mg; Calcium 18mg; Fibre 1.5g; Sodium 34mg.

BRAISED TOFU <u>WITH</u> MIXED MUSHROOMS

FOUR DIFFERENT KINDS OF MUSHROOMS ARE INCLUDED IN THIS RECIPE AND THEY FLAVOUR THE TOFU BEAUTIFULLY TO MAKE A PERFECT VEGETARIAN MAIN COURSE. THE DISH HAS AN UNMISTAKABLY CHINESE TASTE, THANKS TO THE FLAVOURS OF SOY SAUCE, GINGER AND CHINESE RICE WINE.

SERVES FOUR

INGREDIENTS
  350g/12oz tofu (bean curd)
  2.5ml/½ tsp sesame oil
  10ml/2 tsp light soy sauce
  15ml/1 tbsp vegetable oil
  2 garlic cloves, finely chopped
  2.5ml/½ tsp grated fresh root ginger
  115g/4oz/1 cup fresh shiitake
    mushrooms, stalks removed
  175g/6oz/1½ cups fresh oyster
    mushrooms
  115g/4oz/1 cup drained, canned
    straw mushrooms
  115g/4oz/1 cup button mushrooms,
    cut in half
  15ml/1 tbsp Chinese rice wine or
    dry sherry
  15ml/1 tbsp dark soy sauce
  90ml/6 tbsp vegetable stock
  5ml/1 tsp cornflour (cornstarch),
    blended to a paste with a little
    cold water
  salt and ground white pepper
  2 spring onions (scallions),
    shredded

1 Put the tofu in a dish and sprinkle with the sesame oil, light soy sauce and a large pinch of pepper. Leave to marinate for 10 minutes, then drain and cut into 2.5 x 1cm/1 x ½in pieces.

2 Heat the vegetable oil in a wok. When it is very hot, fry the chopped garlic and ginger for a few seconds, taking care to stir it and prevent it from burning. Add all the mushrooms and stir-fry for 2 minutes.

COOK'STIP
In Asian dishes, aim to use a good, light vegetable oil for frying rather than a fruity or heavy variety such as extra-virgin olive oil. Corn, soya, peanut or pure olive oil are all good for stir-frying as they can be heated to high temperatures without smoking and tainting the food.

3 Stir in the wine or sherry, soy sauce and stock, with salt, if needed, and pepper. Simmer for 4 minutes.

4 Stir in the cornflour paste and cook, stirring, until thickened.

5 Carefully add the pieces of bean curd, toss gently to coat thoroughly and simmer for 2 minutes. Scatter the shredded spring onions over the the mixture, transfer to a serving dish and serve immediately.

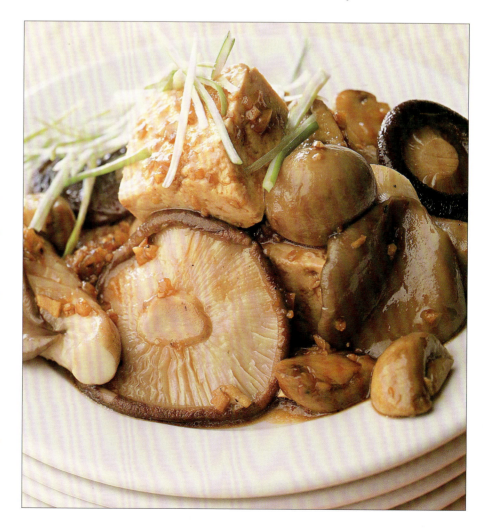

Per portion Energy 116Kcal/483kJ; Protein 9.6g; Carbohydrate 1.7g, of which sugars 1g; Fat 7.5g, of which saturates 1g; Cholesterol 0mg; Calcium 456mg; Fibre 1.4g; Sodium 456mg.

ROASTED VEGETABLES WITH PEANUT SAUCE

SERVED AS A VEGETABLE SIDE DISH OR AS A MAIN COURSE, A SELECTION OF BLANCHED, FRIED, GRILLED OR ROASTED VEGETABLES IN A PEANUT SAUCE, ENHANCED BY THE USUAL CHILLIES, SOY SAUCE AND OTHER FLAVOURINGS, IS A GREAT FAVOURITE THROUGHOUT SOUTH-EAST ASIA, ESPECIALLY WITH THE MALAYS AND PERANAKANS, WHO OFTEN EAT IT AS A SNACK WITH BREAD.

SERVES FOUR

INGREDIENTS

    1 long, slender aubergine (eggplant),
      partially peeled and cut into long
      strips
    2 courgettes (zucchini), partially
      peeled and cut into long strips
    1 thick, long sweet potato, cut into
      long strips
    2 leeks, trimmed, halved widthways
      and lengthways
    2 garlic cloves, chopped
    25g/1oz fresh root ginger, peeled
      and chopped
    60ml/4 tbsp vegetable or groundnut
      (peanut) oil
    salt
    30ml/3 tbsp roasted peanuts,
      coarsely ground, to garnish
    fresh crusty bread, to serve
For the sauce
    4 garlic cloves, chopped
    2–3 red chillies, seeded and
      chopped
    5ml/1 tsp shrimp paste
    115g/4oz/1 cup roasted peanuts,
      crushed
    15–30ml/1–2 tbsp dark soy sauce
    juice of 1 lime
    5–10ml/1–2 tsp Chinese
      rice vinegar
    10ml/2 tsp palm sugar (jaggery) or
      clear honey
    salt and ground black pepper

COOK'S TIP
Aim to cut all the vegetables to a similar size and shape, so that they cook in roughly the same time. Long thin strips look good and give lots of sharp edges that will draw in the heat and brown and crisp appetizingly while the centres are still deliciously soft. The final peanut garnish adds extra crunch: the nuts should not be ground too fine.

1 Preheat the oven to 200°C/400°F/Gas 6. Arrange the vegetables in a shallow oven dish. Using a mortar and pestle or food processor, grind the garlic and ginger to a paste, and smear it evenly over the vegetables. Sprinkle with a little salt and pour over the oil.

2 Place the dish in the oven for about 45 minutes, until the vegetables are tender and slightly browned – toss them in the oil halfway through cooking.

3 Using a mortar and pestle or food processor, grind the garlic and chillies to a paste then beat in the other ingredients, with salt and pepper to taste. Blend with water to pouring (half-and-half) cream consistency.

4 Arrange the vegetables on a serving dish and drizzle the sauce over them. Sprinkle the ground peanuts over the top and serve warm with crusty bread.

Per Portion Energy 361Kcal/1502kJ; Protein 11.9g; Carbohydrate 22.7g, of which sugars 11.1g; Fat 25.4g, of which saturates 4.1g; Cholesterol 0mg; Calcium 76mg; Fibre 6.9g; Sodium 292mg.

POTATO CURRY WITH YOGURT

VARIATIONS OF THIS SIMPLE INDIAN CURRY ARE POPULAR AT THE MALAY AND MUSLIM STALLS, AND AT THE ROTI STALLS, WHERE IT IS SERVED WITH FLATBREAD. SOME SINGAPORE COFFEE SHOPS EVEN SERVE IT FOR BREAKFAST. MALAYS AND INDIANS USUALLY EAT IT WITH A MEAT CURRY AND RICE, BUT IT IS ALSO DELICIOUS ON ITS OWN, SERVED WITH YOGURT AND A SPICY PICKLE OR CHUTNEY.

SERVES FOUR

INGREDIENTS

6 garlic cloves, chopped
25g/1oz fresh root ginger, peeled
  and chopped
30ml/2 tbsp ghee, or 15ml/1 tbsp oil
  and 15g/½oz/1 tbsp butter
6 shallots, halved lengthways and
  sliced along the grain
2 green chillies, seeded and
  finely sliced
10ml/2 tsp sugar
a handful of fresh or dried
  curry leaves
2 cinnamon sticks
5–10ml/1–2 tsp ground turmeric

15ml/1 tbsp garam masala
500g/1¼lb waxy potatoes, cut into
  bitesize pieces
2 tomatoes, peeled, seeded
  and quartered
250ml/8fl oz/1 cup Greek (US
  strained plain) yogurt
salt and ground black pepper
5ml/1 tsp red chilli powder, and fresh
  coriander (cilantro) and mint leaves,
  finely chopped, to garnish
1 lemon, quartered, to serve

COOK'S TIP
This recipe also works well with sweet potatoes, butternut squash or pumpkin, all of which absorb the flavours.

1 Using a mortar and pestle or a food processor, grind the garlic and ginger to a coarse paste. Heat the ghee in a heavy pan and stir in the shallots and chillies, until fragrant. Add the garlic and ginger paste with the sugar, and stir until the mixture begins to colour. Stir in the curry leaves, cinnamon sticks, turmeric and garam masala, and toss in the potatoes, turning them over to make sure they are well coated in the spice mixture.

2 Pour in just enough cold water to cover the potatoes. Bring to the boil, then reduce the heat and simmer until the potatoes are just cooked – they should still have a bite to them. Season with salt and pepper to taste.

3 Gently toss in the tomatoes to heat them through. Fold in the yogurt so that it is streaky rather than completely mixed in. Sprinkle with the chilli powder, coriander and mint. Serve immediately from the pan, with lemon to squeeze over it and flatbread for scooping it up.

Per Portion Energy 231Kcal/967kJ; Protein 6.7g; Carbohydrate 26.2g, of which sugars 7.4g; Fat 12.4g, of which saturates 4.1g; Cholesterol 0mg; Calcium 110mg; Fibre 2g; Sodium 63mg.

KAI LAN WITH KING PRAWNS

THIS ASIAN VEGETABLE COMES FROM THE SAME FAMILY AS TENDERSTEM BROCCOLI, AND IT IS A FAVOURITE AMONG THE CHINESE IN MALAYSIA AND SINGAPORE. THE LEAVES ARE DARK GREEN AND THE THICK STALKS HAVE A NICE CRUNCH. THE CLASSIC CONDIMENT IS OYSTER SAUCE, WHICH IS A COMPLETE SEASONING, OBVIATING THE NEED TO ADD ANYTHING ELSE.

SERVES TWO

INGREDIENTS
- 200g/7oz kai lan
- 200g/7oz king or tiger prawns (jumbo shrimp)
- 2 garlic cloves, crushed
- 30ml/2 tbsp oil
- 30g/2 tbsp oyster sauce
- ½ tsp ground black pepper
- 90ml/3fl oz/¼ cup water

1 Trim off the hard ends of the kai lan stalks and slice into diagonal pieces about 7.5cm/3in long. Wash and dry.

2 Shell the prawns, wash and pat dry. Remove the dark veins by making a slit down the back of each prawn.

3 Heat the oil in a wok or large, heavy pan until it is smoking and throw in the kai lan. Stir-fry for 2 minutes, then add the prawns.

COOK'S TIP
A good splash of Chinese wine adds a lovely flavour: add this at any time.

4 Continue to stir-fry for 2 minutes while adding oyster sauce, pepper and water.

5 When the leaves wilt a little, the vegetables are done. Serve at once.

Per portion Energy 225Kcal/939kJ; Protein 22.3g; Carbohydrate 6.1g, of which sugars 5.7g; Fat 12.5g, of which saturates 1.6g; Cholesterol 195mg; Calcium 137mg; Fibre 2.8g; Sodium 443mg.

AVIAL WITH ROASTED COCONUT

ORIGINALLY FROM SOUTHERN INDIA, THIS DELICIOUS DISH HAS FOUND ITS WAY INTO MANY MALAY HOMES. IN SINGAPORE, IT IS SERVED IN SOME COFFEE SHOPS AND AT THE INDIAN AND MALAY STALLS, WHERE IT IS OFTEN AMONG A SELECTION OF DISHES OFFERED TO ACCOMPANY RICE. FOR VEGETARIAN HINDUS, IT IS A POPULAR EVERYDAY DISH OR A TASTY SNACK, SERVED WITH INDIAN FLATBREAD. MADE WITH FIRM VEGETABLES, ROOTS AND GOURDS, ALL CUT INTO LONG BITESIZE PIECES, IT IS SUBSTANTIAL AND FLEXIBLE — CHOOSE YOUR OWN ASSORTMENT OF VEGETABLES, SUCH AS PUMPKIN, BUTTERNUT SQUASH, WINTER MELON, YAMS, AUBERGINES OR BEANS.

SERVES FOUR

INGREDIENTS
- 2–3 green chillies, seeded and chopped
- 25g/1oz fresh root ginger, peeled and chopped
- 5–10ml/1–2 tsp roasted cumin seeds
- 10ml/2 tsp sugar
- 5–10ml/1–2 tsp ground turmeric
- 1 cinnamon stick
- 5ml/1 tsp salt
- 2 carrots, cut into bitesize sticks
- 2 sweet potatoes, cut into bitesize sticks
- 2 courgettes (zucchini), partially peeled in strips, seeded and cut into bitesize sticks
- 1 green plantain, peeled and cut into bitesize sticks
- a small coil of long (snake) beans or a handful of French or green beans, cut into bitesize lengths
- a handful fresh curry leaves
- 1 fresh coconut, grated
- 250ml/8fl oz/1 cup Greek (US strained plain) yogurt
- salt and ground black pepper

1 Using a mortar and pestle or food processor, grind the chillies, ginger, roasted cumin seeds and sugar to a paste.

2 In a large, heavy pan, bring 450ml/15fl oz/scant 2 cups water to the boil. Stir in the turmeric, whole cinnamon stick and salt.

3 Add the carrots and cook for 1 minute. Add the sweet potatoes and cook for 2 minutes. Add the courgettes, plantain and beans and cook for a further 2 minutes.

4 Reduce the heat and stir in the spice paste and curry leaves.

5 Cook gently for 4–5 minutes, or until the vegetables are tender – but not soft and mushy – and the liquid volume has greatly reduced.

COOK'S TIPS
• Choose live yogurt if you can find it – the beneficial bacteria help to maintain good digestion.
• Plantains may be found in larger supermarkets, but a better selection of fruit and vegetables for cooking non-European cuisine is often available in small Caribbean or Asian stores.

6 Gently stir in half the grated coconut. Take the pan off the heat and fold in the yogurt. Season to taste with salt and pepper.

7 Quickly toast the remaining grated coconut in a heavy pan over a high heat, until nicely browned. Meanwhile, heat serving plates in the oven.

8 Sprinkle a little toasted coconut over the vegetables in the pan, then divide the avial between individual plates.

9 Serve hot, with the rest of the coconut and warmed flatbreads on the side for people to help themselves.

Per Portion Energy 419Kcal/1753kJ; Protein 9.9g; Carbohydrate 47.7g, of which sugars 19.4g; Fat 23g, of which saturates 16.9g; Cholesterol 0mg; Calcium 176mg; Fibre 9g; Sodium 104mg.

ULAM VEGETABLES

THE TERM ULAM REFERS TO THE PREPARATION OF FRESH VEGETABLES TO BE EATEN RAW WITH SPICES, A THROWBACK TO THE DIETARY HABITS OF MALAYSIAN JUNGLE DWELLERS, WHO ATE WITH THEIR FINGERS. THIS METHOD EVOLVED INTO THE MAINSTREAM MALAY STYLE OF EATING, AND ENTERED THE NONYA CULINARY REALM. ULAM IS ALWAYS SERVED COLD BUT CAN BE EATEN WITH WARM RICE.

SERVES FOUR

INGREDIENTS
    130g/4½oz long (snake) beans
    1 cucumber
    130g/4½oz cabbage
    2 stalks lemon grass
    2 red chillies
    30ml/2 tbsp vegetable oil
    small bunch of sweet basil
    5m/1 tsp salt
    5ml/1 tsp sugar
    30ml/2 tbsp lime juice
    500g/1¼lb cooked rice,
        cold or warm
For the spice paste
    30ml/2 tbsp dried shrimp
    3 red chillies
    15ml/1 tbsp shrimp paste
    3 garlic cloves, chopped
    4 shallots, chopped

1 Cut the long beans into small dice. Peel and seed the cucumber and cut it and the cabbage into similar-sized dice. Finely slice 5cm/2in of the root end of the lemon grass stalks and the chillies.

2 Grind together all the ingredients for the spice paste until fine. Heat the oil in a small pan and fry the paste for 3 minutes, until fragrant.

3 Put the prepared vegetables in a large bowl. Toss with the cooked rice and fried spices and add the salt, sugar and lime juice.

4 For an authentically rustic touch, serve the vegetable mixture on a banana leaf and get everyone to eat it with their fingers. Provide finger bowls, with a squeeze of lemon.

Per portion Energy 287Kcal/1211kJ; Protein 12g; Carbohydrate 45.1g, of which sugars 4.3g; Fat 7.8g, of which saturates 1.1g; Cholesterol 57mg; Calcium 197mg; Fibre 2.3g; Sodium 984mg.

CUCUMBER AND SHALLOT SALAD

IN MALAYSIA AND SINGAPORE, THIS LIGHT, REFRESHING SALAD IS SERVED WITH INDIAN FOOD ALMOST AS OFTEN AS COOLING MINT-FLAVOURED CUCUMBER RAITA. THE MALAYS ALSO ENJOY THIS SALAD WITH MANY OF THEIR SPICY FISH AND GRILLED MEAT DISHES. IT CAN BE MADE AHEAD OF TIME AND KEPT IN THE REFRIGERATOR. SERVE IT AS A SALAD OR A RELISH.

SERVES FOUR

INGREDIENTS
  1 cucumber, peeled, halved
    lengthways and seeded
  4 shallots, halved lengthways and
    sliced finely along the grain
  1–2 green chillies, seeded and sliced
    finely lengthways
  60ml/4 tbsp coconut milk
  5–10ml/1–2 tsp cumin seeds,
    dry-roasted and ground to a powder
  salt
  1 lime, quartered, to serve

1 Slice the cucumber halves finely and sprinkle with salt. Set aside for about 15 minutes. Rinse well and drain off any excess water.

2 Put the cucumber, shallots and chillies in a bowl. Pour in the coconut milk and toss well. Sprinkle most of the roasted cumin over the top. Just before serving, toss the salad again, season with salt, and sprinkle the rest of the roasted cumin over the top. Serve with lime wedges to squeeze over the salad.

Per Portion Energy 17Kcal/68kJ; Protein 0.7g; Carbohydrate 3.3g, of which sugars 2.7g; Fat 0.1g, of which saturates 0g; Cholesterol 0mg; Calcium 19mg; Fibre 0.7g; Sodium 15mg.

FRIED TOFU SALAD <u>WITH</u> A TANGY SAUCE

A GREAT FAVOURITE AT THE HAWKER STALLS, FRIED TOFU CAN EITHER BE STUFFED WITH BEANSPROUTS AND CUCUMBER AND THEN DRIZZLED WITH A SAUCE, OR ARRANGED AS A SALAD ON A PLATE. EITHER WAY, TAHU GORENG, AS THIS SALAD IS KNOWN, IS TANGY AND REFRESHING, AN IDEAL ACCOMPANIMENT TO GRILLED MEATS AND STIR-FRIED NOODLES. THE MALAYS, PERANAKANS AND EURASIANS ALL ENJOY THIS DISH, SO THE SAUCE VARIES FROM STALL TO STALL ACCORDING TO TASTE.

SERVES FOUR

INGREDIENTS
- vegetable oil, for deep-frying
- 450g/1lb firm tofu (bean curd), rinsed, patted dry and cut into thick rectangular slices
- 1 small cucumber, partially peeled in strips, seeded and shredded
- 2 spring onions (scallions), trimmed, halved and shredded
- 2 handfuls of fresh beansprouts rinsed and drained
- fresh coriander (cilantro) leaves, to garnish

For the sauce
- 30ml/2 tbsp tamarind pulp, soaked in water until soft
- 15ml/1 tbsp sesame or groundnut (peanut) oil
- 4 shallots, finely chopped
- 4 garlic cloves, finely chopped
- 2 red chillies, seeded
- 2.5ml/½ tsp shrimp paste
- 115g/4oz/1 cup roasted peanuts, crushed
- 30–45ml/2–3 tbsp kecap manis
- 15ml/1 tbsp tomato ketchup

COOK'S TIP
If you cannot find kecap manis, which consists of soy sauce sweetened with palm sugar (jaggery), you could switch to ordinary soy sauce and increase the tomato ketchup to achieve a balance of sweet and sour in the sauce.

1 First make the sauce. Squeeze the tamarind pulp to soften it in the water, and then strain through a sieve. Measure 120ml/4fl oz/½ cup of the tamarind liquid. Discard the pulp.

2 Heat the oil in a wok and stir in the shallots, garlic and chillies, until fragrant. Stir in the shrimp paste and the peanuts. Add the kecap manis, ketchup and tamarind liquid and mix to a thick sauce. Leave to cool.

3 Heat enough oil for deep-frying in a wok or heavy pan. Slip in the blocks of tofu and fry until golden brown all over.

4 Remove the tofu from the pan and pat dry on kitchen paper. Cut each block into long, thin slices.

5 Arrange the tofu slices on a serving plate with the cucumber, spring onions and beansprouts.

6 Spoon the sauce over the tofu or serve it separately in a bowl. Garnish the salad with the coriander leaves.

Per Portion Energy 423Kcal/1749kJ; Protein 17.9g; Carbohydrate 7.8g, of which sugars 4.5g; Fat 35.8g, of which saturates 5.3g; Cholesterol 0mg; Calcium 607mg; Fibre 2.8g; Sodium 296mg.

BRIDAL SALAD

ACTUALLY MORE A FIERY SAMBAL THAN A SALAD, DESPITE ITS NAME, THIS DISH IS DE RIGUEUR AT TRADITIONAL PERANAKAN AND MALAY WEDDINGS. IT HAS MUCH SYMBOLIC MEANING TO ENSURE THAT THE BRIDE WILL GO ON TO HAVE A GOOD, FERTILE LIFE AND BEAR HER HUSBAND MANY OFFSPRING. IT MAKES VERY GOOD EATING AT ANY TIME, EVEN IF IT IS TONGUE-SEARINGLY HOT.

SERVES FOUR

INGREDIENTS
    10 fresh red chillies
    10 fresh green chillies
    45ml/3 tbsp vegetable oil
    4 kaffir lime leaves
    350ml/12fl oz/1½ cups
      coconut milk
    30ml/2 tbsp lime juice
    5ml/1 tsp salt
    5ml/1 tsp sugar
For the spice paste
    ½ large onion, chopped
    4 garlic cloves, chopped
    15ml/1 tbsp shrimp paste
    6 candlenuts

COOK'S TIP
You can add 200g/7oz of shelled prawns (shrimp) for a richer dish.

1 Remove the stalks from the chillies and slice each into two lengthways. Scoop out the seeds and remove some of the pith, where most of the heat is concentrated.

2 Heat the oil in a wok or heavy pan and fry the chillies for 2 minutes until they are slightly shrivelled. Remove them and set aside to cool.

3 Grind the ingredients for the spice paste until smooth. In the remaining oil, fry the spice paste for 2 minutes. Add the lime leaves, coconut milk, lime juice, salt and sugar and stir over medium heat for 3 minutes.

4 Return the fried chillies to the pan and stir for 1 minute. Serve with plain steamed rice.

Per portion Energy 137Kcal/570kJ; Protein 5.8g; Carbohydrate 8g, of which sugars 7g; Fat 9.3g, of which saturates 1.2g; Cholesterol 19mg; Calcium 106mg; Fibre 0.4g; Sodium

WINTER MELON PACHADI

Some varieties of pachadi and raita dishes, originating in southern India, are designed to cool the palate and aid digestion when eating hot, spicy food. These yogurt-based dishes are made with cooling vegetables and herbs, such as okra, courgette, spinach, pumpkin, cucumber with mint, and this refreshing winter melon.

SERVES FOUR

INGREDIENTS

225g/8oz winter melon, peeled, seeded and diced
5ml/1 tsp ground turmeric
5ml/1 tsp red chilli powder
300ml/½ pint/1¼ cups Greek (US strained plain) yogurt
2.5ml/½ tsp salt
2.5ml/½ tsp sugar
15g/½oz fresh root ginger, peeled and grated
1 green chilli, seeded and finely chopped
15ml/1 tbsp vegetable oil
1.5ml/¼ tsp ground asafoetida
5ml/1 tsp brown mustard seeds
8–10 dried curry leaves
1 dried red chilli, seeded and roughly chopped

COOK'S TIP

In Malaysia and Singapore, cooling Indian dishes like pachadi are often served at the Indian and Malay stalls and coffee shops to balance the hot curries and spicy grilled dishes. In many Indian households, the pachadi is made a day or two in advance, so that the flavours mingle.

1 Put the diced winter melon in a heavy pan with the turmeric and chilli powder and pour in enough water to just cover it. Bring to the boil and cook gently, uncovered, until the winter melon is tender and all the water has been absorbed or evaporated.

2 In a bowl, beat the yogurt with the salt and sugar until smooth and creamy. Add the ginger and green chilli, and fold in the warm winter melon.

3 Heat the oil in small heavy pan. Stir in the Asafoetida and the brown mustard seeds.

4 As soon as the mustard seeds begin to pop, stir in the curry leaves and dried chilli. When the chilli darkens, add the spices to the yogurt and mix thoroughly.

5 Allow the pachadi to reach room temperature before serving.

Per Portion Energy 127Kcal/527kJ; Protein 5.1g; Carbohydrate 5.3g, of which sugars 5.3g; Fat 10.5g, of which saturates 4.2g; Cholesterol 0mg; Calcium 120mg; Fibre 0.2g; Sodium 316mg.

KERABU

Kelantan in the north of Malaysia is well known for its rich traditional Malay cuisine, particularly nasi kerabu, the famous blue rice dish, and this beansprout salad, kerabu, which is served with it. In the Kota Bharu markets, up near the Thai border, the blue rice is wrapped in a banana leaf with kerabu and eaten as a snack – the first or last Malay snack when crossing the border. Kerabu is also served as a refreshing salad to accompany many of the highly spiced Malay dishes.

1 Dry-roast the coconut in a heavy pan until it is lightly browned and emits a nutty aroma. Using a mortar and pestle or a food processor, grind the roasted coconut to a coarse powder. Drain the soaked dried prawns and grind them coarsely too.

2 Put the vegetables, herbs and chillies into a bowl. Mix the lime juice with the sugar and pour it over the salad. Season with salt and pepper. Scatter the ground coconut and dried prawns over the salad, and toss well until thoroughly mixed.

SERVES FOUR

INGREDIENTS

115g/4oz fresh coconut, grated
30ml/2 tbsp dried prawns (shrimp),
 soaked in warm water until soft
225g/8oz beansprouts, rinsed
 and drained
1 small cucumber, peeled, seeded
 and cut into julienne strips
2–3 spring onions (scallions),
 trimmed, cut into 2.5cm/1in
 pieces and halved
 lengthways
a handful of young, tender
 mangetouts (snow peas),
 halved diagonally
a handful of green beans,
 halved lengthways
a handful of fresh chives,
 chopped into 2.5cm/1in pieces
a handful of fresh mint leaves,
 finely chopped
2–3 red chillies, seeded and sliced
 finely lengthways
juice of 2 limes
10ml/2 tsp sugar
salt and ground black pepper

Per Portion Energy 230Kcal/947kJ; Protein 12.6g; Carbohydrate 15.9g, of which sugars 13.9g; Fat 12.9g, of which saturates 10.2g; Cholesterol 0mg; Calcium 151mg; Fibre 7.8g; Sodium 24mg.

ROJAK

ORIGINALLY FROM INDONESIA, ROJAK HAS BEEN SO WELL INTEGRATED INTO THE CUISINE OF MALAYSIA AND SINGAPORE THAT THERE IS EVEN AN INDIAN VERSION MADE WITH HARD-BOILED EGGS, FRIED TOFU, SLICED FISH CAKES AND A SPICY SAUCE. THE CHINESE, PERANAKANS AND MALAYS ALL HAVE THEIR OWN VERSIONS, BUT ALL INCLUDE A SELECTION OF FRUIT AND VEGETABLES, BATHED IN A TANGY SAUCE. AS THIS RECIPE IS SO FLEXIBLE, YOU CAN REALLY USE ANY COMBINATION OR FRUIT AND VEGETABLES AND MAKE THE SAUCE AS PUNGENT AND FIERY AS YOU LIKE.

SERVES FOUR TO SIX

INGREDIENTS

1 jicama (sweet turnip), peeled and
   finely sliced
1 small cucumber, partially peeled
   and finely sliced
1 green mango, peeled and
   finely sliced
1 star fruit (carambola), finely sliced
4 slices fresh pineapple, cored
half a pomelo, separated into
   segments, with membrane removed
a handful of beansprouts, washed
   and drained
fresh mint leaves, to garnish
For the sauce
225g/8oz/2 cups roasted peanuts
4 garlic cloves, chopped
2–4 red chillies, seeded and chopped
10ml/2 tsp shrimp paste, dry-roasted
   in a pan over a high heat
15ml/1 tbsp tamarind paste
30ml/2 tbsp palm sugar (jaggery)
salt

1 First make the sauce. Using a mortar and pestle or food processor, grind the peanuts with the garlic and chillies to a coarse paste. Beat in the roasted shrimp paste, tamarind paste and sugar. Add enough water to make a thick, pouring sauce, and stir until the sugar has dissolved. Add salt to taste.

2 Arrange all the sliced fruit and vegetables on a plate, with the beansprouts scattered over the top.

3 Drizzle the sauce over the salad and garnish with mint leaves. Serve as an accompaniment to grilled (broiled) meats and spicy dishes, or on its own as a healthy snack.

Per Portion Energy 330Kcal/1381kJ; Protein 12.9g; Carbohydrate 28g, of which sugars 25.1g; Fat 19.3g, of which saturates 3.4g; Cholesterol 13mg; Calcium 114mg; Fibre 6.3g; Sodium 416mg.

SWEET SNACKS AND DRINKS

The abundant tropical fruit available at all times of year is often eaten to end a meal or as a refreshing snack during the day, either as it is or turned into cooling water ices or juices. The inhabitants of Malaysia and Singapore also enjoy a variety of very sweet snacks, oozing palm sugar, rich with coconut cream and eggs and fragrant with pandan and spices. Baked, fried or steamed, they are sold at the hawker stalls and eaten freshly made and still warm.

ROASTED COCONUT ICE CREAM

THE POPULARITY OF ICE CREAM IN MALAYSIA AND SINGAPORE ENSURES THAT, IN THE CITIES AT LEAST, YOU WILL NOT HAVE TO SEARCH FOR IT FOR VERY LONG. ICE CREAM TRUCKS SET THEMSELVES UP AT BUSY STREET CORNERS, IN SHOPPING CENTRES AND ENTERTAINMENT PARKS, SELLING AN EXOTIC SELECTION, WITH FLAVOURS RANGING FROM FRUITY PASSION FRUIT, MANGO, SOUR PLUM AND DURIAN TO RICH AND CREAMY COCONUT, AVOCADO AND CORN.

SERVES FOUR TO SIX

INGREDIENTS

    115g/4oz fresh coconut, finely
      chopped in a food processor
    4 large (US extra large) egg yolks
    115g/4oz/generous ½ cup sugar
    900ml/1½ pints/3¾ cups coconut
      milk
    250ml/8fl oz/1 cup double
      (heavy) cream
    25ml/1½ tbsp rice flour, blended
      with 30ml/2 tbsp coconut milk
      or cream
    salt

1 Roast the coconut in a heavy frying pan over a medium heat until nicely browned and emitting a nutty aroma. Transfer to a plate and leave to cool.

2 In a bowl, whisk the egg yolks with the sugar until pale and creamy. In a heavy pan, heat the coconut milk with the cream and a generous pinch of salt to scalding point. Gradually pour the hot coconut milk into the egg yolk mixture, whisking vigorously at the same time to form a smooth custard. Strain the custard into a clean heavy pan and stir it gently over a low heat, until slightly thickened.

3 Beat the rice flour mixture into the custard until it coats the back of a wooden spoon. Pour the custard into a bowl or freezer-proof container and leave to cool.

4 Stir most of the roasted coconut (reserve a little for decorating) into the cooled custard and put it in the freezer until frozen, taking it out and stirring after about half an hour. Alternatively, churn in an ice cream maker according to the manufacturer's instructions.

5 To serve, sprinkle the ice cream with the reserved roasted coconut.

Per Portion Energy 448Kcal/1863kJ; Protein 4.1g; Carbohydrate 32.5g, of which sugars 29.1g; Fat 34.3g, of which saturates 21.9g; Cholesterol 192mg; Calcium 95mg; Fibre 1.8g; Sodium 191mg.

LYCHEE SORBET

SORBETS ARE LOVELY ALTERNATIVES TO ICE CREAM, ESPECIALLY FOR THOSE WHO ARE WATCHING THEIR WEIGHT. THEY ARE EASY TO MAKE AND YOU CAN USE ANY SOFT FRUIT. THEY MAKE DELIGHTFUL TASTE CLEANSERS BETWEEN COURSES BUT ARE EQUALLY SATISFYING AS A DESSERT AT THE END OF A MEAL. MANY KINDS OF TROPICAL FRUIT MAKE SUCCESSFUL SORBETS, INCLUDING LIMES, MANGOES AND PAPAYAS, BUT FRAGRANT LYCHEE SORBET REMAINS A FAVOURITE.

SERVES FOUR

INGREDIENTS
    500g/1¼lb lychees, peeled and
      stoned (pitted)
    500ml/17fl oz/generous 2 cups
      lychee syrup
    juice of 2 limes
    fresh mint leaves, to decorate

COOK'S TIPS
Lychee syrup is available from supermarkets. If fresh lychees are not available you can make this sorbet using canned lychees and the syrup from the can. You can add 250ml/8fl oz/1 cup of single (light) cream or natural (plain) yogurt when processing the second time for an even smoother sorbet.

1 Process the lychees in a food processor with half the syrup until you get a smooth purée. Mix in the remaining syrup and the lime juice.

2 Pour into a large plastic container or ice cream tub, cover and place in the coldest part of the freezer.

3 Freeze the mixture for several hours until slushy. Return to the processor and blend until light and creamy. Return to the container and re-freeze until firm, preferably overnight.

4 Serve in individual bowls, decorated with a mint leaf or two.

Per portion Energy 249kcal/1064kJ; Protein 1.4g; Carbohydrate 64.7g, of which sugars 64.7g; Fat 0.1g, of which saturates 0g; Cholesterol 0mg; Calcium 31mg; Fibre 0.9g; Sodium 4mg.

SWEET PURÉED AVOCADO

THIS SWEET AVOCADO SNACK IS THOUGHT TO HAVE ORIGINATED WITH THE DUTCH IN MELAKA, BUT NOW IT IS ALSO SERVED IN PENANG AND SINGAPORE, WHERE IT IS POPULAR WITH THE SWEET-TOOTHED MALAYS, INDIANS, EURASIANS AND, OF COURSE, TOURISTS. IT CAN BE SERVED AS A THICK PURÉE OR BLENDED WITH COCONUT MILK UNTIL IT IS THE CONSISTENCY OF THICK POURING CREAM. IT CAN ALSO BE ENJOYED AS A DRINK WITH A COUPLE OF ICE CUBES STIRRED IN.

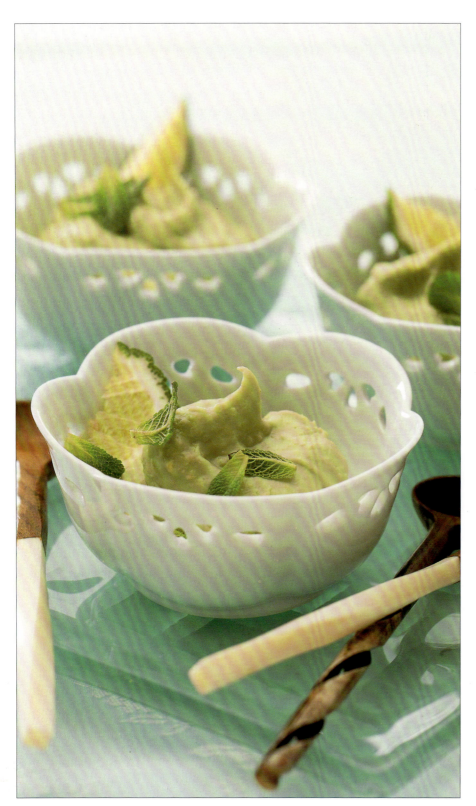

SERVES TWO

INGREDIENTS

    1 avocado, stoned (pitted)
    juice of ½ lime
    30ml/2 tbsp sweetened
      condensed milk
    30ml/2 tbsp coconut cream
    a pinch of salt
    fresh mint leaves, to decorate
    ½ lime, halved, to serve

1 Put the avocado flesh into a food processor and purée it with the lime juice. Add the condensed milk, coconut cream and salt and process until the mixture is smooth and creamy.

2 Spoon into individual bowls or glasses and chill over ice. Decorate with a few mint leaves and serve with lime wedges to squeeze over it.

VARIATION
This recipe works equally well with other soft-fleshed fruit, such as bananas, mango and papaya.

Per Portion Energy 243Kcal/1006kJ; Protein 3.2g; Carbohydrate 10.3g, of which sugars 9.2g; Fat 21.2g, of which saturates 8.5g; Cholesterol 5mg; Calcium 54mg; Fibre 2.6g; Sodium 421mg.

JELLIED MANGO PUDDINGS

LIGHT AND SOPHISTICATED, THESE INDIVIDUAL JELLIED MANGO PUDDINGS MAKE DELIGHTFUL AND ATTRACTIVE DESSERTS. SERVED WITH A SELECTION OF TROPICAL FRUITS SUCH AS THOSE SUGGESTED BELOW, THEY ADD A REFRESHING TOUCH TO THE END OF A SPICY MEAL. YOU ARE MORE LIKELY TO FIND ELEGANT LITTLE PUDDINGS OF THIS KIND IN THE DIM SUM RESTAURANTS OF SINGAPORE AND KUALA LUMPUR THAN AS A SWEET SNACK AT A HAWKER STALL.

SERVES FOUR

INGREDIENTS
    750ml/1¼ pints/3 cups
        coconut milk
    150g/5oz/¾ cup sugar
    15ml/1 tbsp powdered
        gelatine
    1 egg yolk
    1 large, ripe mango, stoned (pitted)
        and puréed
    4 slices ripe jackfruit or pineapple,
        quartered
    1 banana, cut into diagonal slices
    1 kiwi fruit, sliced
    4 lychees, peeled
    2 passion fruit, split open,
        to decorate

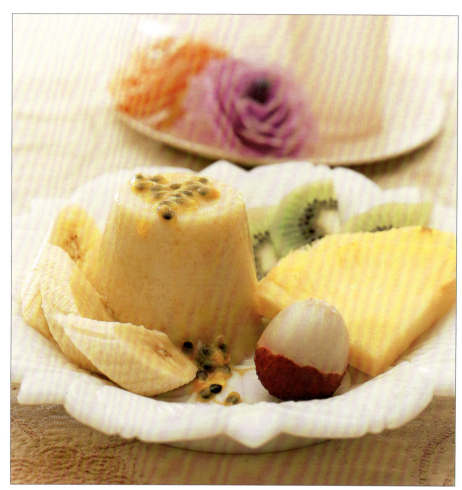

1 In a heavy pan, heat the coconut milk with the sugar, stirring all the time, until it has dissolved. Add the gelatine and keep stirring until it has dissolved. Remove from the heat. Beat the egg yolk with the mango purée.

2 Add the purée to the coconut milk and stir until smooth. Spoon the mixture into individual, lightly oiled moulds and leave to cool. Place them in the refrigerator and leave for 2–3 hours, until set.

VARIATION
The tangy fruitiness of mango is particularly delicious in these jellied puddings, but you could substitute papaya, banana, durian or avocado.

3 To serve, arrange the fruit on individual plates, leaving enough room for the jellies. Dip the base of each mould briefly into hot water, and then invert the puddings on to the plates. Lift off the moulds and decorate with passion fruit seeds.

Per Portion Energy 305Kcal/1300kJ; Protein 2.9g; Carbohydrate 72.6g, of which sugars 72g; Fat 2.4g, of which saturates 0.8g; Cholesterol 50mg; Calcium 109mg; Fibre 3g; Sodium 216mg.

SAGO PUDDING WITH PALM SUGAR SYRUP

IN SABAH AND SARAWAK, SAGO IS THE MAIN STAPLE AND THE SAGO PALM IS KNOWN AS THE "TREE OF A THOUSAND USES", AS IT SUPPLIES NOT ONLY FOOD BUT BUILDING AND CRAFT MATERIALS AND MEDICINE. SAGO PEARLS ARE USED IN BOTH SAVOURY AND SWEET DISHES, SUCH AS THIS ONE. THIS SWEET PUDDING, SAGU GULA MELAKA, IS ALSO ENJOYED IN MANY MALAY HOMES THROUGHOUT THE PENINSULA. THE INTENSE SWEETNESS OF THE PALM SUGAR SYRUP IS AN ESSENTIAL ACCOMPANIMENT.

SERVES FOUR

INGREDIENTS
    1 pandan (screwpine) leaf, tied
      in a knot
    250g/9oz pearl sago, picked over,
      washed and drained
    400ml/14fl oz/1⅔ cups coconut
      milk, lightly beaten
    salt
For the syrup
    250ml/8fl oz/1 cup water
    175g/6oz/¾ cup palm sugar (jaggery)

VARIATIONS
Alternatively, you could keep the sago hot in a steamer and heat up the coconut milk, so that the whole pudding is hot. If you cannot find pandan leaves, use a vanilla pod (bean) to flavour the pudding instead.

1 Bring a deep pan of water to the boil. Drop in the pandan leaf and let the sago pour into the water through the fingers of one hand, while you stir with a wooden spoon, to prevent the pearls from sticking.

2 Boil for 5 minutes, then remove from the heat, cover and leave the sago to steam for about 10 minutes – the sago pearls will go swollen and translucent.

3 Drain the sago through a sieve (strainer) and rinse under cold running water.

4 Reserve the pandan leaf. Put the sago in a bowl and stir in 15–30ml/1–2 tbsp of the coconut milk with a pinch of salt.

5 Spoon the sago into a lightly greased mould, or four individual moulds, packing it down gently, and leave at room temperature to set.

6 Meanwhile, make the syrup. Put the water and palm sugar into a heavy pan and stir over a high heat until the sugar dissolves.

7 Bring to the boil and boil for 2 minutes. Drop in the reserved pandan leaf, reduce the heat, and simmer for 10 minutes, stirring from time to time.

8 Beat the rest of the coconut milk with a pinch of salt. Turn the mould, or moulds, upside down in a shallow bowl and slip them off the pudding.

9 Spoon the coconut milk over the top, allowing it to flow down the sides and form a pool in the dish.

10 Pour the hot syrup all over the pudding, allowing plenty for each person. Serve the dessert immediately, while the syrup is still hot.

Per Portion Energy 416Kcal/1777kJ; Protein 0.7g; Carbohydrate 109.4g, of which sugars 50.6g; Fat 0.4g, of which saturates 0.2g; Cholesterol 0mg; Calcium 59mg; Fibre 0.3g; Sodium 115mg.

EGG CUSTARD IN PUMPKIN

THIS UNUSUAL DESSERT HAS ARRIVED IN MALAYSIA FROM THAILAND, WHERE IT IS CALLED SANGKAYA FAKTONG AND IS TRADITIONALLY MADE WITH DUCK EGGS. MALAYSIAN COOKS HAVE ADOPTED THE IDEA WITH GUSTO, AND IT MAKES A SPECTACULAR DESSERT FOR A PARTY. YOU DO NOT SPECIFICALLY HAVE TO USE EITHER PUMPKIN OR DUCK EGGS TO MAKE THIS RECIPE. ANY GOOD-LOOKING SQUASH CAN BE USED AS THE "BOWL" FOR THE CUSTARD, AND HENS' EGGS ARE PERFECTLY SATISFACTORY.

SERVES FOUR

INGREDIENTS

6 large (US extra large) eggs
250ml/8fl oz/1 cup coconut cream
150g/5oz palm sugar (jaggery)
1 pumpkin, about 20cm/8in
  in diameter.

1 Grate the sugar. Beat the eggs lightly and whisk in the coconut cream and sugar. Cut off the top of the pumpkin and scoop out seeds and fibres.

2 Pour in the frothy custard mixture, cover with the pumpkin top and place the pumpkin in a steamer.

3 Cover the steamer and steam for 25 minutes until the custard is set. Allow to cool and cut into slices to serve, but do not eat the pumpkin skin.

COOK'S TIP
If you use only egg yolks (for this, increase the number to 8), the results will be even richer.

Per portion Energy 217Kcal/907kJ; Protein 4.6g; Carbohydrate 16.3g, of which sugars 15.7g; Fat 15.4g, of which saturates 11.9g; Cholesterol 71mg; Calcium 71mg; Fibre 1.3g; Sodium 88mg.

PUMPKIN, SWEET POTATO AND BANANA IN COCONUT MILK

THIS DISH OF SWEET VEGETABLES COOKED WITH BANANAS IN COCONUT MILK IS A FAVOURITE AMONG MANY RURAL MALAYS AND INDONESIANS. SERVED AS A SWEET SNACK, OR FOR BREAKFAST, IT IS BOTH NOURISHING AND WARMING. IT IS ALSO A POPULAR SWEET FOOD IN THE JUNGLES AND FIELDS OF SARAWAK, SABAH AND THE RURAL AREAS OF THE MALAYSIAN PENINSULA, WITH THE RECIPES DIFFERING BY THE INCLUSION OF GOURDS SUCH AS YAM, BUTTERNUT SQUASH AND WINTER MELON.

SERVES FOUR TO SIX

INGREDIENTS

900ml/1½ pints/3¾ cups
    coconut milk
½ small pumpkin, seeded and cut
    into bitesize cubes
2 sweet potatoes, cut into
    bitesize pieces
1 pandan (screwpine) leaf
150g/5oz/¾ cup palm sugar (jaggery)
2.5ml/½ tsp salt
3 bananas, cut into thick
    diagonal slices

1 Bring the coconut milk to the boil in a heavy pan. Stir in the pumpkin, sweet potatoes and pandan leaf.

2 Continue to boil for 1 minute, then reduce the heat and simmer for about 15 minutes, until the pumpkin and sweet potato are tender but retain their shape well.

3 Using a slotted spoon, lift the pumpkin and sweet potato pieces out of the coconut milk and put them on a plate.

4 Add the sugar and salt to the coconut milk and stir until the sugar has dissolved. Bring the sweetened coconut milk to the boil, then reduce the heat and simmer for 5 minutes.

5 Add the bananas to the sweetened coconut milk and simmer for 4 minutes.

6 Put the pumpkin and sweet potato back into the pan and gently mix all the ingredients together.

7 Remove the pandan leaf and serve the dessert warm.

Per Portion Energy 249Kcal/1063kJ; Protein 2.6g; Carbohydrate 61.4g, of which sugars 51.7g; Fat 1g, of which saturates 0.5g; Cholesterol 0mg; Calcium 97mg; Fibre 2.8g; Sodium 187mg.

STEAMED GINGER AND COCONUT MILK CUSTARDS

DELICATE AND WARMING, GINGER CUSTARD IS A FAVOURITE AMONG THE CHINESE AND PERANAKANS IN SINGAPORE. OFTEN SERVED WARM, STRAIGHT FROM THE STEAMER, THE INDIVIDUAL CUSTARDS ARE ENJOYED AS A SWEET MID-AFTERNOON SNACK OR EVEN LATE AT NIGHT. THEY ARE EQUALLY DELIGHTFUL SERVED COLD AS A DESSERT. TOAST A LITTLE SHREDDED GINGER OR SOME COCONUT SHAVINGS TO DECORATE THE TOP OF THIS DELICIOUS CONCOCTION.

SERVES FOUR

INGREDIENTS
  115g/4oz fresh root ginger, chopped
  400ml/14fl oz/1⅔ cups coconut milk
  60ml/4 tbsp sugar
  2 egg whites

1 Using a mortar and pestle or food processor, grind the root ginger to a fine paste. Press the ginger paste through a fine sieve (strainer), or twist it in a piece of muslin (cheesecloth), to extract the juice. Discard the pulp.

2 Fill a wok one-third of the way up with water. Place a bamboo steamer in the wok, bring the water to the boil and reduce the heat to low.

3 In a bowl, whisk the coconut milk, sugar and egg whites with the ginger juice until the mixture is smooth and the sugar has dissolved.

4 Pour the custard into four individual heatproof bowls and place them in the steamer. Cover and steam for 15–20 minutes, until set.

5 Remove the bowls from the steamer and leave the custards to cool. They can be served while still slightly warm. Alternatively, cover them with clear film (plastic wrap) once they are completely cool and place in the refrigerator overnight to firm up. Serve the custards chilled or at room temperature.

Per Portion Energy 89Kcal/380kJ; Protein 2g; Carbohydrate 20.8g, of which sugars 20.8g; Fat 0.4g, of which saturates 0.2g; Cholesterol 0mg; Calcium 50mg; Fibre 0.3g; Sodium 159mg.

MASHED BANANA FRITTERS

A REALLY MEMORABLE DISH FROM RURAL MALAYSIA, THIS IS NOT TO BE CONFUSED WITH THE BANANA FRITTERS COMMONLY SERVED IN CHINESE AND MALAYSIAN RESTAURANTS. THIS RECIPE USES MASHED BANANAS, WHICH ARE THICKENED WITH RICE FLOUR AND FRIED IN ROUGH SPOONFULS UNTIL BROWN, THEN DIPPED IN CASTER SUGAR. ANY TYPE OF BANANA WILL DO.

SERVES FOUR

INGREDIENTS
4 large bananas
130g/4½oz rice flour
1 egg, lightly beaten
oil for deep-frying
caster (superfine) sugar, for dusting

1 Peel the bananas and mash them with a fork to a pulp. Sift the rice flour over and blend with the banana mash. Beat in the egg to bind the mixture.

2 Heat the oil for deep-frying in a wok or large pan. Drop in a heaped tablespoonful of mash at a time until golden brown. Lift out with a slotted spoon and drain on kitchen paper.

3 Spread some caster sugar on a large plate. Drop the fritters into it and dust liberally with sugar while still warm. Serve immediately.

COOK'S TIP
These rustic banana fritters are delicious with coconut or vanilla ice cream.

Per portion Energy 204Kcal/855kJ; Protein 3.9g; Carbohydrate 26.7g, of which sugars 14.8g; Fat 9.8g, of which saturates 4.4g; Cholesterol 48mg; Calcium 48mg; Fibre 1.7g; Sodium 75mg.

DEEP-FRIED BANANAS WITH COCONUT

PERHAPS THE MOST COMMON OF ALL THE SWEET SNACKS, DEEP-FRIED BANANAS ARE POPULAR THROUGHOUT SOUTH-EAST ASIA, AND ARE A HAWKER-STALL FAVOURITE IN MALAYSIA AND SINGAPORE. VERSATILE AND DELICIOUS, THEY ARE OFTEN MUNCHED ON THEIR OWN, SPRINKLED WITH SUGAR, OR THEY CAN BE SERVED WITH SWEET STICKY RICE, ICE CREAMS OR STEAMED CAKES AND BUNS.

SERVES FOUR TO SIX

INGREDIENTS
115g/4oz/1 cup plain (all-purpose) or rice flour
5ml/1 tsp baking powder
2 eggs
750ml/1¼ pints/3 cups coconut milk
30ml/2 tbsp palm (jaggery) or granulated (white) sugar
90g/3½oz fresh coconut, grated or desiccated (dry unsweetened shredded) coconut
3 large bananas, halved widthways and lengthways
vegetable oil, for deep-frying
salt
caster (superfine) or icing (confectioners') sugar, for sprinkling

1 Sift the flour with the baking powder and a pinch of salt into a bowl. Make a well in the centre and drop in the eggs. Gradually pour in the coconut milk, beating all the time, until the batter is thick and smooth.

2 Beat in the sugar and fresh dessicated coconut and add the banana pieces, coating each completely with the batter.

3 Heat enough oil for deep-frying in a wok or large heavy pan. Check the oil is the right temperature by dropping in a cube of bread – if it sizzles and turns golden brown, the oil is ready.

4 Lift the pieces of banana out of the batter with tongs or chopsticks and lower them into the oil. Fry two or three pieces at a time, until crisp and golden, and drain on kitchen paper. Repeat with the remaining banana pieces.

5 Sprinkle caster or icing sugar over the banana fritters and serve while they are still warm.

Per Portion Energy 377Kcal/1571kJ; Protein 5g; Carbohydrate 39.6g, of which sugars 22.7g; Fat 22.5g, of which saturates 9.9g; Cholesterol 63mg; Calcium 26mg; Fibre 3.2g; Sodium 30mg.

STICKY COCONUT RICE IN BANANA LEAVES

Sweet and savoury sticky rice cooked in banana leaves is common fare in the markets and at the hawker stalls throughout South-east Asia. In this recipe, sliced banana is added to steamed rice to make this sweet treat particularly moist and delicious.

SERVES FOUR

INGREDIENTS

 115g/4oz/generous ½ cup white
  sticky rice, well rinsed in several
  changes of water, soaked in plenty
  of water for 6 hours and drained
 400ml/14fl oz/1⅔ cups coconut milk
 60ml/4 tbsp palm sugar (jaggery)
 banana leaves, cut into pieces,
  roughly 20cm/8in square
 2 bananas, cut into diagonal slices
 salt
 coconut cream and icing
  (confectioners') sugar, to serve

1 Fill a wok one-third of the way up with water and place a bamboo steamer inside it. Bring the water to the boil. Alternatively use an electric steamer.

2 Place a piece of muslin (cheesecloth), dampened in warm water, over the steamer rack.

3 Spread the sticky rice on the muslin, leaving a gap at the edges for the steam to come through. Fold over the edges of the muslin, place the lid on the steamer, and leave to steam for 20 minutes until the rice is tender but still firm.

4 Meanwhile, heat the coconut milk in a heavy pan with the sugar and a pinch of salt, stirring all the time until the sugar has dissolved. Stir in the steamed sticky rice until well mixed.

5 Remove from the heat, cover the pan and leave the rice to sit for 10–15 minutes until it has absorbed the sweetened coconut milk.

6 Place the banana leaf squares on a flat surface. Spread 30ml/2 tbsp of rice in the centre of each, in the shape of a rectangle. Place a few overlapping banana slices on top and form a sandwich with another 30ml/2 tbsp rice. Fold in the two short ends, and then fold over the wider flaps to form a bundle. Secure the bundle with string or a cocktail stick (toothpick).

7 Refill the wok one-third of the way up with water. Place the bundles in the bamboo steamer, cover with the lid and steam for 1 hour. Serve the bundles hot, straight from the steamer, with a spoonful of coconut cream and a dusting of icing sugar, or leave them to cool in the banana leaves and serve at room temperature as a sweet snack.

COOK'S TIP
In the north of Peninsular Malaysia, where much of the rice is grown and the influence from Thailand is strong, these banana leaf bundles are popular snacks. They are also in great demand at the Malay hawker stalls in the fast-paced cities of Kuala Lumpur and Singapore.

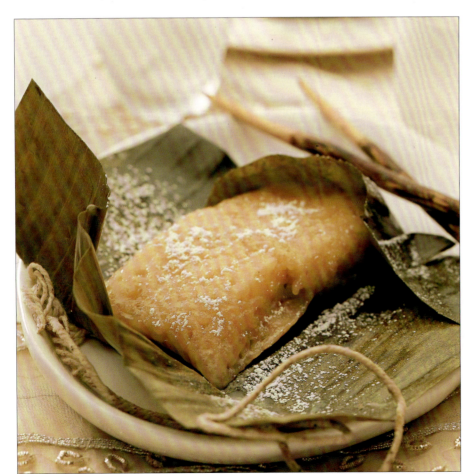

Per Portion Energy 232Kcal/981kJ; Protein 3.1g; Carbohydrate 55.1g, of which sugars 31g; Fat 0.6g, of which saturates 0.3g; Cholesterol 0mg; Calcium 46mg; Fibre 0.6g; Sodium 112mg.

BLACK GLUTINOUS RICE PUDDING

ALSO KNOWN AS BLACK STICKY RICE, BLACK GLUTINOUS RICE HAS LONG DARK GRAINS AND A NUTTY TASTE REMINISCENT OF WILD RICE. THIS BAKED PUDDING HAS A DISTINCT CHARACTER AND FLAVOUR ALL OF ITS OWN, AS WELL AS AN INTRIGUING APPEARANCE.

SERVES FOUR TO SIX

INGREDIENTS
    175g/6oz/1 cup black or white
      glutinous rice
    30ml/2 tbsp soft light brown sugar
    475ml/16fl oz/2 cups coconut milk
    250ml/8fl oz/1 cup water
    3 eggs
    30ml/2 tbsp granulated (white) sugar

1 Combine the glutinous rice and brown sugar in a pan. Pour in half the coconut milk and the water.

2 Bring to the boil, reduce the heat to low and simmer, stirring occasionally, for 15–20 minutes, or until the rice has absorbed most of the liquid. Preheat the oven to 150°C/300°F/Gas 2.

3 Spoon the rice into a large ovenproof dish or divide it among individual ramekins.

4 Beat the eggs with the remaining coconut milk and sugar. Strain the egg mixture into a jug (pitcher), then pour it evenly over the par-cooked rice.

5 Place the dish or ramekins in a roasting pan. Carefully pour in enough hot water to come halfway up the sides of the dish or ramekins.

6 Cover with foil and bake for about 35–60 minutes, or until the custard has set. Serve warm or cold.

COOK'S TIP
Throughout South-east Asia, black glutinous rice is usually used for sweet dishes, while its white counterpart is more often used in savoury recipes.

Per portion Energy 135Kcal/568kJ; Protein 1.7g; Carbohydrate 31.8g, of which sugars 17.4g; Fat 0.3g, of which saturates 0g; Cholesterol 0mg; Calcium 247mg; Fibre 0g; Sodium 2mg.

GLUTINOUS RICE <u>WITH</u> COCONUT

AT PERANAKAN WEDDINGS AND OTHER SPECIAL OCCASIONS, THIS DESSERT IS INVARIABLY FEATURED. IN MALAY IT IS CALLED PULUT INTI, WHICH IS A LITERAL TRANSLATION OF "RICE AND DESICCATED COCONUT". IT IS TRADITIONALLY WRAPPED IN BANANA LEAVES BUT THIS IS NOT NECESSARY IF YOU CANNOT GET THE LEAVES. INSTEAD, MAKE IT IN A TRAY AND CUT IT INTO WEDGES TO SERVE.

3 Cut the pandan leaf into small pieces and distribute all over the tray, pushing a few pieces into the rice. Steam the rice for about 20 minutes. Check to see if it is cooked by tasting a few grains.

4 Put the palm sugar into a small pan and add the water. Stir over a gentle heat until all the sugar has dissolved, then remove from heat and blend with the coconut. Mix well.

SERVES FOUR TO SIX

INGREDIENTS

  200g/7oz glutinous rice, soaked in
    water for 3 hours
  2.5ml/½ tsp salt
  1 pandan (screwpine) leaf
  125g/4¼oz palm sugar (jaggery)
  200ml/7fl oz/scant 1 cup water
  200g/7oz desiccated (dry
    unsweetened shredded) coconut

1 Drain the glutinous rice from the soaking water, rinse in a sieve (strainer) under running water and drain again.

2 Place in a bamboo steaming tray with enough water to moisten it and stir in the salt. There should be no surplus water as the rice will already have absorbed a sufficient amount for the steaming process.

5 Remove the rice from the steamer and press the desiccated coconut on top, spreading it evenly all over the surface of the rice. Cut into wedges to serve cold.

Per portion Energy 457Kcal/1947kJ; Protein 8.6g; Carbohydrate 102.4g, of which sugars 50.8g; Fat 4.4g, of which saturates 1.3g; Cholesterol 0mg; Calcium 92mg; Fibre 0.5g; Sodium 381mg.

RED BEAN PUDDING

CHINESE IN ORIGIN BUT POPULAR THROUGHOUT SOUTH-EAST ASIA, TINY RED ADUKI BEANS ARE OFTEN SERVED AS A SWEET SNACK. RED, YELLOW AND GREEN BEANS ARE USED IN MANY CHINESE SWEET DISHES, SUCH AS THE SYRUPY SOUPS OR SPONGY DUMPLINGS FILLED WITH BEAN PASTE. AT SOME OF THE HAWKER STALLS, THIS PUDDING IS PRESENTED ON A BANANA LEAF WITH A DRIZZLE OF COCONUT MILK.

SERVES FOUR TO SIX

INGREDIENTS
115g/4oz dried red aduki beans, soaked in water for 2 hours
1.2 litres/2 pints/5 cups water
4 pandan (screwpine) leaves
150g/5oz/¾ cup sugar
150ml/¼ pint /⅔ cup thick coconut milk, fresh or canned, beaten until smooth, or fresh coconut cream

VARIATION
Generally, pandan leaves are used to flavour the syrup in this dish but you could easily use a flavouring of your choice, such as fresh root ginger, bay or lime leaves, lemon grass or vanilla.

1 Drain the soaked beans and put them in a deep pan. Add the water and bring it to the boil. Add the pandan leaves and reduce the heat. Simmer, uncovered, for about 40 minutes until the beans are tender and the water has greatly reduced. Stir in the sugar.

2 Allow the sugar to dissolve, and simmer for a further 10 minutes. Remove the pandan leaves and spoon the beans into individual bowls. Serve hot or leave to cool and chill before serving. Serve the coconut milk or cream separately, to pour over.

Per Portion Energy 155Kcal/661kJ; Protein 4.4g; Carbohydrate 35.8g, of which sugars 27.8g; Fat 0.4g, of which saturates 0.1g; Cholesterol 0mg; Calcium 40mg; Fibre 3g; Sodium 33mg.

ROSE-FLAVOURED LASSI

Sweet and savoury lassi is always in demand at Indian and Malay coffee shops, restaurants and hawker stalls. Soothing and cooling, this Indian yogurt-based drink is an ideal partner to spicy food. Savoury lassi is often salty and flavoured with mint, whereas the sweet drink is fragrant with the traditional essences of rose or pandan leaf.

SERVES TWO

INGREDIENTS
    300ml/½ pint/1¼ cups natural
      (plain) yogurt
    5–10ml/1–2 tsp rose essence
    10ml/2 tsp sugar
    6 ice cubes, to serve
    rose petals, to decorate

1 In a jug (pitcher), beat the yogurt with 150ml/¼ pint/⅔ cup water, until smooth. Add the rose essence and sugar, adjusting the sweetness to taste, and mix well.

2 Divide the ice cubes between two glasses and pour in the lassi. Decorate with a few rose petals and serve.

Per Portion Energy 104Kcal/438kJ; Protein 7.7g; Carbohydrate 16.5g, of which sugars 16.5g; Fat 1.5g, of which saturates 0.8g; Cholesterol 2mg; Calcium 288mg; Fibre 0g; Sodium 125mg.

MANGO AND LIME LASSI

INSPIRED BY THE CLASSIC INDIAN DRINK, THIS TANGY, FRUITY BLEND IS GREAT FOR BREAKFAST OR AS A DELICIOUS PICK-ME-UP AT ANY TIME OF DAY. SOFT, RIPE MANGO BLENDED WITH YOGURT AND SHARP, ZESTY LIME AND LEMON JUICE MAKES A WONDERFULLY THICK, COOLING DRINK THAT'S PACKED WITH ENERGY. IT CAN ALSO BE ENJOYED AS A MELLOW SOOTHER WHEN YOU NEED TO UNWIND.

MAKES 2 TALL GLASSES

INGREDIENTS

  1 mango
  finely grated rind and juice of 1 lime
  15ml/1 tbsp lemon juice
  5–10ml/1–2 tsp caster
  (superfine) sugar
  100ml/3 1/2fl oz/scant ½ cup natural
  (plain) yogurt
  mineral water
  1 extra lime, halved, to serve

1 Peel the mango and cut the flesh from the stone (pit). Put the flesh into a blender or food processor and add the lime rind and juice.

2 Add the lemon juice, sugar and natural yogurt. Blend until the mixture is completely smooth, scraping down the sides of the bowl once or twice, if necessary. Stir in a little mineral water to thin it down.

3 Serve immediately, with half a lime on the side of each glass so that more juice can be squeezed in, if desired.

Per portion Energy 81Kcal/344kJ; Protein 3.1g; Carbohydrate 17g, of which sugars 16.7g; Fat 0.7g, of which saturates 0.4g; Cholesterol 1mg; Calcium 106mg; Fibre 2g; Sodium 43mg.

CONDIMENTS

The essential condiments of South-east Asia add delicious flavours and textures to many dishes. Although they are often thought of as aromatic spicy dips or side dishes, they are in fact more than optional extras, often imparting the heat or flavour that really makes the meal. Wonderfully simple to prepare, the condiments in this chapter are exquisitely tasty and lift a feast of Malaysian or Singaporean dishes to memorably flavoursome heights.

SAMBAL BELACAN

This is the ubiquitous condiment of the Malays and Peranakans. As they have such a penchant for strong, fiery tastes, this punchy condiment graces their tables on a daily basis. A little bowlful seems to go with everything: chunks of bread, rice, grilled foods and stir-fried vegetables. The pungent shrimp paste, belacan, is made from tiny shrimp mashed to a paste and buried for several months to ferment.

SERVES FOUR

INGREDIENTS
    15ml/1 tbsp shrimp paste
    4 fresh red chillies, seeded (reserve
    the seeds)
    2 kaffir lime leaves, spines removed,
    and chopped
    2.5ml/½ tsp sugar
    1.5ml/¼ tsp salt
    juice of 1 lime
    1 lime, quartered, to serve

COOK'S TIP
The fermented shrimp paste, belacan, is available in Asian markets. If you cannot get hold of it, replace it with the more readily available Thai shrimp paste.

1 In a small, heavy pan, dry-roast the shrimp paste until it is aromatic and crumbly. Using a mortar and pestle or food processor, grind the roasted shrimp paste with the chillies to form a paste. Grind in half the chilli seeds and the lime leaves.

2 Add the sugar and salt, and stir in the rest of the chilli seeds. Moisten with the lime juice. Spoon the sambal into little dishes and serve with wedges of lime to squeeze over it.

Per Portion Energy 17Kcal/69kJ; Protein 2.8g; Carbohydrate 0.8g, of which sugars 0.8g; Fat 0.3g, of which saturates 0g; Cholesterol 19mg; Calcium 53mg; Fibre 0g; Sodium 312mg.

SAMBAL SERONDENG

A QUINTESSENTIAL DRESSING FOR CURRIES IN MALAYSIA AND SINGAPORE, SERONDENG ORIGINATED IN INDONESIA, WHERE IT WAS EATEN WITH RIJSTAFEL, A MOUTHWATERING MELANGE OF DISHES BUILT AROUND RICE, WHOSE DUTCH NAME LITERALLY MEANS "RICE TABLE". THE PERANAKAN COMMUNITY IN MALAYSIA ADOPTED THIS IDEA FOR THEIR FESTIVE TOK PANJANG, OR "LONG TABLE", AND ALSO BORROWED THE RECIPE FOR SAMBAL SERONDENG, OF WHICH THERE ARE SEVERAL VERSIONS.

SERVES SIX TO EIGHT

INGREDIENTS
   2 stalks lemon grass
   5 shallots
   4 garlic cloves
   3 fresh red chillies, seeded
   (optional)
   50g/2oz tempeh (fermented soy
   bean cake)
   30ml/2 tbsp vegetable or groundnut
   (peanut) oil
   175g/6oz fresh coconut, grated or
   100g/3½oz desiccated (dry,
   unsweetened, shredded) coconut
   2.5ml/½ tsp salt
   2.5ml/½ tsp sugar

1 Trim the lemon grass stalks and slice the 7.5cm/3in at the root end into very thin rounds. Peel and slice the shallots and the garlic. Slice the chillies diagonally into thin pieces.

2 Cut the tempeh into small dice, and fry it in oil in a wok or heavy pan until light brown. Crush it coarsely.

3 Heat another wok without oil and dry fry the lemon grass, shallots, garlic and chillies until just sizzled. Add the coconut, and stir-fry with a to and fro motion until all the ingredients are golden brown.

4 Add the crushed tempeh, salt and sugar and fry, stirring, until well-mixed. Remove from the heat and leave to cool before storing in an air-tight container, if not serving immediately. Keep the serondeng in the refrigerator and eat within a week.

COOK'S TIPS
Serondeng is delicious sprinkled over dishes like beef rendang, coconut milk kormas and curries or over plain rice as a relish. Use freshly grated coconut for the best flavour as store-bought desiccated coconut is over-dehydrated. Good serondeng should be succulent and softly moist.

Per portion Energy 120Kcal/494kJ; Protein 1.7g; Carbohydrate 4.1g, of which sugars 3.3g; Fat 10.8g, of which saturates 7g; Cholesterol 0mg; Calcium 44mg; Fibre 2.2g; Sodium 128mg.

SOUR MANGO SAMBAL

ANOTHER MALAY FAVOURITE IS SAMBAL ASAM, SOUR SAMBAL, MADE WITH GREEN MANGO OR PAPAYA.
IT IS SERVED IN SMALL QUANTITIES AS A RELISH TO ACCOMPANY FRIED FISH AND SHELLFISH, SPICY
GRILLED FOODS AND FIERY CURRIES, BUT IT CAN ALSO BE SERVED ON ITS OWN AS A REFRESHING SNACK.

SERVES FOUR

INGREDIENTS
    5ml/1 tsp shrimp paste
    4 fresh red chillies, seeded
    7.5ml/1½ tsp salt
    5ml/1 tsp sugar
    1 green mango, peeled and shredded
    juice of ½ lime

1 In a small, heavy pan, dry-roast the shrimp paste over a low heat until it is aromatic and crumbly.

COOK'S TIP
Mangoes are widely available, but for this recipe you need an unripe fruit, in which the flesh is just starting to turn yellow.

2 Using a mortar and pestle or food processor, grind the chillies with the salt to form a paste. Add the shrimp paste and sugar and pound into the spicy paste. Toss in the shredded mango and moisten with the lime juice. Mix well and serve in little bowls.

Per Portion Energy 34Kcal/143kJ; Protein 1.7g; Carbohydrate 6.5g, of which sugars 6.4g; Fat 0.3g, of which saturates 0.1g; Cholesterol 6mg; Calcium 28mg; Fibre 1g; Sodium 794mg.

PINEAPPLE PICKLE

THIS SPICY SWEET-AND-SOUR PICKLE IS IDEAL TO SERVE WITH GRILLED FOODS OR AS A FRUITY ACCOMPANIMENT TO CURRIES OR VEGETABLE DISHES. MALAYS LIKE THEIR PICKLES HOT, BUT YOU CAN ADJUST THE AMOUNT OF CHILLI IN THIS RECIPE TO SUIT YOUR TASTE.

SERVES SIX TO EIGHT

INGREDIENTS

15ml/1 tbsp brown mustard seeds
2 dried chillies, soaked in water until
 soft, squeezed dry and seeded
15g/½oz fresh root ginger, peeled
 and chopped
1 garlic clove, chopped
5ml/1 tsp ground turmeric
200ml/7fl oz/scant 1 cup white wine
 vinegar or rice vinegar
15ml/1 tbsp palm sugar (jaggery)
1 ripe pineapple
salt

1 In a small, heavy pan, dry-roast the mustard seeds until they pop.

2 Using a mortar and pestle or food processor, grind the chillies, ginger and garlic to a paste. Stir in the mustard seeds and ground turmeric. Add the vinegar and sugar, stirring until the sugar has completely dissolved.

COOK'S TIP

Malays and Indians often serve a selection of condiments with every meal. The Malay sambal, the Nonya acar and myriad Indian pickles can all be interchanged with the food of these cultures.

3 Peel and core the pineapple and dice the flesh. Put the pineapple in a bowl and pour over the pickling sauce. Add salt to taste. The pickle will keep for 2–3 days in the refrigerator.

Per Portion Energy 56Kcal/238kJ; Protein 0.7g; Carbohydrate 12.5g, of which sugars 12.2g; Fat 0.2g, of which saturates 0g; Cholesterol 0mg; Calcium 20mg; Fibre 1.3g; Sodium 4mg.

LIME PICKLE

This Indian pickle is popular among Malays, Eurasians and Peranakans, as well as the Indian communities of Malaysia and Singapore. Often sold in jars at hawker stalls, the pickle is eaten mainly as an accompaniment to fiery curries. Commercial varieties of this famous pickle are widely available, but cannot compare with this freshly made version.

SERVES EIGHT TO TEN

INGREDIENTS
  8–10 limes
  30ml/2 tbsp salt
  150ml/5fl oz/⅔ cup sesame or
    groundnut (peanut) oil
  10–15ml/2–3 tsp brown
    mustard seeds
  3–4 garlic cloves, cut into thin sticks

25g/1oz fresh root ginger, peeled
  and cut into thin sticks
5ml/1 tsp coriander seeds
5ml/1 tsp cumin seeds
5ml/1 tsp fennel seeds
10ml/2 tsp ground turmeric
10ml/2 tsp hot chilli powder
  or paste
a handful of fresh or dried
  curry leaves

1 Put the whole limes in a bowl. Cover with boiling water and leave to stand for 30 minutes. Drain and cut into quarters. Rub the lime pieces with salt and put them into a sealed sterilized jar. Leave the limes to cure in the salt for 1 week.

2 Heat the oil in a wok and stir in the mustard seeds. When they begin to pop, stir in the garlic, ginger, spices and curry leaves. Cook gently for a few minutes to flavour the oil, then stir in the lime pieces and the juices from the jar. Reduce the heat and simmer the pickle for about 45 minutes, stirring from time to time.

3 Pour the pickle into sterilized jars and store in a cool place for 1–2 months.

COOK'S TIP
This pickle is delicious served with grilled (broiled) or fried fish, and spicy stir-fried noodles. You can make it as fiery as you like by adding more or less chilli powder.

Per Portion Energy 96Kcal/395kJ; Protein 0.3g; Carbohydrate 0.9g, of which sugars 0.6g; Fat 10.1g, of which saturates 1.5g; Cholesterol 0mg; Calcium 25mg; Fibre 0.2g; Sodium 1185mg.

NONYA ACAR

THERE ARE NUMEROUS VERSIONS OF ACAR, A PICKLE CREATED IN NONYA KITCHENS. PENANG ACAR, ACAR KUNIN AND ACAR AWAK ALL CONSIST OF A MEDLEY OF VEGETABLES THAT CAN BE SERVED AS A RELISH OR SIDE DISH. MORE ELABORATE THAN MALAY AND INDIAN PICKLES, NONYA ACAR RECIPES VARY FROM ONE HOUSEHOLD TO ANOTHER, SO YOU CAN EXPERIMENT WITH DIFFERENT VEGETABLES.

SERVES SIX TO TEN

INGREDIENTS

   450g/1lb carrots, peeled and cut into matchsticks
   450g/1lb daikon (mooli or white radish), peeled and cut into matchsticks
   2 small cucumbers, halved lengthways, seeded and cut into matchsticks
   6 dried red chillies, soaked in warm water to soften, squeezed dry and seeded
   6 garlic cloves, chopped
   50g/2oz fresh root ginger, peeled and chopped
   50g/2oz fresh turmeric, chopped
   30ml/2 tbsp vegetable or groundnut (peanut) oil
   6 shallots, sliced
   2 lemon grass stalks, halved and bruised
   45–60ml/3–4 tbsp rice or white wine vinegar
   30ml/2 tbsp sugar
   45ml/3 tbsp roasted peanuts
   30ml/2 tbsp roasted sesame seeds
   salt

1 Put the vegetables into a bowl, sprinkle with salt and set aside for about 15 minutes. Rinse the vegetables, drain and pat dry.

2 Using a mortar and pestle or a food processor, grind the chillies, garlic, ginger and turmeric together until they form a smooth paste.

3 Heat the oil in a wok. Stir in the shallots and lemon grass and fry until golden. Stir in the spice paste and fry until fragrant. Add the vegetables, tossing them around the wok to coat them in the spices. Add the vinegar and sugar and continue to cook the vegetables until they are tender, with just a little bite to them.

4 Season to taste with salt and put the vegetables into a large serving bowl. Leave the mixture to cool, then toss in the peanuts and sesame seeds. The pickle can be stored in a non-metallic container in the refrigerator, or a cool place, for 3–4 days.

Per Portion Energy 96Kcal/398kJ; Protein 2.3g; Carbohydrate 9.6g, of which sugars 8.8g; Fat 5.6g, of which saturates 0.9g; Cholesterol 0mg; Calcium 52mg; Fibre 2.3g; Sodium 18mg.

LIME <u>AND</u> CHILLI DIP

FOR THIS MALAY DIP, SAMBAL LIMAU, IT IS BEST TO USE CALAMANSI (ALSO KNOWN AS KESTURI) LIMES, WHICH ARE INDIGENOUS TO SOUTH-EAST ASIA AND HAVE VERY THIN SKINS THAT CAN BE GRATED TO ADD TO THE SAUCE. WEST INDIAN LIMES CAN BE USED PROVIDED YOU GRATE THE SKIN VERY THINLY, OTHERWISE THE SAUCE WILL HAVE A BITTER EDGE. CALAMANSI OR KESTURI LIMES ARE OCCASIONALLY AVAILABLE IN THAI AND FILIPINO MARKETS.

SERVES FOUR TO SIX

INGREDIENTS
    6 calamansi limes
    4 red chillies
    2 garlic cloves
    2 spring onions (scallions)
    2 kaffir lime leaves
    15ml/1 tbsp fish sauce
    5ml/1 tsp sugar
    30ml/2 tbsp water

1 Finely grate the rind of one lime into a bowl. Squeeze the juice from all the limes into the bowl and, with a spoon, scoop out the flesh. Discard the seeds.

2 Finely chop the chillies, garlic and spring onions. Shred the lime leaves finely. Mix these ingredients into the lime juice and add the sugar, fish sauce and water. Stir everything together.

3 Taste and adjust the proportions if necessary, adding more water or lime juice as needed. Serve the dip with fish and chicken dishes or salads.

Per portion Energy 9Kcal/38kJ; Protein 0.6g; Carbohydrate 1.6g, of which sugars 1.3g; Fat 0.1g, of which saturates 0g; Cholesterol 0mg; Calcium 6mg; Fibre 0.1g; Sodium 179mg.

CHILLI, GARLIC AND GINGER SAUCE

REGARDED AS THE HOLY TRINITY OF HERBS, CHILLIES, GARLIC AND GINGER HAVE AN EXTRAORDINARY AFFINITY WHEN THEY ARE COMBINED IN THE CORRECT PROPORTIONS. FIRST, THE CHILLIES MUST BE ABSOLUTELY FRESH, RED, AND AS HOT AS TASTE DICTATES. THE GARLIC SHOULD BE FRESH AND PLUMP WITH NO WRINKLY SKINS. THE BEST GINGER ROOTS FOR THIS SAUCE ARE THE TENDER YOUNG STEMS, IDEALLY WITH SHORT PALE GREEN STALKS STILL ATTACHED TO THEM.

MAKES ABOUT 300ML/½ PINT/1½ CUPS

INGREDIENTS
    10 fresh red chillies
    10 cloves garlic
    50g/2oz fresh root ginger
    200ml/7fl oz/scant 1 cup rice
        wine vinegar
    2.5ml/½ tsp salt
    30ml/2 tbsp vegetable oil
    2 spring onions (scallions)
    2.5ml/½ tsp sugar

1 Wash the chillies and pat them dry. It is important that you do not introduce moisture into the sauce as it will encourage bacterial growth and the sauce will not keep well. Do not remove the seeds of the chillies in this case as the sauce is intended to give sweet, sharp fire to dishes. Chop roughly.

2 Peel the garlic and wipe dry with kitchen paper: do not wash it. Chop the flesh roughly.

3 With a sharp paring knife, peel or scrape off the thin outer skin of the ginger. If the roots you are using have any green stems attached, do not discard these. Roughly chop the ginger.

COOK'S TIP
When ready to eat, scoop out as much as is needed with a clean dry spoon and add more rice wine vinegar and sugar to the sauce to taste.

4 Place all three ingredients in a mortar and pestle or food processor and process until fine, but be careful not to reduce it to a purée consistency. To facilitate the grinding, add a spoonful or two of the vinegar.

5 Turn the mixture into a bowl and combine with the remaining vinegar and the salt. Heat the oil in a small pan or wok and add to the sauce. Finely chop the spring onions and mix them in well. Keep in a jar with a screw-top lid.

Per portion Energy 339Kcal/1405kJ; Protein 13.9g; Carbohydrate 18.1g, of which sugars 3.5g; Fat 23.9g, of which saturates 2.7g; Cholesterol 0mg; Calcium 100mg; Fibre 4.6g; Sodium 1070mg.

GINGER AND GARLIC SALT

This is a classic dip for Cantonese deep-fried chicken. It is very easy to make. If you can find coarse-grained sea salt, it is ideal for this mixture, as it has a fuller flavour and an appetizingly flaky texture, as well as a lower sodium content.

MAKES ENOUGH AS A DIP FOR 1 CHICKEN

INGREDIENTS

    50g/2oz fresh root ginger, peeled
    4 garlic cloves
    30ml/2 tbsp vegetable oil
    15ml/1 tbsp sesame oil
    2.5ml/½ tsp sugar
    5ml/1 tsp salt
    2.5ml/½ tsp freshly ground
      black pepper
    1 spring onion (scallion)

COOK'S TIP

If you don't have a microwave, heat the mixture in a small pan for 2 minutes.

1 Grate the ginger and finely chop the garlic. Blend in a small bowl and mix in the oils, sugar, salt and pepper. Microwave for 1 minute to cook the oil so the sauce will not have a raw taste.

2 Chop the spring onion very finely and stir it into the sauce. Leave the sauce to cool and store it in a jar with a screw top, in the refrigerator, if you are not using it immediately.

Per portion Energy 401Kcal/1650kJ; Protein 0.5g; Carbohydrate 0.8g, of which sugars 0.7g; Fat 44.1g, of which saturates 5.8g; Cholesterol 0mg; Calcium 27mg; Fibre 0.7g; Sodium 1996mg.

DRIED SHRIMP AND CHILLI CONDIMENT

LOOK FOR DRIED SHRIMPS THAT ARE LARGE, UNBROKEN AND A DULL PINKISH BROWN. THEY ARE MUCH EASIER TO PROCESS WHEN SOAKED BRIEFLY IN WARM WATER UNTIL JUST SOFT BUT NOT MUSHY. DRAIN THEM TO REMOVE ANY DUST, WHICH IS INVARIABLY PRESENT. THAI AND LAOTIAN COOKS ALWAYS GRILL OR CHAR THEIR SPRING ONIONS TO IMPART A SMOKY FLAVOUR TO THIS SAUCE.

SERVES FOUR

INGREDIENTS
    2 spring onions (scallions)
    50g/2oz dried shrimps
    6 shallots
    4 garlic cloves
    30ml/2 tbsp water
    30ml/2 tbsp lime juice
    5ml/1 tsp sugar

1 Hold the spring onions by their green tops and run the white parts briefly over a gas flame until they are lightly charred and frizzled. Trim and cut into short lengths.

2 Peel and slice the garlic and shallots. Grind them together with the spring onions in a mortar and pestle or a food processor to a coarse paste. Remove the paste to a bowl, then grind the soaked dried shrimps finely. Add them to the bowl and mix all the ingredients together thoroughly.

3 Add the lime juice, sugar and water and blend well.

Per portion Energy 59kcal/247kJ; Protein 8.1g; Carbohydrate 6g, of which sugars 4.1g; Fat 0.5g, of which saturates 0.1g; Cholesterol 63mg; Calcium 166mg; Fibre 1g; Sodium 543mg.

INDEX